Praise for

And the Good News Is . . .

"AND THE GOOD NEW IS...is an antidote to despair about politics. It's a proposal for—and witness to—something better, from someone who has learned along the way and in her gratitude wants to share and help others....Whether she's discussing the presidential-primary trail, Twitter, or marriage, she shares the joys and practical benefits of actual human encounter: prioritizing, humility, and encouragement."

Kathryn Lopez, *National Review*

"Part autobiography, part memoir of a press secretary in the White House, part career and life guidance, and part appeal to civility, Dana Perino's AND THE GOOD NEWS IS...is all parts captivating."

Donna Brazile

"With this delightful blend of the political, personal, and professional, Dana Perino gives us a useful glimpse into one of the most remarkable workplaces in the world, the White House. Political junkies will revel in her insider tales but every reader will come away knowing more about the human dimension of working in the most powerful place on the planet."

Mike McCurry, former White House Press
Secretary to President Bill Clinton

"Congrats to Dana Perino! It's a great read. *Little House on the Prairie* meets *West Wing*."

Chris Stirewalt, Digital Politics Editor, Fox News

"This book is perfect for anyone interested in politics, media or simply advice about taking courageous chances in life, love and work. Dana has written a book that is as accessible for those who are just starting out on their career path as for those who are long-time students of current events and history."

Julie Roginsky, Fox News Contributor

"The book is a study in character, and why surrounding one's self with people of good character (from Dana's husband, parents and grandparents to Tony Snow and George W. Bush) leads to a life well lived."

Doug Brunt, author of *The Means* and
Ghosts of Manhattan

"If you want to be inspired by a successful woman who goes from ranching in the West, to the White House, to helping in Africa, to a fine marriage and a loving dog, you will find it in this book. You will also find the kind of honest advice about life, politics and the Presidency that makes you feel good. Now there's a rarity."

Marlin Fitzwater, former White House Press Secretary
to Presidents Ronald Reagan and George H.W. Bush

"This book is a gem—modest and moving, clear and unpretentious. It gives the kind of practical and even ethical advice everyone starting out needs, but it's also funny and full of great stories. Dana is a true role model."

Peggy Noonan

"A lovely memoir, both charming and wise, studded with invaluable life lessons garnered on her fascinating journey to the highest levels of media and government. A wonderful read."

Charles Krauthammer

And the Good News Is...

LESSONS AND ADVICE FROM THE BRIGHT SIDE

〜〜〜

Dana Perino

TWELVE

New York   Boston

Twelve
Hachette Book Group
1290 Avenue of the Americas
New York, NY 10104
twelvebooks.com
twitter.com/twelvebooks

Originally published in hardcover by Twelve, April 2015
First Trade Paperback Edition: April 2016

Twelve is an imprint of Grand Central Publishing.
The Twelve name and logo are trademarks of Hachette Book Group, Inc.

The publisher is not responsible for websites (or their content)
that are not owned by the publisher.

The Hachette Speakers Bureau provides a wide range of authors for speaking
events. To find out more, go to www.hachettespeakersbureau.com or call
(866) 376-6591.

Library of Congress Cataloging-in-Publication Data has been applied for.

ISBNs: 978-1-4555-8491-8 (trade), 978-1-4555-8489-5 (ebook)

Printed in the United States of America

LSC-C

Printing 2, 2021

To my Bush Administration colleagues

Contents

*And the
Good News Is…*

Introduction

The Black Eye of Baghdad

I knew the job of a White House press secretary would be hectic and demanding, but I never expected I'd come to physical harm. I'd almost finished the job without a scratch when a top-secret trip to Baghdad, six weeks before President George W. Bush left office, changed all of that.

It was December 2008, and a very small team at the White House was assigned to work on a covert trip to Iraq and Afghanistan. It would be the President's last overseas trip on Air Force One, and we had to be extra careful to keep it all under wraps because the press was already nosing around. Reporters that covered the President suspected that he'd want to see the troops one last time. They knew his style.

I was in charge of the press part of the trip, and I worked with Gordon Johndroe, my deputy press secretary for national security, to figure out our piece of the puzzle. Thankfully, Gordon has a good poker face. It was awkward to tell white lies to our colleagues about our weekend plans, and we had to sneak out "to get coffee" so we could talk without being overheard. I didn't like keeping secrets from my team, but I understood why we had to.

We put together a group of reporters, photographers, and a

camera crew to make up the press pool. Only the editor and the journalist of each organization could know about the trip. And in turn, the reporter could only tell one family member (also sworn to secrecy). Just one leak and the trip would be canceled.

I was under the same rules—only my husband, Peter, was aware of where I was going. He was concerned—not about the flight, as there's no safer plane than Air Force One—but about potential hostile action on the ground. He knew that once we landed, the enemy might try to take a shot at disrupting our plans or even harming the President. And we had another problem. That weekend, Peter was to be the best man at a friend's wedding at the United States Naval Academy in Annapolis, Maryland. He'd have to make up an excuse for me. He ended up apologizing for my absence by saying that I had to work, which was true but a lame excuse for missing a wedding.

As the sun was setting in Washington on December 13, the handful of us going on the trip were picked up from our homes in unmarked cars and driven to Andrews Air Force Base. There we waited for the President and National Security Advisor, Steve Hadley, to fly in from Camp David. The President was wearing a black baseball cap that said "43" and a tan canvas jacket. At the bottom of the ladder to the plane, he paused and, grinning, said, "Who's ready? Let's go!" before bounding up the steps.

As soon as we got on board, I made a beeline for the conference room near the front of the plane and set down my bag. That room has a large oval table with big swivel chairs all around it, and a video screen for secure teleconferences or watching TV. Most of the senior staff liked to sit in there to work, have a chat, and sometimes play cards. Along the side of the room is a comfortable bench that curves around in a semicircle shape under the video screen. Since there weren't beds for all of us to lie down on, I staked out that spot because I was the smallest person on the staff and could fit there comfortably. We settled in for the thirteen-hour flight.

A couple of hours before our arrival in Iraq, we got up and took turns getting ready in the small restrooms and making ourselves presentable. I was pretty good at changing clothes in a space that was only slightly bigger than a phone booth. I washed, put on a bit of makeup, and brushed my hair in ten minutes.

For safety's sake, Air Force One's pilot, Colonel Mark Tillman, descended quickly in a tight spiral over the protected airspace. The President watched from the cockpit, and after a couple of minutes, we settled gently onto the runway. Our first stop: Baghdad.

President Bush and Prime Minister Nouri al-Maliki spent the day in meetings on everything from troop training to insurgents to economic reform. The most important issue on the agenda was the Status of Forces Agreement that President Bush was trying to finalize with the Iraqis. Unfortunately, Maliki didn't fully accept the agreement, but they agreed to keep working on it. Then we headed into the press conference at another location. The motorcade ride was bumpy, but aside from being jostled we got there in one piece.

I went in the back door, ahead of the leaders. This was an historic moment—it was the last time that President Bush and the Prime Minister of Iraq would appear together. The room was full of security guards and about two dozen journalists, including our press pool. We took our seats on the side of the room. To my left was Ed Gillespie, the counselor to the President, and on my right was the interpreter, with a boom microphone that was set on a steel arm. The room was relatively small and filled with technical equipment—cameras, lights, and cables wedged in around all of the people.

I felt some solidarity with the Iraqi reporters who were seated in the first two rows. I told Ed they grew up thinking they'd never get the chance to ask their leader a question, let alone the President of the United States. I silently cheered them on—but not for long.

President Bush and Prime Minister Maliki stepped up to their podiums and began their opening remarks. Out of the corner of my eye, I saw one of those "journalists" reach down and yank off his shoe and hurl it hard and fast at President Bush's head. He ducked and the shoe hit the wall. BAM! Immediately, the shoe thrower took another shot. BAM! Thankfully, the President dodged that shoe, too, and he didn't seem angry or afraid, but bemused. His look said, "What is *wrong* with you?"

I, however, was whimpering, but not in fear. As the second shoe was being thrown, the President's Secret Service agent charged forward to protect him, and he knocked the mic stand. The steel arm whipped around and hit me in the face on my upper cheekbone, just under my right eye. I didn't see it coming because I'd been looking the other way toward the leaders. I yelped and fell into Ed. The pain pierced, and I was like a cartoon character seeing stars.

I also had a fleeting thought that we were about to be blown up, and that the shoe throwing was a distraction for a bigger and deadlier attack. I looked to the back of the room, where all of the camera equipment and empty cases were stacked—a perfect place to hide a bomb—and thought, "Here we go."

Luckily, shoes were the only weapons being used.

Ed held my head to his chest and I clamped my hand over my eye. We waited for instructions to leave through the back door. While I bit the inside of my cheeks to defer the pain, the shoe thrower was learning a little something about manners from the Iraqi security forces. They had him on the ground, and he was screaming much louder than I had.

Through the commotion, President Bush was assuring his security that he was okay, and he waved them back. He said into his microphone, "Don't worry, it's fine. Everyone calm down. We're going to finish this." He locked eyes with the agent in charge and nodded—that was his final answer.

Prime Minister Maliki, on the other hand, was wobbly. He was embarrassed by the security breach and that one of his countrymen had actually thrown shoes at his guest. Maliki assumed, as I did, that the event would have to be canceled. But President Bush wasn't going to let a two-bit shoe thrower run him out of the room, and he kept Maliki at the podiums and proceeded to call on the reporter that had been interrupted. The reporter was a bit flustered, but he tried to follow the President's lead and proceed as normal.

My face was screaming in pain, but I was silent. When I realized that we weren't leaving right away, I looked for a way out. I wasn't sure what kind of damage the microphone stand had done, but it couldn't be good. I knew the White House medical team was nearby and I needed to get to them. A U.S. Marine came to my rescue. He'd seen me get hit and reached out his hand to pull me up and over the chairs to the door.

But I was still trapped. The Iraqis had shut down the exits and wouldn't let anyone out of the room. They were following orders to secure the crime scene. I took my hand away from covering my eye to show them I needed help. I said, "I need a doctor."

The Iraqi security guard blocking my way lit up with a smile, thumped his chest, and said, "Oh! I am doctor!" wanting to help. (He was one of many professional Iraqis—engineers, physicians, and lawyers—that had taken good-paying security jobs during the war.) He meant well, but I was starting to panic and feel claustrophobic in the small room, the pain throbbing under my eye.

"Um...*my* doctor?" I pleaded. The Marine kept his hand on my back to protect me.

Dr. Richard Tubb, the White House's chief medical officer, was looking for me, too. He'd heard from the President and his agents that I'd been hurt but they didn't know how. He'd quickly checked out the President, and then the President asked him to go find me because he'd seen me crying but didn't know why. In the chaos, Dr. Tubb saw me and got a Secret Service agent to help ease my way into the hall.

Dr. Tubb took a quick look and said, "Oh my," and gave me a plastic bag filled with ice and told me to hold it on the spot. He didn't think the bone was broken, but it was swollen like a robin's egg and he couldn't be sure. I saw the bag was labeled DIARRHEA. I joked with the doctor, "What the heck was in this bag before you put ice in it?" We laughed but it hurt when I smiled. "Ouch," I said and put the bag back up to my eye.

I didn't get to rest for long. A few minutes later when my heartbeat slowed, I suddenly remembered that President Bush was going to be interviewed by ABC's Martha Raddatz. For the same reasons the President wanted to continue the press conference—to project normalcy—I wanted to keep the interview on time despite the chaos. I thought the President needed to be on record as soon as possible to show the folks back home that he was fine, calm, and unbothered by having shoes thrown at his head.

Before I could brief the President, I needed to do his TV makeup. On trips like that with a skeletal staff, I doubled as the makeup artist. I carried a set of powders that he tolerated but wiped off as soon as the cameras were off. I got my kit ready and waited for him in a hold room with the bag of ice still pressed onto my eye.

The President rushed into the room to find me after the press conference. He leaned down and put his arm around me and asked, "What happened? I saw you were crying but I thought it was just because the guy threw a shoe at me." I leaned into him and let myself be comforted for a second, but I tried to lighten the mood and said, "You know I love you, Mr. President—but I grew up out West, and I'm a little tougher than that!"

Then I made him sit down so that I could powder his forehead and nose and run the comb over his hair, asking him mock questions that I thought Martha might ask. He seemed ready to go, "This isn't my first rodeo," he said jokingly. He got through the interview just fine, of course.

After dinner with the Iraqis and U.S. military and embassy personnel, we finally said good-bye and motorcaded to Air Force One. "So, that went *very well*," I said to Gordon, and we just looked at each other, shook our heads, and giggled nervously. We'd planned for everything but flying shoes.

The plane felt like home—and it was safe. The nurse gave me some more Advil and told me to keep the ice on the bruise on the flight to Kabul, Afghanistan. But no one told me not to lie down.

My colleagues wanted to work in the conference room, so I gave up my sofa spot and headed to the staff cabin, which had ten chairs, five on each side of a table where people could eat or work. The chairs were big enough for me to curl up in, but since they'd already turned down the lights and I couldn't see, I grabbed one of the floor mats and a fleece blanket and lay down, huddled against the wall. It was just a few hours to our next stop.

The floor was cold, but I didn't want to move. It hurt when I moved my head, and the area under my eye still throbbed, though not as badly. When the crew served breakfast, I smelled the coffee and started to get up. I returned my mat and blanket to the storage closet and walked into the conference room. I hadn't seen myself yet, but my colleagues' reaction let me know it was bad. They gasped and Mark Thiessen, a Presidential speechwriter and hockey player, put his hands over his mouth. "Oh no, did you lie on your side? All the blood pooled there!" I checked the mirror in the bathroom next door. My eye was pitch-black and the right side of my face was swollen like E.T.

Makeup was useless. Nothing covered the bruise, and my cheek was tender to the touch. I did what I could to look presentable with a sponge bath using the tiny bathroom sink. I put my hair in a clip and changed into warmer clothing. As we were settling into our seats for the landing, the President came to find me and winced when he saw my face. He knew it had to hurt, and it looked terrible. I smiled, though, and said, "I'm fine, no problem, nothing to see here, sir!" I wanted to be tough.

Kabul was freezing. The wind was bitter when we landed around 4:30 a.m. local time at Bagram Air Base, but that didn't stop hundreds of troops from gathering there to greet their Commander in Chief. Watching the troops, I forgot about my eye for a while. They cheered during the President's speech and many of them participated in the reenlistment ceremony right there and then, pledging another four years of military service to their country. They are such remarkable men and women.

We couldn't linger with them, though. We rushed onto Marine One, which was already on the base and was a safer and faster way to travel than by motorcade, to fly to the President's meetings with President Hamid Karzai. Looking out of the window, I saw and smelled lots of cooking fires across the city, which burned my nose and my eyes. Everything looked gray and still. It was like watching a movie in black and white—there were almost no colors.

After we'd flown awhile, a castle suddenly came into view: the Arg (Turkish for "Citadel"). It was built by a king in 1880 and it's where Afghanistan's rulers—both kings and presidents—have resided since. The bricks were a gray color, crumbling in some parts, and there was a moat all around it (but sadly, no dragon). The outside looked medieval, like a castle you'd see in a storybook, yet the inside had been modernized. There were silk-covered sofas, chandeliers, historical artifacts, and artwork by famous Afghans.

Outside the castle, the tallest man I'd ever seen was actually rolling out the red carpets by himself and hurling them up over the castle walls for decoration. We had given them only a few hours' notice that we were coming because of security, so the residence wasn't ready for a visit from the American President. The man looked like Andre the Giant, and I learned he indeed had gigantism just like Andre. He'd been working at the castle since he was a child. His traditional dress would have reached the ground on anyone else, but he was so tall it came up above his knees. I myself barely came up to his waist.

President Bush asked me to walk with him to greet President Karzai. I'd met Karzai before at the White House, and while I knew to be wary of him and of the accusations of corruption, he was quite charming in person. I remembered something General Colin Powell had told me once when we were watching an event at the White House. "Beware of dictators that speak very good English." That was good advice I never forgot.

Karzai had seen the news about the President's trip to Iraq and the shoe throwing, but he hadn't heard that I'd been hurt. When he saw my face, he gasped and grabbed my hands and asked if they could get me anything.

"Don't worry, Mr. President—you should see the other guy," I said.

Karzai threw back his head and laughed, and President Bush rolled his eyes and patted me on the shoulder.

We spent several hours at the palace and the President met

with military commanders, diplomats, and tribal leaders. When the meetings wound down, President Bush asked to see Karzai privately, and I went to find our press pool. I caught up with some of my favorites—three photojournalists I'd worked with for years. They told me about a pact they'd made not to release any photographs of my injury—out of respect for me. That was very kind, and it reflected the good relations my office had with the White House press corps (with only a couple exceptions who shall not be named!).

Of course, when we got back to Washington and I stepped off Marine One, those photographers hadn't agreed to any pact, and the cameras clicked away. By then my black eye looked like a well-earned battle wound, and they got a good look at it before I walked into the West Wing, where the press office staff was gathered to give me hugs and hear all about the trip.

My black eye stayed with me for the last six weeks of the administration, going from black to purple to blue to green to yellow. For many months, my upper cheekbone would ache, especially in the cold. It took a long time to heal.

Other press secretaries have been much more heroic than me, including James S. Brady, who was shot and paralyzed when John Hinckley Jr. tried to kill President Ronald Reagan in 1981. The White House briefing room is named for him. Brady continued a life of public service focusing on proposals for gun control until he died in August 2014.

His injury was real and lasting. I, on the other hand, have the meager distinction of getting the Black Eye of Baghdad. To this day, I'm still the only press secretary that's ever taken a boom mic for the President (and I hope I'm the last), but in a way, it's what all press secretaries do on occasion—take black eyes for the boss. And even on my worst day on the job, the experience of working for the Bush Administration was the very best time of my life.

And the Good News Is...

This book explains the unlikely story of how I became the White House press secretary, the things I witnessed and learned in that job, and how those experiences eventually led me back to what I wanted to do originally—television commentary on politics, policy, and culture.

I was the first and only Republican woman to be the press secretary, and I served during a time of terror threats, two wars, several hard-fought domestic policy debates, mass shootings, Supreme Court nominations, natural disasters, and a major financial crisis. I spoke for the country and the President and was very privileged to do so.

During that time, my goal was to represent America and the President with honor, grace, and dignity. I was cautious in choosing my words and my tone—if I thought President Bush would frown at something I said or how I said it, then I didn't say it. Being prepared, forthcoming, and gracious was important to me. What I said then is a matter of public record, but what I was thinking, feeling, and seeing is what this book is about. These are my personal reflections, the things I remember.

I chose the title *And the Good News Is...* because I say it all the time. I'm an optimistic person, and I want people to realize that in America, nothing is ever as bad as it seems because we have the opportunity and capabilities to fix problems (though we don't always have the will). Optimism has been my coping mechanism for any adversity. "Shoulders back, chin up, smile—you can handle this" is a voice in my head, and that's helped me deal with all sorts of challenges.

My instinct to find the positive in any situation might be found in my DNA. I grew up with a ranching family in Wyoming, a tough, unpredictable life where you rely on a certain faith that everything is going to be all right. Those instincts attracted me to other optimistic people. As a kid, I remember hearing Ronald Reagan and how his words made me feel safe. When he talked about living on the sunshine side of the mountain, I liked that image—it fit me. I was drawn to his approach to leadership and life.

Years later, my own positive outlook served me well when I started briefing the President. He knew that on some days we'd be dealt a tough hand, and he was less interested in hearing how bad it was than how we were going to play it. Over the years that I worked for him he became much more to me than my boss or even the President of the United States. He became like a second father, a friend, and a confidant.

In this book, I write about the strange twists that led me to the Oval Office. Many people assume I grew up active in Republican politics and that I must have known the Bushes or the Cheneys in order to end up in that job. But I never met any of them until after the 9/11 terrorist attacks. I was born in Wyoming, raised in Colorado, and planned to go into television journalism. Instead, in a theme repeated throughout my life, my tendency to plan out my life was disrupted by chance opportunities and my openness to them. How I got my first press secretary job on Capitol Hill, returned to Washington, and ended up as the co-host of *The Five* on Fox News were all because I was at the right place at the right time, prepared, and willing to take a risk. That's the same approach I took when I made the most consequential decision of my life—to talk to a guy I was sitting next to on an airplane (he became my husband).

A section of *And the Good News Is . . .* reveals stories from the Bush Administration that you've not heard before. These are things that I experienced, my eyewitness accounts and my feelings about them—such as how the President stood up for America when there were no cameras to capture it, shared tender moments with wounded warriors, and made decisions based on principle instead of popularity. I recount stories about things that humbled me and others that still make me laugh. I recall the President teaching me how to pass on taking credit for an accomplishment so that someone else could achieve a goal, conspiring with me to make a point when a young woman reporter was treated unfairly, and helping me get over feelings of bitterness by forgiving a betrayal by a former colleague. As I wrote this, I loved reliving those moments.

I also include my reflections on the importance of civility that I learned from my childhood and then from the Bushes, and how it's being lost in politics and pop culture. I worry about how aggressive and vicious our discourse has become. I don't think all is lost, however. I believe that there are ways that we can get our public debates back on track, because civility and manners are a matter of choice. We don't have to own each other's comments, but we are responsible for whatever we say. In America, we are blessed with the freedom to speak our minds—and we should do so thoughtfully. We also have to recognize that people who disagree with us are not enemies. We're all in this together—and we should act like it.

In addition to those sections, this book is an opportunity to share the best work and life advice that I've used in my own career. Because of the high-profile jobs I've held, I'm often asked what I'd suggest young people do in order to be successful (many would like to be the White House press secretary one day). In particular, I've found that young people and their parents are hungry for this type of advice, and across the country the questions are similar: Should I go to graduate or law school? How do I make the transition from being someone's assistant to a management role? What can I do if my boss is a jerk or asks me to do something that I think is unethical? How do you find the perfect work-life balance?

The problem I've had in responding to these questions is that there's never enough time or resources to reach every person one-on-one, and yet I feel guilty if I don't respond. I believe that anyone who has achieved some success is obligated to help others do the same. I had people guide me along the way, and I've got a lot of pent-up advice to give, so this book helps me address that supply and demand problem. I've added as many of the best tips as I can in three sections that can be applied immediately at work, throughout a career, and during a lifetime. If I were a parent, educator, or employer, I'd want my kids and employees to read this section—advice that will stick with them and help them to be more successful, productive, and content.

I believe that a positive outlook and treating others with respect, dignity, and graciousness lead to professional and personal success. It's a no-lose formula. I also learned that my best-laid Type A personality plans have been disrupted for better things—plans I didn't make, but ones I chose to embrace, no matter how difficult or crazy they seemed to be.

I hope that readers of *And the Good News Is...* will conclude that it doesn't matter where you come from—whether you went to an Ivy League school or grew up in a city or on a farm, you can end up advising a President in the Oval Office. No one should think they can't make it to the top because they didn't go to Harvard. I hope people will be inspired by stories of my upbringing, my years in the White House, and my transition to television. It wasn't all sunshine—there have been adverse and humbling experiences that have kept me grounded. But I've had the opportunity to travel the world and to realize just how blessed I am to have been born in America with a family that loves me. As a bonus, I am the proud mother of Jasper, America's Dog—he gets his due in Chapter 4.

And so, let the good news begin....

CHAPTER 1

~~~~~~

Wide-Open Spaces

"Excuse me, ma'am," the Secret Service agent whispered in my ear. "The President needs you at Marine One in ten minutes." No one else in the crowd of fifteen thousand heard him. We were in Norfolk, Virginia, for the commissioning of the USS *George H. W. Bush*, the latest American aircraft carrier in our military's fleet. I wasn't expecting the summons because I thought we had time to watch the speeches. I was trying to soak up the moment—the January air was cold and dry, but the sun was shining so we could all be outside to celebrate the life accomplishments of President George H. W. Bush, the father of the President I worked for, George W. Bush. I was nostalgic because it was one of the last events we'd attend before he left office. The agent's words snapped me out of it.

I didn't want to raise suspicions by a quick reaction, especially not with the media, so I didn't race for the exit. I nodded to the agent and smiled, trying to look unconcerned. It's a good thing I had big sunglasses on because I was worried. Our intelligence had picked up terrorist chatter that the enemy wanted to disrupt events before the Inauguration of President Barack Obama, and what better place to attack than where the major leaders, public servants, and friends and family of the Bushes were gathered? We had an obligation to be paranoid.

Still I played it cool. I waited about thirty seconds before I slipped back into the ship and followed the agent through the steel hallways and out a door that I hadn't seen. I tried to walk at a normal pace. I have short legs, but I've always walked fast—I had to keep up with my mom or I'd be left behind.

Marine One was ready to go. Secretary of State Condi Rice arrived when I did; we climbed aboard and buckled in. A few minutes later, President Bush jogged up the few steps of the chopper. "Let's go see the SEALs," he said before taking his seat and buckling on his seat belt.

Then I got it—this wasn't an emergency. The President just wanted to see his guys one last time as their Commander in Chief. They'd been through a lot together—he'd asked so much of the SEALs, and they'd exceeded his expectations. Few people knew he was coming to visit, and it was closed to the press. This would be their last moment alone together.

Navy SEALs are so cool, and a hangar full of them is awesome. Our staff snuck into the building from a side door and made our way to the back of the crowd as the President got ready to take the stage. The SEALs were listening to a speech by Vice President Dick Cheney when all of a sudden he introduced President Bush. The President hopped up onto the stage, shook hands with the Vice President, and took in the scene. The SEALs hooted and hollered with patriotism and appreciation.

The President addressed the crowd—the East Coast SEALs including DEVGRU (aka SEAL Team Six). He thanked them for all of the missions they'd completed after the attacks on 9/11. He spoke without notes and from the heart. He finished with "God bless you, and may God continue to bless America," and they cheered for a long time, ignoring his pleas to stop. That was an order they didn't have to obey. The President had tears in his eyes, and so did I.

After his speech, President Bush shook hands with every one of them and posed for pictures they could send to their families and friends. All of the young men had really long beards, so it wasn't hard to figure out where in the world they were about to be deployed (and it wasn't Indiana). The jackets and ties they were wearing for the President's visit would soon be switched out for their combat uniforms.

It's very humbling to be around Navy SEALs. Their courage and bravery surpasses anything I'd ever thought of doing. They're remarkably unselfish, honorable, strong, and courageous. They made me feel safe. I loved watching their interaction with President Bush. There's nothing like the bond that can develop between a Commander in Chief and his troops. That day, as the President was about to turn over his command to President-elect Obama, the SEALs were giving President Bush as much gratitude and encouragement as he was trying to give to them.

I faded into the background, but two SEALs came over to me and said, "Pardon us, ma'am, but are you the press secretary?" I was honored they even recognized me. I stuck out my hand to introduce myself and thanked them for serving, and they asked if they could get their picture taken with me.

As one of their guys got his camera phone ready, I tried making some small talk.

I asked the first guy, "So what was it that made you want to become a Navy SEAL—chance for adventure? Family tradition? Physical challenge? Desire to see the world?"

"Oh no, ma'am. Chicks dig it," he said.

"Even with the beard?" I asked.

"Oh yeah...they get it," he said. He was confident of that, and I believed him.

I then asked the second SEAL, "When you get ready to go...
wherever it is you may be going...do you have to take a lot of language courses?"

"Oh no, ma'am, we're really not there to talk," he said. Indeed.

We laughed and smiled for the cameras. They thanked me for
my service, a compliment I accepted but it didn't compare to theirs.

We got back on Marine One, and I told President Bush what
the SEALs told me about chicks and language classes. He threw his
head back and laughed. Then he looked out the window, bit the side
of his cheek, and jutted out his jaw a little to the side—an expression
I saw him make when he was letting a feeling or a thought settle in.

"God, I love those guys," he said.

To President Bush, those guys were the true celebrities. He felt a
responsibility for and a kinship to them. They understood the global
war on terror and were in sync with him as their leader. He asked for
their sacrifices, and they were eager to fulfill their pledge and commitment to their country. They would miss each other.

That was my last flight on Marine One. I was thirty-six, and it was
as unlikely a place I ever thought I'd be. I'd grown up modestly in
rural America with clear blue skies and lots of sunshine. I was raised
to believe that America was a force for good in the world and that it
should take its leadership role seriously. I understood early on that
the freedom of America is what made our way of life possible, and
that we should help other people live in freedom, too.

My upbringing in the West can sound very unusual, as if from
another place and time, and my path to the White House wasn't
exactly a straight line. My family didn't donate a lot of money to
campaigns, nor did they have any connections that helped me get
my first job in media or politics.

I didn't have a plan to be the White House press secretary, but looking back, I can see how my life experiences built up to that career achievement. So when I try to explain how someone like me ended up working in a place like that, I have to start at the beginning—on a ranch.

Wyoming and Origins

I was born in Evanston, Wyoming. Most people have never been to my home state or even heard of my hometown. And most people in Wyoming prefer to keep the state's beauty their little secret.

My parents, Leo Ernest Perino and Janice Marie Brooks, were born in Wyoming, too. When I was nearly two years old, they moved to Denver, Colorado, but they took us to Wyoming so often that when I'm asked where I'm from, I say Colorado and Wyoming, as if it were one state. Colorado-Wyoming is a place that makes me feel grounded, steady, and content. Far from shedding my Western roots since I moved away at twenty-two, I've clung to them.

The West is where I learned about independence, self-reliance, patriotism, and the blessings of freedom. It's where I first galloped on a horse on a cattle drive and watched my family brand their cows, make hay bales, and farm fields of oats. We knew we had a special life experience that most people in America could never imagine. We felt sorry for city dwellers, the poor fellas.

In the Black Hills, the canyons are filled with big black pines that grow tall and sturdy despite wicked winds, nasty blizzards, and raging forest fires. They dig way down deep into the red dirt and hold on no matter what—one season is too dry, the next too wet. That's how Wyoming life is, too—you learn to adapt in order to thrive. And people that live that kind of life wouldn't have it any other way.

The Black Hills are ancient but they shaped my family's future early in the twentieth century. Leaving their homes in Italy, my great-grandparents walked into one side of the American Dream and just over a hundred years later, I walked out of the other side as the White House press secretary. They never would have imagined that.

My surname, Perino, is Italian. My great-grandparents on my father's side were born in the Piemonte Province, near Torino. They were poor farm workers with little hope of a better lifestyle. They were part of a wave of Italian immigrants who left Italy in the late 1800s, escaping poverty for an opportunity to take a chance, start over, and have something to show for their hard work.

They didn't speak English well—in fact, my great-grandmother, Rosi, spoke very little and had almost no formal education. She relied on the kindness of people to get her from Ellis Island to Coal City, Illinois, in late 1901, where her sister ran a boardinghouse. When she arrived in the States, she told authorities that she was a maid from Mezze, Italy, and reported that she had $15 to her name. She eventually moved to Cambria, Wyoming, and met my great-grandfather, Jacinto "Matteo" Perino, where he worked as a coal miner. They'd actually lived only three miles from each other in Italy, but never met.

They married in 1904 and pledged to work a homestead in Newcastle, Wyoming, under the government's Enlarged Homestead Act, where you could get 320 acres for free if you built a structure that had four walls and at least one glass window and agreed to farm the land for five years. On weekends, my great-grandfather dug a mile-long channel from a spring to the homestead and fixed the place up enough to move his bride to their new home.

Distant relatives and new friends and family moved into neighboring areas in the Black Hills. They farmed and raised a few cattle, but most of them also worked in the coal mines called Cambria Camp. At the same time, my great-uncle Pete reportedly had a full-scale moonshine operation in a box canyon (a ravine with three steep walls) on his place and would smuggle it in wagons to Deadwood, South Dakota, to sell. My great-grandfather would buy a load of grapes every year and make his own wine, too. I don't know if he sold any, but I'm sure it was a nice vintage by Wyoming standards.

While my great-grandfather worked the mines, my great-grandmother ran the ranch. She was strong of heart, mind, and body. She gave birth to seven children and six survived—a daughter died of pneumonia at six months. It's said that people in the area relied on my great-grandmother and that she helped with many births in Newcastle. My great-grandfather died of black lung in the 1960s, and she must have felt sad and lonely after their major life adventure moving to the frontier together and building such a good life for their family.

My great-grandmother lived to be 100 years old, so I got to know her. She always sent us birthday cards that had $2 bills inside—we kept them for good luck. In her later years, my grandparents set her up with a house in town and she would visit with friends and family, watch soap operas, and braid throw rugs out of Wonder Bread plastic sacks. She had a garden in the backyard, and when we visited, she made sure we ate a lot. "STRONG!" she would say, making a muscle. From her front porch we could watch the Weston County parades on the Fourth of July and race around trying to get as much candy as we could that was thrown from the cowboys on horseback and rodeo queens in fancy pickup trucks.

I had a lot of pride in my great-grandmother, even though because of the language gap, we didn't really communicate that much. We lived 350 miles away from one another and I didn't think of her daily, but we had a special connection. When I was fourteen, I had a dream right before I woke up one morning that I can still remember. In the dream, my great-grandmother was with my sister and me in an office building in Denver. She went to get into an elevator, and I tried to pull her back because I knew the elevator had no floor. But I didn't reach her in time and she stepped into the space and I watched her fall all the way down. She didn't scream.

The next morning, I started to tell my mom about my dream and she interrupted me and said, "Your dad just got a call—your great-grandmother died in the night." I believe Great-Grandma Rosi was saying good-bye to us in that dream—nothing else can explain it.

My grandpa, Leo Perino Sr., was born at the homestead in 1921, the second youngest. His childhood sounded like one out of a storybook—one with a good ending. Up at the ranch they had cold winters and hot summers, and he spent his time riding horses, studying, and doing chores. He spoke Italian at home and English at school. Once when we asked him for more chewing gum, he told us about how when he was a kid they could make gum last for months by placing it on the bedpost at night (it wasn't exactly walking uphill both ways to school, but the message was the same). But he always gave us more.

As a young man, he served in the Marines in World War II and he fought in the Pacific. Surviving war on tropical islands, he contracted some type of skin rash. My dad remembers in the 1950s going with him as a young boy to VA hospitals in Cheyenne and Denver. Each time it took forever for him to get an appointment. His ailment was bad and the only thing that helped was Baby Magic Lotion, but I never heard him complain about it.

The war ended, and my grandfather sailed through the Panama Canal and pulled into port at his base in Philadelphia. His first night back, some friends wanted to set him up on a blind date with this nursing student they knew. He said no to a blind date. She similarly refused the suggestion. But the friends prevailed and a great love story began. Within a couple of months of that first date, my grandmother, who had never been west of the Mississippi River, left Philadelphia for a ranching life in the rural countryside of the Black Hills.

My grandmother's name was Victoria Thelma Potts Smith Perino, and she went by Vicky. She was born in Pennsylvania and her dad worked in a coal mine. When she was very young, he hurt his back at work and could no longer take care of all the children. To help the family, the Methodist minister got involved and arranged an adoption by the Smith family of my grandmother and her sister. They were well taken care of, and she and her sister remained close all their lives. My grandmother decided to become a nurse and was finishing her training when she met my grandfather.

Love at first sight wasn't in her plan, and she was a bit concerned about taking my grandpa home to meet her parents because Italians at the time were distrusted and disliked. However, her parents were very supportive of the match, and with their blessing, my grandfather asked her to marry him. She said yes.

The East Coast was not for him. Having felt like he'd traveled and seen enough, my grandpa wanted to go home to the ranch in Wyoming. Vicky readily agreed, even without knowing what ranching life would be like. They took the train back to Newcastle to introduce her to the Perinos.

My great-grandparents must have liked Vicky because after the wedding at the Methodist church they met the newlyweds at the ranch gate and gave them $100 (quite a lot of money in those times). But some of the other family members and people in the area were concerned that my grandfather had just brought in someone they basically considered a foreigner and "Weren't the local girls good enough for him?" I see it as kind of a Wyoming version of *Romeo and Juliet*—they were meant to be together even if some didn't think so. Over time, my grandmother more than earned her place among the hardworking women of Wyoming and became a local girl. She worked as a nurse in town and helped run the ranch in the mornings, evenings, and every weekend.

Through the years, my grandfather and his siblings grew the ranch in acreage. There was a homesteader who acquired a great deal of land throughout the Depression. After he died, his ranch was to be sold but no one in his family had the money to buy it all. Many families went in on a transaction to buy the ranch and parcel it out.

That's when Rosi and Matteo's children, Aunt Dora, Uncles Joe and Fred, and my grandfather bought a large part of that ranch and formed "the outfit," a Western term that encompasses everything on a ranch and its owners. The outfit stayed together for quite some time, but as happens in families, disagreements occurred and it was split up in the mid-1960s or so. My grandpa had started moving away from farming as the mainstay and converted to ranching—cattle and horses for the most part. At its largest, through my uncle Matt's work, the ranch was 50,000 acres, almost three times the size of Manhattan, where I live now.

My grandparents had three sons—my dad, Leo Jr., and my uncles Matt and Tom. Today, my dad lives in Denver. Matt continues to ranch in Newcastle, with his high school sweetheart, Donna, and their two sons, Wade and Preston. My uncle Tom, the very picture of an American cowboy, died from cancer in 2006, and his part of the ranch is still worked by his widow, Janet, and their family.

The ranch house sat at the bottom of a red-dirt hill at the end of a canyon. It was above the other structures—an old-fashioned red barn, a series of white-painted fenced corrals, a cellar for potatoes and other vegetables, a chicken house, and storage sheds. The soil around the ranch was red, almost like clay.

I loved the barn. It was large with several stalls for horses or cows, and a hayloft on the second level. It had been painted red with white trim years before I was a kid so the color was slightly faded. Tools, whips, and halters hung on the walls by the workbench. In the winter, sometimes my grandpa and uncles had to go down and help a cow that was having difficulty giving birth. They'd wrap chains around the legs of the calf and pull, doing all they could to ensure that the mother cow and the calf were healthy at the end of their ordeal. It was messy but rewarding work. My sister and I never had to muck out the stalls, and we felt bad that we weren't expected to, but we never volunteered for the job either.

I used to go down the hill to the barn and climb up to the top of the fence that lined the barnyard and take a look around. I knew it was a special place, and it's where I was most content. We were the center of our own universe, and the adults reminded us over and over to be appreciative of what we had.

It wasn't all work on the ranch. Morning chores gave way to afternoon fun. Under the porch of the house, my cousins and I played with mini versions of the trucks, combines, and tractors the adults used on the ranch. Some of the toys were so old that my dad and uncles remembered them from when they were kids.

We had other amusements, too—my grandfather bought us an Olympic-sized trampoline that he set up in the storage shed while the big combine was used in the summer. My uncle Tom was the best jumper—he could do tons of tricks and he'd bounce us as high as we wanted until our moms threatened to scream if he didn't stop. Then he'd bounce us one more time just to drive them crazy.

The real magic of the ranch, however, was in the other residents—the animals. Quarter horses, cattle, chickens, goats, pigs, dogs, and kittens—all under my grandparents' care—and then there were the coyotes and snakes that we learned to avoid. For years, peacocks roamed the area, and my grandmother had a vase that held all of the big feathers that we picked up for her around the property.

And always there were dogs. My grandfather mostly raised collies and Australian shepherds, but also the occasional mutt or housedog. My family trained the dogs themselves, to obey, work, and even do some neat tricks. My grandpa had several whistles that the dogs understood and they'd signal what job they were expected to do next (gather the mares, round up the cows, hop in the back). The livestock learned what the whistles meant, too, especially if there was cake involved (like a PowerBar but for cows and horses).

One of the most majestic of the shepherds was Blue. He never stepped inside the house even if it was 40 degrees below zero and he was invited to come in from the cold. He was too proud to go in (quite a different life from Jasper's in Manhattan). The other dogs cut him a wide berth and let him eat first.

My uncle Matt and my aunt Donna owned another family favorite, a tricolored Australian shepherd named Robin. She had only one blue eye because when she was a puppy a horse had kicked out the other one. One time we grandkids were playing with Robin outside our uncle Tom's double-wide trailer on a summer afternoon. All of a sudden Robin yelped and howled. A rattlesnake had bitten her.

Matt and Donna tried to save her and raced down the gravel road to get to a vet in Sundance, but Robin died on the way. Meanwhile, Tom got his rifle and blew the rattlesnake's head off so that no one else would be hurt by it. I felt so sad for my aunt and uncle because Robin was like one of their children—she had been their first baby. I was also frightened because the snake could have bitten any of us.

My grandpa's last dogs were Ray and Floyd. They ran as a pair.

They'd just sit in the yard waiting to be asked to work, and they'd beat you to the pickup if they saw you leave the house. They hated to be left behind. If their services weren't needed, they'd run off and have an adventure. When they came back, they'd be filthy and panting. Lord knows what they got up to out there. They didn't seem to be afraid of anything, but why would they be when they had my grandfather's permission to rule the hills?

We made our dogs a part of our games, like hide-and-seek. We'd sit in the back of the pickups with them and hold on to their collars while they put their heads over the sides and sniffed the air as we rolled down the road. I was taught the simple pleasures of the love of a dog from early as a kid—and the dogs I've raised with Peter—Henry and Jasper—have given me some of the greatest joys and best memories of my life.

Even after we moved, to keep the connection to Wyoming, my mom and dad would take my sister and me to the ranch several times a year. From Denver, it was about a seven-hour drive. We spent every Christmas and Easter holiday and our summer vacations there.

Since my sister and I didn't live at the ranch full-time, we didn't have specific chores. My cousins, on the other hand, had a lot of responsibilities. We'd helped them out by filling the water tanks, feeding calves in the winter, and opening or closing gates. I'd do anything to get out of having to pick eggs. The chicken coop scared me—it was dark and smelly and the hens would peck me when I reached my hands in to get the eggs. To keep our cousins happy, we found that the best way for us to help was to either take specific direction from them or stay out of their way.

There were also ancient creatures to check out. As a kid, I loved learning about dinosaurs, so in the summers my dad would take us digging for belemnite fossils in a canyon road about a mile from the ranch. Belemnites were squid-like creatures that lived when the Black

Hills were under an ocean over 250 million years ago. They were long-tailed and bullet-shaped. When we found one of their fossils, we would put it in a tin Folgers coffee can to take back to the ranch house to show my grandparents. They always seemed impressed.

In the winter when it snowed, my grandfather would put the wooden sleds into the back of one of his pickups (he was a Chevy man), and we'd pile into the cab. Then he'd drive us to the top of one of the big hills not far from the house. We'd get on our uncles' sleds because they were heavy enough to give us a real ride, and we'd land in a big gulley that had double the snow. It was like flying and probably quite dangerous by today's standards.

My grandpa didn't make us walk up the hill to have another go; instead, he watched us slide down and then he'd drive down to the bottom to pick us up and take us back to the top. When we'd had our fun and started to feel the cold, my grandpa would get on the CB radio and call my grandma to tell her to get the hot chocolate and marshmallows ready.

When I was really young, my walkie-talkie handle was Big Bird and my sister's was Cookie Monster. Sometimes a trucker driving in the area would hear us on the radio and call out to us. With our grandpa's permission, we'd ask where he was headed, what he was hauling, and wish him a safe journey.

While we played with the radio, my family used it for work—it kept them informed about what was happening in the area. In the hot dry summers, they'd listen for reports of lightning strikes because one hit could turn into a full-blown forest fire. All of the neighbors pitched in to help one another contain or put out fires when they started.

My grandfather had a yellow fire truck that the Weston County firefighters acquired from the U.S. military as surplus equipment.

My grandpa let my sister and me go with them as long as we stayed in the backseat. It was such a privilege that we didn't dare move, and what I learned on those emergencies came in handy later at the White House when I was the spokesperson for the President's Healthy Forests Initiative. I was one of the few people in Washington that had actually seen the problem of overgrown brush up close.

In the evenings, my grandpa would make us root beer or Pepsi floats, or we'd have some watermelon from his garden. We ate well, always a salad of cucumbers, onions, and tomatoes with olive oil and vinegar dressing and beef of some cut—usually cooked well without marinade. Sometimes there was a chocolate cake my grandma made or vanilla ice cream that was delivered by the Schwan Man, a grocery catalog delivery service.

The noontime meal was called "dinner," and it was the main meal of the day. A big bell next to the gate leading to the house alerted the family that the food was ready. After eating, my uncles would take a bit of a nap with their hats covering their faces on the couch in the winter and out in the front yard in the summer. After about thirty minutes, they'd be back outside baling hay, gathering cows, shoeing horses, or fixing a tractor. No wonder they were so fit.

If the ranch seems like a bit of Americana to you, I would agree. And we weren't the only ones who thought so. In the 1970s, a couple of men scouting locations for some ads for Marlboro cigarettes drove up to the ranch. They were hoping to find an outfit that had cattle and horses that they could work with to film the ads. My family agreed to help them and everyone worked in the background to help during the photo shoots.

My uncle Matt recalls that the Marlboro Men weren't just models with pretty faces who wore a pair of Wranglers well—they were good cowboys, too, with skills and experience. My aunt Donna would feed them when they were visiting and she even gave them haircuts out on location. I got to hang with them one day, but I wasn't smart enough to get their autographs.

As a part-time city slicker, I could still ride a horse, and that was my favorite thing to do. When my grandpa knew I was coming up for a visit, he'd have my uncles go get Sally, my pony, so that she'd be in the corral when I arrived. The first thing I did was climb on her back, hold on to her mane, and kick her gently in the ribs to get going. She'd walk slowly around the arena where my uncles and cousins practiced their rodeo skills. My grandpa said I was a pretty good horsewoman, and that was the highest of compliments in my book.

Sally was just a pony, but there were majestic horses, too. Jet was my grandpa's pride and joy. He was a Triple AAA racehorse from southeast Texas that my grandpa wanted to cross with his quarter horse mares to give his colts some additional size and speed. The plan worked very well. My grandpa had his annual horse auction for around forty years and sold horses to people in every state in America and even to folks in a couple of foreign countries.

Once after taking Jet for one of his planned liaisons with a mare, my grandparents stopped at our house in Denver and Jet got to eat some city grass in our backyard. I was the envy of every neighborhood kid, and I lapped it up. When Jet died at nearly thirty years old, he got a special burial up on the hill that you could see from the picture window in the kitchen.

But not every animal was a pet. My uncles Matt and Tom were always trying to toughen up my cousins—Wade, Preston, Jill, Jared, and Logan—and every so often during dinner they'd remark on the steak we were eating, and say, "Well, Wade, your ol' steer Biscuit sure turned into some good eatin'!" I never knew if they were serious, but I felt bad for my cousins who, younger than me, bit their lips and tried hard not to react. Cowboys and cowgirls don't cry (much).

That was the reality of ranching life, and so was care for the animals—even the undomesticated ones. In the summers, my grandfather would create big slash piles of timber and brush that he cleared out of the forest. Those piles were supposed to be burned down, but my grandfather in his later years didn't set the fires because he didn't want the critters to be homeless. I loved that about him—he even protected the bunnies.

I'll admit, it all sounds very Laura Ingalls Wilder. But it wasn't always that way. We had to learn the hard lessons of ranching life, too. Once when I was about eight years old and my sister was only four, we were passengers in my grandpa's pickup along the gravel road that led back to the ranch house. We liked to tell him all about the Smurfs and he pretended he could see little blue creatures with white hats up in the hills. I knew he was kidding and I went along with it for my sister's benefit. We were having a great time, but when we came to a cattle guard along the road, he saw that one of his quarter horses had fallen through and broken its leg. The horse was in great pain and whimpering, his eyes rolling back into his head.

My grandfather pulled over and was reaching for the rifle that hung securely in the back window before he came to a full stop. He told my sister and me to get down on the floorboards of the pickup, locked eyes with me, and said, "And don't look up, okay?" I nodded.

I made sure my sister was covering her eyes and looking down, but I didn't completely obey. I knew I wasn't supposed to, but I stole a glance at him. Framed in the window of the pickup, I saw his profile—strong nose, cowboy hat, tanned skin, blue eyes, and glasses. A tear rolled down his cheek right before he pulled the trigger.

I choked back a cry and swallowed it so that I didn't make anything worse or get in trouble for looking up. When he got back into the vehicle, he made us stay down until we'd passed the herd. As we drove up the road, he called ahead on the radio to my uncles to let them know what happened. Then he rested his hand on my knee and gave it a squeeze, and I felt a bit of his character seeping into me. I learned from him that strength and gentleness go hand in hand.

My grandfather was slow to anger, but one winter my cousin Wade really got into trouble. The temperatures had been below zero for days and the grandkids were responsible for mixing up formula, putting the milk into bottles, and carrying them down to feed the calves whose moms had rejected them or died during the birth. We poured the leftover warm milk into huge cast-iron skillets and placed it on the barn floor for the cats. We repeated this process in the afternoon.

One day just before sunset when we got to the barn, we found that a little kitten had climbed into the warm milk and sunk down to his shoulders like a Calgon bath. The problem was that during the day the milk had frozen around him and the kitten was stuck by the time we arrived. Wade was really young and he picked up the skillet and started twirling it around his head making whooping sounds. Well, just then my grandpa came around the corner into the barn-yard and saw what was happening.

Wade got in so much trouble. He ended up with extra chores for a week, but the most awful part for Wade was letting down my grandfather. That was the worst punishment. My grandpa's lesson to us that day was that every beating heart deserved respect, especially the vulnerable that are in our care. Even when we killed a spider, he told us to make it quick and never let it suffer. Like most country people I've known, he had a real bond with the animals under his care. He knew his own life—his family's livelihood—was tied to the animals' safety and well-being. And he was a bit of a softy.

My favorite time of year was the cattle drive. It was better than anything you've ever seen in a movie. Every June, my family and friends from the community gathered together to take the little calves and their mothers up to the green pastures in South Dakota for summer grazing. My grandpa had to coordinate with the train conductor to make sure that we had enough time to get all the cattle across safely.

We departed the ranch at 4 a.m. As he and I sat on our horses watching the last coal train go by before we started the drive, he said, "There they go again, carting off Wyoming's resources for all the people back East." My grandpa was a real conservationist—people who work the land usually are.

I returned to the ranch as often as I could after college, though my visits were fewer than I'd have liked. It takes an entire day to travel to the old homestead, and once I started working, I had few vacation days to take. One June after Peter and I were married, we went for one of the spring cattle drives. At the end of it, we finished scattering the calves and their mamas around the pasture and we headed back, galloping in a line, like the opening of *Bonanza*. It felt like freedom: blue sky, tall green grass, and working the land with love for one another and patriotism toward our country. Even my British husband felt more American that day than any other. Plus he earned faint praise from my uncles, who said, "Peter's a good hand... from the wrist down."

The truth was Peter really could ride and he took direction well. He enthusiastically volunteered for the hardest chores, including barreling into the forest to find a lost calf and going out to break ice for the cattle's watering holes in the middle of the winter. They liked how he didn't let the hazing get to him. He gave back as many barbs as he got and had all of us laughing with his English accent. "Move along, ladies!" he yelled at the cows, and it all sounded so proper. And every time he left the house, he'd toss a little bit of cat food into Preston's boots. "Damn you, Peter!" he'd yell when he slipped his foot in and stepped on the kibble. Once we took a friend with us on a drive, and after a couple of hours she asked, "Is everyone's middle name God Dammit?!"

As I got older, I started to learn more about economics and politics from my grandpa Perino. He served as a county commissioner and was on the local Weston County Fair Board, which oversaw the Junior Rodeo. I saw him on more than one occasion bid up a youngster's steer so that he could boost their confidence. Sometimes he ended up paying more than he intended.

My grandpa didn't like the taste of alcohol and told me that at meetings he'd accept a drink and then pour it into a plant when no one was looking. Every day he recorded his observations about the weather—temperature, precipitation, wind, and anything else of note, which he'd then compare to the *Farmer's Almanac*. In the evenings, he'd flip through the newspapers or quarter horse catalogs and he'd try to teach me things. He was the first to tell me about bovine spongiform encephalopathy, commonly known as mad cow disease, because he was worried that some practices other ranchers were using could lead to its spread. When news of a BSE outbreak hit the papers years later, I was the only staffer in my Capitol Hill office that had ever heard of it. My ranching background often helped me in my work in Washington.

I watched all of the news with my grandparents when I visited the ranch—*Good Morning America*, *Today Show*, *CBS This Morning*, and then any local news from Rapid City, South Dakota, or Denver (which wasn't very local but it provided a good weather forecast for the region). I would hear the TV early in the mornings and knew it was time to get up before I was yelled at by my uncles for sleeping in. The sun never rose before my family did, and everyone hit the hay soon after the sun went down, too. I've kept an early bedtime ever since, even though I've lived in cities and worked in jobs that required lots of late nights.

In the 1980s, I recall listening to political discussions—about death taxes and government spending, foreign oil, communism, the Bureau of Land Management and the Endangered Species Act, the mining companies and the EPA, the USDA, and on and on. I learned by absorbing thoughts and observing the arguments. I suppose that's where the conservative values I hold now took root.

In Wyoming, you learned quickly that everyone had to pull his or her own weight, and that paying attention was key to protecting everyone's safety. You were no better than anyone else, and showing off was the surest way to lose friends. Helping out a neighbor was second nature, and the kindness went both ways. At the ranch, you were the blessed recipient and the cursed landowner depending on what Mother Nature had in store. No one sat at a desk all day—the saddle was the office chair.

I also grew up watching a true love story. My grandpa adored my grandmother. He called her Mother and she called him Dad. She didn't mind that he snored like crazy at night. They didn't snap or bicker. They were kind to each other and accepting of flaws. She'd run him a bath and set out his clothes for his meetings in town, and he'd rub her shoulders and tease her to make her laugh. They adored their grandchildren and on Sundays we'd sit between them in the pickup and take a drive all around the ranch.

On the last cattle drive before my grandfather died, I remember seeing them sitting off to the side under a tree during our stop for a picnic lunch. After all those years, they still only wanted to spend some time alone. I'd been married only a short while, and I thought if I could just capture that for a few minutes now and then with my husband, Peter, then I'd have a good marriage, too.

For years, my grandfather had heart trouble and he carried around a little Bayer pill in his cowboy shirt pocket, just in case he needed it. It sat next to his Life Savers mints, Big Red gum, and Jolly

Ranchers. But on the day after Thanksgiving in 2001, my grandfather was moving cows from one pasture to the next when he had a major heart attack. The Bayer pill never would have helped at that point, and despite my cousin's efforts to revive him, my grandfather died, just two miles from where he was born.

Two months later I got a job at the White House. He never knew I went on to be the press secretary, but I think he would have approved. It was by his example that I kept in mind that speaking with graciousness, class, and poise was the most effective way to communicate and to keep your self-respect.

My grandmother died in 2010, after suffering from dementia and diabetes. But what really led to her death was being a widow. Her heart gave out emotionally after my grandpa died. She loved us all very much, but she lived for him.

The life my grandparents had was thoroughly American. They built a small ranch into a huge operation and fulfilled my great-grandparents' dreams. Theirs was a different era—not without its problems and mistakes—but a simpler time of contentment and patriotism. And that was just on my father's side.

My mom's family history is a little less clear to me because her grandparents died before she was born. But we know that one grandmother, Lena Marie von Pertz, left Germany at age fourteen to come to America. She was a pianist and passed on that talent to my mom. The rest of her grandparents were born in America in the Midwest—Kansas, Missouri, and Illinois.

As with many people during the Depression, my grandmother Dorothy ("Dot") was orphaned at age fourteen in Kansas and eventually sent to live with an aunt and uncle in Rawlins, Wyoming, where she met my grandfather, Thomas Brooks. He was born "Thomas Texas

Ranger Brooks" in Port Lavaca, Texas (I love that). He changed his name to Thomas Raymond Brooks when he went into the military.

After my maternal grandfather moved to Wyoming, he joined the Army in 1943 to fight in World War II. He fought in Germany, where his mother had been born. Back in the States, my grandmother worked as a "Rosie the Riveter" and darned wool socks to send to the soldiers. Those must have been cold and lonely winters while she waited for news from the front lines about his safety. She saved enough money to buy a car, and when he got home from the war, they drove to Niagara Falls for their honeymoon in 1946. My mom was born in 1947. So I'd say it was a successful trip.

My grandfather had good business sense. He first worked for City Steam Laundry after the war and then was a banker with Rawlins National Bank. Later, he owned a business, the Thomas R. Brooks Insurance Agency. He was the sole proprietor of a gas station and an apartment building. The last business he owned was the Uptown Motel, which was on I-80 and got a lot of trucking traffic. He was on the school board and there's a street named after him out by the town cemetery. My mom said her father taught her to have a firm handshake, repeat folks' names and look into their eyes, and to ask questions and be interested in their lives. She said that was the key to all the marketing she did in her career.

When we didn't go to the ranch on holidays or school breaks, we went to see my mom's parents in Rawlins, Wyoming. Rawlins is on I-80, and it doesn't really draw you outside. It's one of the windiest places in the country. And since we didn't have video games or computers, we played a lot of cards at the kitchen table—Kings in the Corner, Crazy Eights, Slap Jack, and War. Occasionally we went to eat at the Lariat, the best Mexican food for miles. There was a theater on Main Street that only showed one movie at a time, which was changed maybe every month. My aunt Patty Sue would take us to see movies like *Back to the Future* and *Crusoe*. We shopped the sidewalk sales on Main Street and took drives to the Snowy Range in the summers.

We watched a lot of TV in my grandmother's living room. She called the sofa a "davenport," the cushions were like bricks, and the fabric pricked at our legs when we wore shorts. My sister and I chose to share one of the large La-Z-Boy recliners and she took the other. When the news was on, my grandmother often remarked on President Reagan's good looks. "He sure has a good head of hair," she sighed (my grandfather did not).

The little things that I remember about my grandmother left a strong impression on me. I loved how she signed her name, Dorothy, on a card with just a dot. She let us pick out all of the marshmallows from the Lucky Charms box and throw away the cereal. She always made pies and would bake an extra crust with cinnamon sugar for us to share. Cookie dough was our weakness, and she'd let us scrape the bowl and alternated which one of us got to lick the spoon.

At Christmas, my grandmother carefully decorated scores of cookies that she gave away. She was detail-oriented and every Santa had blue eyes, a silver bell, and a coconut beard. She had a big showing at the school carnival, and people would make a beeline for her cookies, pies, and cakes, which were the prizes for a game called Musical Pies. (We gotta bring this game back...Music was played while people walked around the table, and when the music stopped, whatever was by their side was what they won.)

My grandmother may have been in a one-and-a-half-horse town, but she knew fashion. When she dressed up for a special occasion in a black dress, hose, heels, and her fur coat (which I now have), she looked great. She kept up with beauty trends through *Better Homes and Gardens* and *Woman's Day* magazines. On her dressing table she kept Jergens Rose Milk Lotion, a glass jar of Oil of Olay, and White Shoulders perfume. My grandfather kept her supplied with that, and my mom has her last bottle, unopened.

She also made sure my mom and aunt's dolls were in style, sewing a complete wardrobe for every doll they ever received. She sewed after her daughters went to bed so that they'd get a morning surprise in the light blue trunk that held all of their doll clothes. She made my mom's clothes, too, including her wedding dress.

My grandma loved to sing to my mom's piano playing and she danced the Charleston in the kitchen while she waited for a pot to boil, holding a wooden spoon as her dancing partner. When my parents moved from Wyoming to Denver when I was just two years old, my mom would set the timer on the oven and let us make an expensive long-distance phone call to talk with her. Hers was the second telephone number I memorized after our own and I still know it.

My grandfather died when I was around ten years old, and unfortunately many of my memories of him are of when he was getting cancer treatment. He used to let my sister and I grind up his pills in the mortar and pestle that they kept on the kitchen table. I don't remember him ever complaining—he seemed resigned to his illness. He was on oxygen for a while and after one surgery had to use a device held to his throat when he wanted to say something because radiation had made it difficult to talk. He sounded like Yoda. He liked having us around, and he was generous to his daughters. He used to slip $20 bills into my mom's pockets that she'd find later.

My grandparents had a traditional relationship—old-fashioned in a good way. For example, my grandfather had been the book-keeper of the family, and by the time he died, my grandmother had never written a check. That was natural in their partnership— he took care of paying the bills and she ran the house and helped manage the businesses. Far from being overly dependent, she put her trust in him. I learned from that example that there is freedom in sharing a responsibility and not trying to control everything. That's one of the ways that Peter and I have made our marriage work, too.

My grandmother was a sad widow, but she rallied by visiting us a lot and taking ceramics and knitting classes. She was a talented artist and even surprised herself with her results. We still have the blankets, chip and dip bowl, cookie jar, and a pie plate that she made for us.

She also spent a lot of time visiting the senior citizens home in Rawlins called "The Manor." She and four friends from ceramics class formed the "Popcorn Gang," a group that would make popcorn every week and eat and talk with the residents. The Popcorn Gang was such a fixture in the community that it got a mention in my grandmother's obituary. She died from cancer in 1988 when I was still in high school.

I believe that the war affected my grandparents' approach to life, and I learned from them to appreciate how good America is compared with the rest of the world. Their patriotism was subtle. My grandfather didn't talk much about the war, and in fact, most of what we know about his bravery we learned about after he died and went through his trunks. But I remember how he stood with his cap over his heart during the parades through town, and I've always been proud to be the granddaughter of two World War II veterans.

The war perhaps changed my grandparents, but mostly for the good. Grandma and Grandpa had the confidence to risk their savings to start small businesses in Rawlins, and they invested wisely. It was clear they relied on each other to help raise their family and keep the customers happy at the same time. Because of hard work, they moved up solidly to the middle class. But I don't think money motivated them. From what I remember, they mostly enjoyed the little things— eating my grandma's pot roast and cherry pie and then playing cards at the kitchen table, where we knocked to let the next person know it was their turn. Those are the best memories from Rawlins. They're the best kind of memories—the ones that remind you that there were strong, caring people who helped make you who you are.

Mom and Dad

My mom, Janice Marie Brooks, was the older of two. Her younger sister is my aunt Patty Sue. They pitched in to help at the motel my grandparents owned, but they had a lot of time for school and play. My mom liked sports and played basketball, softball, and tennis—she'd try anything. She was also a clarinet player in the marching band.

One of my favorite stories of her childhood was about when the Rawlins High School football team had traveled to another town to play a game and the band went with the athletes. On the way home, the school bus stopped at a diner in Rock Springs, Wyoming, and everyone went in, but the owners would not serve the one black student that played on the team. So instead of eating there, they refused. The entire group stood up, walked out, and got back on the bus. I loved that my mom did that. That was a lesson I learned from an early age; she was insistent about not allowing us to hear any insensitive or racist talk.

My mom took piano lessons for years and still plays everything from classical to hymns to hits from the fifties and sixties. Christmas music was her specialty. She used to play for us every morning before school—like a private concert. She went to Casper College in 1965 when women still had to wear skirts to class. She started working at a physician's office in Wyoming and continued her career in hospital admissions and marketing in Colorado, which included managing hospice care for dying patients.

When we were in junior high and high school, she took on additional work transcribing medical records. She could type 105 words per minute—with accuracy—and so smoothly that the sound was hypnotic and I could fall asleep to the rhythm. She also took shorthand, so she could take dictation at 100 to 120 words per minute and then transcribe it. Sometimes the notes she'd leave in our lunch boxes would be in shorthand and we'd have to try to figure out what she was trying to say. I wish I would have learned shorthand better—it would have come in handy.

At one point, my mom worked for Lutheran Family Services and one of its national programs called Refugee Services. There were about ten offices across the United States. Each office had a certain number of refugees to resettle per year, which was determined by the government. These refugees sometimes stayed in camps for two years or more before getting a visa to enter the United States.

My mom helped the families settle in—she organized volunteers that set up the household with dishes, towels, cribs—whatever they needed. Then she'd teach them how to do things like ride the bus so that she wouldn't have to go to the grocery store with them every day. She did the trip with them a few times until she was sure they knew the route. On occasion, my mom would take my sister and me with her and also my dad to deliver a washer and dryer to a home. Most of the families were from the former Soviet Union or Eastern Europe (getting to know them I learned how difficult, oppressive, and scary life was under communist rule). My mom included us so we could see how others were able to come to our country for a better life.

As part of her work with Lutheran Disaster Relief, my mom pitched in to help the families of the victims of the Oklahoma City bombing. After that domestic terrorist attack, the trial required a change of venue and was set in Denver. My mom took up the charge of taking care of the family members of the victims who were there to witness the prosecution of the terrorists. She had a group that got up at 4 a.m. to stand in line for seats for the families, and when trial opened for the day, they'd meet in the basement of a nearby church and would take their places in the courtroom if a family member needed a break. Volunteers also helped serve a hot lunch every day for all involved.

After putting in more than her fair share of work over her career, she retired and finally gets to watch me on Fox News every day. I love when she has suggestions for "One More Thing" for *The Five* and when she sends a message during the show that says, "Tell that Bob Beckel to go to his room!"

My dad, Leo Perino Jr., was the oldest of three sons. He grew up as a good ranch hand, excellent bull rider, and smart at school and in business. He and his two brothers, my uncles Matt and Tom, were good-looking boys—towheads with slight builds and chiseled jaws. The Perino boys carried on my great-grandparents' legend in Weston County, Wyoming.

My dad was born into ranching, but he says he knew from an early age that he wanted to have a different career. He had terrible hay fever, which made every summer tough on him and there were few remedies on the market at the time. He loved politics and public affairs, but he wanted to go into business. He was the first member of his family to go to college, and he had a successful career in human resources management.

My dad says that he followed the news in the 1950s and '60s, but Woodstock may as well have been on Mars. The kids in Wyoming were insulated in large part from the political turmoil and cultural changes of the sixties. There weren't many drugs around Wyoming during that time, but some of them knew how to get 3.2 percent beer from South Dakota now and then. You have to drink a lot of that stuff to get a buzz.

College called. My dad met my mom at Casper College in the orientation line. He studied business and eventually transferred to the University of Wyoming at Laramie. He loved to debate, and he and his friends would set up a topic and then argue both sides just to try out their arguments. My parents eloped in 1969, my dad skipping his graduation ceremony that day. Their wedding photo was taken in front of my grandpa's red barn in a reenactment of the *American Gothic* painting.

As newlyweds, my parents lived in town in Newcastle, Wyoming—about twenty miles from the ranch—and my dad cut trees in the forest. Both of them worked on the ranch, haying and branding. They stayed in a slightly run-down rental of my grandparents, and they had to deal with critters coming into the house. Once my mom had had enough with a squirrel that got in, and the next day she decided to deal with this situation once and for all. Still in her pajamas, she took the BB gun and with one shot killed the squirrel. My grandpa heard about it and claimed for years that his daughter-in-law was the best shot in town.

Life was good. And then my dad's number was up—he was being drafted for the war in Vietnam. He'd just graduated from college, married my mom, and his teaching job at the Wyoming State Hospital would start in late August. He was called for a physical exam in Denver in early June. The draftees started on a bus in north central Wyoming and drove it across the state and then south to Denver picking up draftees all the way. The local office asked him to be in charge of the Newcastle group, and he was responsible for the paper meal tickets and hotel vouchers. "What a rip-off! The hotel was a flea-bag and the meals were crap," he says now. My dad was released after his medical exam showed an ulcer. He said he felt bad because he could have handled a desk job during the war; instead, he went home and worked the rest of the summer around the ranch.

After this, my parents packed their stuff in a horse trailer and moved to Evanston, Wyoming, for my dad's new job teaching business classes for emotionally disturbed and socially alienated young patients at the State Hospital. Evanston is a small town in the southwest part of the state near the Utah border.

My dad still wanted more education. In addition to his job, he took graduate-level classes at Utah State University just over the border in Logan. My mom also worked at the hospital. She was the administrative assistant for Dr. Paul Saxon, who ran the clinical division. Two years after they moved to Evanston, I was born in 1972. Dr. Saxon and his wife, Donna, became my godparents and my parents' very good friends.

My only strong memory of Dr. Saxon is that he taught me to tie my shoes and was so proud when I finally got it. He was the kind of guy you wanted to impress. Donna never forgot a holiday or a birthday, and she was there for all the important moments in life, like graduations. The best gifts she sent were tightly wrapped angel food cakes that came in a big box in the mail. A tragic motorcycle accident took the life of Donna's youngest son when he was eighteen, and out of stress and grief, his stepfather, Dr. Paul, died of a heart attack six weeks later. Donna grieved gracefully and went on to remarry and to graduate from divinity school and work as a pastor. She's always made me feel very special—a fairy godmother indeed.

My dad climbed the career ladder quickly. He took the human resources track and moved our family from Wyoming to Denver, Colorado. He was really good at managing people and benefits at Western Farm Bureau Life Insurance Company, and whenever we visited his office, you noticed that people liked working for him. He knew everyone from the big boss to the guys in the mailroom. When the company went through a round of layoffs, I remember how stressed he was about having to tell several employees that they no longer had a job. His compassion was clear and his concern made him physically sick.

Corporate America was a good place to work, but my dad still wanted to be his own boss. He retired from human resources and opened a small neighborhood convenience store where locals could get just about anything they needed. The economic downturn in 2008 made it impossible for the store to succeed. He held on to it as long as he could. Reluctant to retire, he still works a job that he likes—especially because now he gets to see *The Five* (Greg Gutfeld cracks him up).

I was two years old when my dad got that job in the Mile High City. Denver was big-city living for my parents, and they took advantage of it, making sure we visited the zoo and the museums. But they held on to their country ways, too. Because I missed my dad so much when he went to work, he made a recording on a cassette that I played over and over—"What does a cow say? Moooo... What does a horse say? Neigh..." He'd grown up around the animals and was a perfect mimic. A couple of times a year, they would bring back a butchered side of cow from the ranch, mostly steaks and roasts. We had an extra big cooler downstairs filled with meat wrapped in butcher paper and tin foil, and one of my chores was to go down and retrieve what my mom needed to make dinner.

When I was in third grade, my dad started a tradition for the two of us. He asked me to read the *Rocky Mountain News* and *The Denver Post* before he got home from work. I had to pick out at least two articles to discuss with him before my mom served dinner. My dad would read the story and then ask me questions that helped me think through my arguments. I look back on that as when I began to articulate my thoughts and to present my ideas persuasively—a skill that came in very handy years later.

My dad was a voracious news consumer. He subscribed to every political magazine available—*Time, Newsweek, U.S. News & World Report, The Economist, National Review,* etc. We'd dog-ear a page to mark something we wanted to discuss with each other. Every evening we watched the nightly news, either NBC or ABC and then CBS because it came on a half hour later. On Saturdays we had a quick family meeting to plan our Sunday schedule. I drove my sister crazy because I always pushed for the 8:30 a.m. church service because then we'd get home in time to watch the Sunday shows. We topped off our weekend with *60 Minutes,* the tick-tick-tick signaling it was time to come in from the backyard. My dad got me hooked on the news. That was a good thing.

And the Rest...

My sister, Angela Leigh, arrived in 1976. My mom says that the day Angie was born, she kept me home from school and a neighbor took care of me until my parents returned. My mom says she was so excited to see me and introduce me to my new sister, but that when I rounded the corner, I was furious and shooting her dirty looks. She asked what was wrong and I demanded to know why I didn't get to go to school. My mom said it was so I could be home to meet my sister. Apparently, I wasn't impressed and said that I could see my sister every day for the rest of my life but that I couldn't always go to school. I was quite serious about my studies, even when I was four.

In those early years, my aunt Patty Sue and my cousin Michael Jr. lived with us. Patty Sue was sixteen when she had Michael; her first husband joined the Army and they were stationed in Germany for a while. When that marriage ended, Patty Sue and Michael came to live with us. Patty Sue worked as a waitress at Azar's Big Boy. Michael, Angie, and I ran around the neighborhood and attended Ellis Elementary. Michael was more like our brother than our cousin and we're still close.

Patty Sue was a cool aunt. She indulged us more than anyone else. For example, when powder jackets were all the rage in the 1980s—two-toned pullover jackets with a pouch in front—we really wanted those jackets, but they were kind of expensive. I don't know how Patty Sue managed it, but one night she took us to Montgomery Ward at the Buckingham Mall and got us the pullovers. She let us wear them out of the store.

After a while of living in Denver, she moved back to her hometown of Rawlins, Wyoming. She found a good job at the Carbon County Road and Bridge Office and learned firsthand about government and business. After she retired, she ran for mayor and won twice. Patty Sue was frugal with taxpayer dollars and her own campaign money, even recycling yard signs for her next campaigns. She and her husband, Rodney Schuler, continue to serve on the city council while they run Memory Lanes, their bowling alley. Memory Lanes is the first tobacco- and alcohol-free bowling alley in Wyoming—she was told it would never succeed but it's the busiest place in town. She likes to prove people wrong. More than anyone else, Aunt Patty taught me how to live in the moment and not to worry my life away (I don't always succeed).

In Denver we had a small three-bedroom house with a backyard on Elm Street. My mom and dad took advantage of the energy tax credits offered in the late 1970s, and we had a huge solar panel added to our roof and a rock box for warm water heating in our basement. When we drove up to Wyoming for visits or over to South Dakota to see "The Faces" at Mount Rushmore, we had what my dad called 2-55 air-conditioning—two windows down while we cruised at 55 mph. We were back and forth so often to Wyoming that my sister and I knew the towns we passed by heart and which ones had the best rest stops for candy. (Lusk was my favorite—they had the best gas station candy store. I loved candy cigarettes and black licorice.)

When I got bored on the road trips, I tormented Angie by holding my feet in her face while she was sleeping. One day she bravely fought back and grabbed my white sock with the Bert and Ernie faces off my foot and threw it out the window. I couldn't believe she had the nerve to do that. I protested, but we were going fast on the highway and my parents did not stop to go back for my favorite sock. From my seat, I saw my mom smile. I think they were kind of proud of Angie for sticking up for herself. So was I, actually.

As with any other kid, I tried to fit in and I longed to wear the fashions of the day. I wanted jeans with designs on the pockets and Izod shirts. My mom's idea to save money was to iron on decals to the back pockets of my jeans and a Lacoste alligator onto my shirts (she still has that alligator in her jewelry box). It was mortifying. She thought that no one would be able to tell that I was wearing fakes, but I knew and it made me self-conscious around the "cooler kids."

My parents indulged some of my fashion desires, though. I remember when headbands came into style in the 1970s, and while totally superfluous, my dad took me in his yellow Dodge pickup to a store to pick out my favorite. It was just my dad and me—Angie had to stay home. I chose a white satin one that had a rainbow printed on it and threaded with a gold braid. I wore it until it was nearly brown and totally worn out. I loved that father-daughter time and think it's so important for young girls to help them develop confidence.

Aside from clothes, I didn't want for much except books. Weekly library trips were a treat, and I checked out the limit. I'd read two of them in the car on the way home. Once at Target, I finished *Sheila the Great* by Judy Blume while my mom and dad did the shopping. I remember asking if I still needed to pay for the book—I thought that was only fair. After that, my parents found a used bookstore where I could buy as many books as I wanted.

It wasn't all studying for me. My parents put me in a tumbling club at the YMCA as a toddler, and I took to it well. I was fairly good at gymnastics and later was on the junior University of Denver team. I had a floor exercise routine to "The Entertainer" by Scott Joplin, and I could do a few back handsprings in a row that made for a so-so performance (no, I will not be performing this on *The Five*). I loved the balance beam, but struggled on the parallel bars. I was not good enough to take it past an amateur level, and I moved on to the soccer, basketball, and track teams. I wasn't the best athlete, but all of those activities helped me appreciate flexibility and strength, and I have exercised consistently most of my life.

My parents exposed me to music, too. I took piano lessons but my left hand wouldn't keep up with my right. Learning to read music had benefits, though, and I joined the church bell choir (which kills Gutfeld). Though I tried out all of those different sports and activities, I was probably best at talking.

Perhaps my future was foretold in a trip to the East Coast. When I was seven years old in 1979, we visited Washington, D.C. My dad attended a few conferences a year, and back then, the company paid for families to travel, too. My parents decided to make an educational vacation out of it. My sister had to stay behind because she was too young, so I had them to myself. None of us had been to D.C. before. We went to all of the tourist spots: Arlington Cemetery, Ford's Theater, the Lincoln and Jefferson Memorials, the Capitol, the Washington Zoo, and even the White House.

My mom's high school friend worked for Presidents Nixon and

Carter, managing the Air Force One scheduling and manifests. She arranged for all three of us to visit the White House, and because the Carters were at Camp David, I got to see the red phone that would place a call to the Kremlin. (Who knew Beckel was working in the West Wing then?) On our flight home on the Fourth of July, I remember seeing fireworks over the Washington Monument. Maybe that's when I started to think of Washington as a magical place.

According to my parents, that trip made quite an impression on me. When we returned home, they say I stood on the milk box outside the front door with the flag my dad flew and said, "One day I am going to work in the White House."

I have vague memories of that visit, but I still get a jolt whenever I see the panoramic sweep of Washington. I believe that every parent should try to take their kids to D.C. at least twice in their lives—once when they're seven or eight, for the majesty and magic of it all, and then again when they are fifteen, for the understanding of our history and our future. At the very least it gives them a taste of participating in our democracy, and who knows where that early experience may lead.

My sister and I were the first granddaughters born to the family. My dad took that seriously. He told us from an early age that we could grow up to be whatever we wanted. He had given me a yellow T-shirt that had big black block letters that read, ANYTHING BOYS CAN DO GIRLS CAN DO BETTER. I wore the heck out of that shirt—it shows up year after year in family photo albums. The early power of feminist marketing worked (though it was quite a hideous design).

My sister and I would walk to elementary school until the fourth grade. My first grade teacher, Mrs. Rittenbaum, was a genius. She pushed us to read by holding contests and to be better people with a weekly citizenship award.

Mrs. Rittenbaum also used to take us on trips around the world, but only in our imaginations. She had us set up our chairs like we were on an airplane and then she would read to us about where we were going that day. When we "arrived," the class got to eat snacks from that country. One time we went to Madagascar and she served pomegranates. I asked my mom to buy some at the store for us, and then my sister and I made a big mess as we tried to figure out how to eat them. Now they come in liquified form.

I was a well-behaved kid—most of the time. But one memory still stings. In the third grade one of my classmates asked if she could copy from my spelling test. I was nervous but agreed. Hours later I got called up to the teacher's desk.

"Dana, why did you turn in two spelling tests?" she asked.

What I hadn't realized was that the girl didn't just copy down the vocabulary words, but my entire paper—including putting my name up top where hers should have been. I got in as much trouble as the cheater.

While my K–third grade experience was wonderful, my fourth grade year was terrible. Denver started busing kids into different neighborhoods to integrate the schools. I had a 45-minute ride in the morning and was one of five white students in the entire fourth grade. It was a confusing mess of trying to fit in but being bullied and unable to figure out a way to manage it. Even the bus drivers used to call me the "little white princess" and would ridicule me in front of the other kids, warning me about what would happen if I told my dad about it. I held my tongue and worried a lot. I tried not to tattle or complain.

I spent hours praying over and over again, "Please don't let them be mad at me, please don't let them be mad at me," because my classmates were really tough on me. They were often mean, picking on me during recess then asking me to help them with their homework—which felt like a threat, because if I didn't help them,

I'd pay for it later. So I started offering to do their assignments or let them cheat off my tests just to keep on their good side. I always worried that someone was going to be angry, and to this day, I brace myself for someone's bad mood until I see that I'm not in trouble with him or her for anything. The President knew this about me, and if he asked his aide to call me over to the Oval Office, he'd say, "And tell her it's nothing bad." Today, Bill Shine of Fox News does the same. Good managers know how to read their people and to keep them from being paralyzed with fear, even if the initial event was over thirty years ago.

Around that time, I started picking up on subtleties of communications between people. I was sensitive to tension, and I really disliked conflict of any kind. My parents argued just like any other parents, and they eventually divorced when I was twenty-eight years old.

Their arguments used to unnerve me—I shrank from conflict anywhere I could because my school situation was so bad and I was constantly tense. If there was fighting at home, I held my breath. I'd listen for things that might cause irritation and start a fight. I remember thinking, "Why didn't he say it *this* way, then she wouldn't have thought he meant *that*..." or "I wish she would have said *this* instead of *that* and then he wouldn't be mad."

That kind of message manipulation is something I've practiced the rest of my life in so many situations. In my personal life, I'm always telling Peter how he should have said something so that I would feel *x* or *y* (yeah, I know, poor guy). I choose my words carefully, and regret it if I get it wrong. I counsel friends on how to break up with boyfriends or quit a job, and later I'd tell the President what he should say to the world. One day when I corrected Brian Kilmeade about something he said on air on Fox News, he asked, "Do you have to be everyone's press secretary?" And I said, "Yes. I can't help it!"

Out of this anxiety and a need to keep things even and steady came my talents to size up a situation and immediately think of the right thing to say at the right time. Part of that was instinct, but the other part was deciding that I had to be the person who had the most information. That gave me control and I could show two parties why they should get along because they had the same goals—and I had facts to back it up. Being on *The Five* has meant giving up some of that control, but as my co-hosts will attest, I sometimes try to shape their answers by sending articles that may affect their views. I like to know what I'm getting myself into.

My school problem got resolved when my parents pulled out of the city and moved to Parker, Colorado, in the outer Denver suburbs. We had five acres, a three-bedroom ranch house, and a view of the Rocky Mountain Front Range. I caught up quickly at school and made a lot of friends. It was starkly different from my previous two years, and probably made all the difference for me. My experience is the basis for my support for school choice programs—my parents had the means to move to a better school, but other parents don't necessarily have the resources to relocate and so their options are limited by outdated laws.

Moving out to the far suburbs came with a lot of upsides, but my mom and dad had long commutes, and my sister and I were often home alone in the afternoon. As you can imagine, the first thing I did every day after school was...my homework.

My sister, Angie, is four years younger than me and has spent her life in Colorado. I think she was my parents' favorite, and that was okay with me. She was my favorite, too. Angie was the definition of a second child. She rarely got punished and often got her own way, except when she poured her cereal milk on her head right before we needed to leave and my mom made her go to school like that. The milk got crunchy in her hair throughout the day and smelled terrible. But the punishment worked—she never did that again.

I wish I'd been a better older sister. I teased Angie by pretending to melt her blanket in the dryer and by confusing her on the difference between Velma and Daphne on *Scooby-Doo*. She loved Cabbage Patch dolls, and I felt sorry for her when my mom was furious that Angie had painted freckles on such an expensive toy. I should have stopped her. But even when she got in trouble, my sister didn't complain. She didn't mind getting sent to her room—she loved her room!

We didn't fight any more than other siblings, and we were actually pretty close. When my parents got ready for a rare night out, we used to watch them practice their country swing and two-step in the living room. Then we'd set our alarm for 6:30 a.m. on a Saturday so that we wouldn't miss *The Smurfs*.

When I was older, my parents got me a car so that I could help them with shuttling Angie back and forth for her allergy shots. Sometimes after her appointments, I'd take her to see my friends so that she could hang out "with the cool people."

My sister is great in a crisis. She goes into "how can I help" mode. When her good friend died from a drug overdose, she put together a memorable slideshow and paired it with his favorite music for the funeral. When her friend, a mother of two young kids, was in the hospital and close to death, Angie took the kids to McDonald's at 5 a.m. and let them order whatever they wanted. Then she gave them her phone number and said they could text whenever they wanted—and did they ever. She always wrote them back.

And whether there's a tragedy or a celebration, she goes to work in the kitchen and makes homemade chicken noodle soup, beef brisket, lasagna, enchiladas, and her favorite—blueberry bread. It is amazing (and a little unfair) that she's so thin!

Angie also was the classic little sister. She really thought I was the smartest and the coolest; and interesting to me, over the years she never seemed envious of any of my successes. She loved President Bush, too, and on her desk at work in Denver she had a photograph of her visit to Air Force One. One day when her computer was acting up, she called the IT department. Ben Machock came to fix her problem and spotted the picture. They'd both felt a spark—love can hit you at any time—and he asked if the photo was real. She said it was. A few years later, they got married.

Angie is the kind of person I wish I could be. Rarely have I met someone who could be that genuinely happy for someone else, but Angie is like that. I try to remember to be more like her.

Junior high was the confusing mess for me that it is for a lot of early teens. I was kind of in the popular kids group but didn't always fit in. I wanted to succeed and ran for student council, made the cheerleading team, and worked on the yearbook staff.

Academically I was an honor student, but that's when I started doing better in English than in math. I loved my literature courses and even enjoyed diagramming sentences. I was clever enough to avoid having to take higher-level math to keep up my grade point average, but I wish the school hadn't let me get away with that.

I had crushes on boys who I know consumed my thoughts, but for the life of me I can't remember many of their names. I recall once when I was thirteen, my mom and dad were at work in the summertime and they told me, "Whatever you do, don't go on those three-wheelers with those boys." I hadn't intended to, but that afternoon a bunch of my friends came over and one had his ATV. He asked me if I wanted to go for a ride. I didn't want them to think I was a chicken, so I said we could just go down to the cul-de-sac and back.

I had a bad feeling, and I should have listened to my instincts and declined the offer of a ride. He told me to hop on the back and hold on, but I didn't want him to think I liked him, so I didn't grip his sides. When he turned right at the end of our driveway, I fell off the back and the big tire ran over my ankle, breaking it and my big toe. I had gravel rash up my calf muscle. My mom had to rush home from work and take me to the doctor. She didn't have to say anything—I learned my lesson. From then on, I didn't go on the three-wheelers, and as an adult, I always hold on.

High school was better. I had a great range of friends—from the speech team to the football players and cheerleaders. Our parents were suburban moms and dads—some worked in offices in the city and others had successful small businesses like Hoff's Landscape Contractors, which my friend runs today. The father of one of our buddies was our principal, so we kept in line but we tucked in behind him when we tried to get away with something. We had a lot of freedom—perhaps more than we should have—but we also grew up at a peaceful time in a semi-rural area so that cushioned us from harsher realities.

I had some nerd-like tendencies—with one friend I only spoke in haiku. I rarely was in trouble, except once when I tried to play hooky with Tracy Schilling and got caught and had to do detention. I thought my parents had no idea, but come that Christmas one of my presents was a framed detention notice that my mother had received. They knew how to punish me—I was so embarrassed that I didn't think it was funny.

Okay, I was a little like Tracy Flick in the movie *Election*. I was student body president, and during the Perino administration, I was successful in getting some flexibility into the weekly schedule for extra tutoring and studying (and an extra forty-five minutes of downtime for those not inclined to study—so I had support from everyone). I helped arrange the dances, including the prom. But my great love was the speech team. Those were my people. I think about them now when I'm on *The Five* and just know they probably all watch *Red Eye* (that's a compliment).

* * *

When it came to choosing a college, I wanted to go to a big school and have big fun, but my dad suggested a smaller school with a chance of a scholarship. I didn't even want to think about it, but he insisted and I pouted the whole drive to Pueblo, Colorado, to visit the University of Southern Colorado. A small, dinky school wasn't what I had in mind for my first time living away from home. This wasn't in my plans!

But Father knew best. After I met several professors, I realized it was the place for me. I wouldn't be lost in a crowd, and I'd have a chance to work at the public television station for southern and western Colorado, the kind of hands-on experience that would help me get a job. Each of the professors in the mass communications department had to have ten years of practice before they could teach—I didn't know how special that was until I learned more about academia. I also received a four-year tuition scholarship for joining the speech team. So it ended up being quite a good deal.

I loved all of my mass communications classes, especially History of Journalism, Ethics, and Public Relations 101. I did well in other subjects, too. I minored in Spanish and even started dreaming in the language. I liked politics, and years later one of my professors, Pauletta Otis, also worked in the Bush Administration at the Pentagon.

I took Philosophy 101 my freshman year, and when I came home for Thanksgiving, I told my dad I was thinking about becoming a Buddhist. That didn't go over very well, but it was a passing fancy—by Christmas I was happily back in the pews at our Lutheran church. That was a great thing about the college—thinking about new ideas and deciding what worked for me.

At the university, I worked on *Standoff*, which was a debate program—kind of an early version of *The Five*. In my senior year at college, I had a weekly show called *Capitol Journal*, which was a show that provided a weekly roundup of the legislative issues affecting southern and western Colorado. I must have been *terrible*, but at least they gave me a shot. I also worked as an overnight country music DJ on the weekends and as a waitress in any spare time I could find. I graduated with honors, and as soon as the ceremony was over, I was ready to move on.

Just like in high school, my best college friends were on the speech team, but I knew lots of people. I got a kick out of one girl who came from New England—she'd actually believed a brochure that told her our university was near the ski slopes. She was a character who smoked cigarettes on the windowsill of her dorm room and never worried about getting in trouble—I wrote a few papers for her for $20 each (I really should have charged more).

I had a couple of boyfriends in college, one more serious than the other. The first was a basketball player. He was the point guard, so there wasn't much of a height disparity. We dated steadily for a couple of years. I really thought he might be the guy I'd be with for my life—he was cute, funny, and not as dumb as you'd think (but close).

One night when he was supposed to come pick me up, he never showed. He dumped me by never showing up or even calling again. I came down with broken heart flu. I felt sad, betrayed, and foolish. My roommate, Andrea Aragon, saved me. She got me up and walking around and eventually out on Saturday nights to the country and Western bars, where we'd dance with a few fellas and go home alone. We still agree, "Thank God he broke my heart."

I chose graduate school right after college, another small school but this one was far from Colorado, at the University of Illinois Springfield. It was an exclusive program—only eighteen people a year got into the public affairs reporting program. The best part was that it was only a one-year commitment. I was anxious to get a job in the news business, but I thought a master's degree would give me a competitive edge.

I scored an internship with a local CBS affiliate. I thought I'd love it, and in some ways I did. I liked learning about legislation and putting together video packages that explained a complicated issue. But it was 1995, the first time in decades that Republicans were in power, and the people I worked with didn't seem to have much regard for them. I picked up on their hostility to any conservative idea, and I thought it was out of line and unfair. It was my first taste of media bias, and it turned me off of wanting to work in local news. I graduated with honors and hightailed it back to Denver to do what all graduate students seem to do—I lived in my parents' basement and started waiting tables.

In the mornings, I'd call a media hotline that listed the local market TV jobs, and I applied for a few in the Southwest because I thought my Spanish skills would come in handy there. I also thought maybe the people out West wouldn't be so biased (I was mostly wrong).

One job was in Guam—a TV anchor on a U.S. military base. I applied thinking it would be quite an experience. As fate would have it, that night my dad and I were flipping through the channels and we saw part of a documentary about the brown tree snake infestation in Guam. People found them in their bathtubs, their toilets, and their washing machines. One lady talked about how she was just walking along and a brown tree snake fell on her head. So much for Guam. I withdrew my application, which may have been a bit rash. I regret not being adventurous enough to take that job.

While I was waiting tables, I found out about a deputy press secretary job in the Colorado State Senate. I wanted to have a good reference, so I called the chief of staff to U.S. Representative Scott McInnis (R-CO). McInnis had been willing to do interviews with me every week for that PBS show when I was in college. Looking back, I realize most politicians wouldn't have given me the time of day, but he was kind. And keeping in contact with his office was my first professional experience of building a good network because you never know when you might need someone's help.

The Congressman's chief of staff offered me a job instead of a reference. I thought they meant in his Pueblo, Colorado, office, so I backpedaled. But the job they needed me to do was in Washington. That got my attention, though I worried that if I didn't take a job in TV right away, I'd miss my chance to work as a journalist. And I'd just taken out a student loan to pay for my graduate degree—was all that money down the drain?

I fretted for three days and didn't sleep. I owed them an answer and finally prayed I'd wake up with a decision. It worked—look out, Washington.

Capitol Living

My room was a crappy little closet in a run-down rental townhouse on Capitol Hill. The water heater was actually in my room, which meant it was probably supposed to be a utility closet and not where someone slept. My mom bit her tongue as we moved my stuff into the place. My roommates were standoffish and kind of mean (my first brush with Democrats suspicious and disdainful of Republicans). They were both from New England and named Katie. We could not have been more different. One of them was sleeping with a married guy from her office, and I hardly saw her. The other Katie and I tried to find some common ground, but we gave up and settled for politeness over friendship.

Right before Halloween, I stayed in on a Saturday night, and I heard a noise outside. I was just in shorts and a T-shirt and so I slipped my office shoes on and stepped outside. The wind was strong and the door slammed behind me. I was locked out and there was no spare key. I nearly cried in frustration, and I looked ridiculous. Alone, cold, inappropriately dressed, and wearing black loafers with a low heel, I went across the street to where these guys I knew lived in a group house. They let me hang there until one of the Katies came home. A week later, the water heater in my room-closet broke and soaked through my futon and ruined all of my new clothes. After that, I found a different place to live in a house with four other nice and kind young women (I'm still close friends with two of them), and I had a closet all to myself.

Identifying myself as a Republican was more of a gradual awakening than a lightning bolt. The values of limited government, personal responsibility, and a strong national defense were ideas that fit my thinking and instincts. My dad was probably the first Libertarian-minded person I knew, and he loved to play devil's advocate and get me to think through my positions on issues. He and my mom canceled out each other's votes in the Presidential election years—my dad often voted for Republicans and my mom voted for Democrats, though they didn't talk about their political differences very often in front of us. I gravitated more to Reagan and Bush, not Dukakis and Clinton.

But I didn't really understand *why* I was a Republican. That changed with what else—a book. Soon after I moved to Washington, a friend gave me a copy of *What I Saw at the Revolution*, by one of Reagan's best speechwriters, Peggy Noonan. I loved her clear thinking and storytelling, the way she framed an argument, and how she used self-deprecating humor to describe working in the Old Executive Office Building with the worst furniture consigned to her office. From that office she helped craft Reagan's speeches that inspired America and fully embraced our national exceptionalism.

As I read, I started to realize what it meant to be a conservative. To me, conservatism was harder—there are no easy answers, reality

Barnes & Noble Booksellers #1912
1542 Northern Blvd
Manhasset, NY 11030
516-365-6723

STR:1912 REG:001 TRN:1036 CSHR:Aaron B

American Marxism
  9781501135972   T1
  (1 @ 28.00) PROMO 30% (8.40)
  (1 @ 19.60)   19.60
Madam Speaker: Nancy Pelosi and the Less
  9781538750698   T1
  (1 @ 32.50) PROMO 50% (16.25)
  (1 @ 16.25)   16.25
President's Daughter
  9780316540711   T1
  (1 @ 30.00) PROMO 50% (15.00)
  (1 @ 15.00)   15.00

Subtotal   50.85
Sales Tax T1 (8.625%)   4.39
TOTAL   55.24
MASTERCARD   55.24
  Card#: XXXXXXXXXXXX8469
  Expdate: XX/XX
  Auth: 03441Z
  Entry Method: Chip Card Tap

  Application Label: CAPITAL ONE
  AID: a0000000041010
  TVR: 0000008000
  TSI: e800

A MEMBER WOULD HAVE SAVED   2.80

Connect with us on Social

Facebook- @BNNorthernBlvd
Instagram- @bnmanhasset
Twitter-   @BNManhasset

055.01C   08/15/2021 03:01PM

CUSTOMER COPY

Return Policy

With a sales receipt or Barnes & Noble.com packing slip,
a full refund in the original form of payment will be issued from
any Barnes & Noble Booksellers store for returns of new and
unread books, and unopened and undamaged music CDs,
DVDs, vinyl records, electronics, toys/games and audio books
made within 30 days of purchase from a Barnes & Noble
Booksellers store or Barnes & Noble.com with the below
exceptions:

Undamaged NOOKs purchased from any Barnes & Noble Booksellers
store or from Barnes & Noble.com may be returned within 14 days
when accompanied with a sales receipt or with a Barnes & Noble.com
packing slip or may be exchanged within 30 days with a gift receipt.

A store credit for the purchase price will be issued (i) when a gift
receipt is presented within 30 days of purchase, (ii) for all textbooks
returns and exchanges, or (iii) when the original tender is PayPal.

Items purchased as part of a Buy One Get One or Buy Two, Get
Third Free offer are available for exchange only, unless all items
purchased as part of the offer are returned, in which case such
items are available for a refund (in 30 days). Exchanges of the items
sold at no cost are available only for items of equal or lesser value
than the original cost of such item.

Opened music CDs, DVDs, vinyl records, electronics, toys/games,
and audio books may not be returned, and can be exchanged
only for the same product and only if defective. NOOKs
purchased from other retailers or sellers are returnable only to
the retailer or seller from which they were purchased pursuant
to such retailer's or seller's return policy.   Magazines,
newspapers, eBooks, digital downloads, and used books are
not returnable or exchangeable. Defective NOOKs may be
exchanged at the store in accordance with the applicable
warranty.

Returns or exchanges will not be permitted (i) after 30 days or
without receipt or (ii) for product not carried by Barnes &
Noble.com, (iii) for purchases made with a check less than 7
days prior to the date of return.

Policy on receipt may appear in two sections.

Return Policy

With a sales receipt or Barnes & Noble.com packing slip,
a full refund in the original form of payment will be issued from
any Barnes & Noble Booksellers store for returns of new and
unread books, and unopened and undamaged music CDs,
DVDs, vinyl records, electronics, toys/games and audio books
made within 30 days of purchase from a Barnes & Noble

and logic weigh heavy, and there is a definite core set of principles. Peggy helped me understand that it was okay to be a Republican *and* be a woman—the two weren't mutually exclusive. That sounds strange to say now, but think of all the messages sent to young American women, from every angle—Republicans are depicted as evil, mean, and the enemy. Almost every book, magazine, movie, and TV show depicts conservatives negatively—it's rare to read something positive about a Republican woman, and when you do, then it's couched as how they're the rare exception to the rule (note to editors: Being called "the relevant Republican" is not a compliment).

I followed Peggy's work for years, and later when I was at Fox filling in for Mike Huckabee, I invited her on as a guest. It was a Saturday afternoon in the fall, a perfect day for walking in Central Park, but she agreed to come into the studios. I tried not to gush but thanked her on air. To my delight, we became friends. I like that she's a good listener who responds with substance and wit. She smiles with her eyes even when she thinks what she's hearing is total crap. I'm glad I got the chance to tell her what she gave me, which was the ability to find my voice and to speak with confidence. You could say that Peggy's book really helped start a career that I never imagined.

My first job in D.C., however, wasn't very exceptional. I answered phones and greeted people arriving at the Capitol. I volunteered to give constituents tours of the building, so I could get out of the office. I grew out of that job in about eight days, but the rest of Hill life was fascinating. I went to brown-bag lunches on the merits of a national sales tax and implementation of the Contract with America. It was a policy nerd's paradise.

In D.C. you don't just make friends, you establish contacts. It's where you build your network, and because of that first job in Washington, I eventually became the White House press secretary.

It started at a hockey game. Now anyone who watches *The Five* knows that sports aren't my strong suit. But a couple of weeks into my D.C. life, I heard about a night out with a group of folks from my home state who were going to watch the Colorado Avalanche play the Washington Capitals. I joined them—it was free, after all, and I needed to meet some people.

I sat next to Tim Rutten, who worked on the Senate side. He asked me what my dream job in D.C. was, and I told him that I hoped to work my way up to being a House press secretary one day. He said that I was in luck because Representative Dan Schaefer of Colorado needed a new press secretary and preferred someone from his home state with *any* sort of media experience. My stomach sank because I thought it sounded like the perfect opportunity, but the timing was wrong. I'd worked for McInnis for less than two months and thought it would reflect badly on me if I left so soon for another job. Tim said I was crazy and arranged for me to meet Schaefer's office.

He was right. Three weeks later, I was working for Schaefer. Far from being irritated, McInnis was happy for me, and he's been one of my supporters ever since. His reaction taught me to be willing to open doors for others, especially your employees, for promotions or new jobs, no matter how inconvenient it may be for you.

So almost overnight I was an instant press secretary—just add water. I didn't know what I was doing. The good thing was that my chief of staff, Holly Propst, was one of the best managers I've ever had. She taught me how to write statements and press releases, and she made sure I understood the policy so that I didn't screw anything up along the way to passing legislation. She let me listen in on her calls with reporters so that I could hear the way she handled interviews. She gave me enough rope to hang myself but was there to make sure I never did.

Believe it or not, one of my first calls was from the late Mike Wallace of *60 Minutes*. The message came in on a pink "While You Were Out" slip. I had no idea what the call was about, but I knew that if *60 Minutes* is calling, you better alert your boss. Holly said to sit on it and see if he calls back. Sure enough, he called again the next day. This time, Holly told me to return the call, explain that I was new to the job, and find out what he wanted.

When I called the number, Mike Wallace didn't answer the phone. It was Tim Rutten, the guy who helped get me the job, playing a prank on me. I renamed him Tim Rotten.

Working on Capitol Hill was a great way to get my career going, and I recommend it to everyone regardless of whether they want to work in politics. And it turned out the job was also a great way to meet my future husband. On assignment for the Congressman on August 17, 1997, I boarded a flight from Denver to Chicago and my life changed forever.

It's a strange but good thing when you feel closer to some of your loved ones well after they've passed on. And the longer I live on the East Coast, the more I appreciate the West. I'm very grateful for the unique upbringing I had and for attentive parents who made sure my sister and I were exposed to lots of different experiences and ways of life. Really, you would never have picked me out of a crowd and said, "She'll be the White House press secretary one day." And that's what makes America so great—one day you're sitting on a barnyard fence thinking you'll never leave home and the next thing you're sitting on Marine One with the President of the United States after his last visit with the Navy SEALs. God bless America indeed.

CHAPTER 2

Love at First Flight

Quarter Life Crisis

When I turned twenty-five in 1997, I should have felt on top of the world. I was young, healthy, and had a good circle of friends at work and through my church. I was the spokesperson for the House chairman of the Energy and Power Subcommittee and had great relationships with the Hill reporters. I had paid off my student loans, didn't have any credit card debt, and lived on my own in an English basement apartment in a Capitol Hill row house. So why was I so nervous and worried all the time? I didn't know what it was called, but I was having what many young women go through: a quarter life crisis.

Looking back, it seems ridiculous that I had such a lack of confidence. By almost every measure, things were going my way, but I couldn't enjoy the moment because I was so worried about the future. I loved my job, though after a couple of years I'd learned enough about being a Hill press secretary that I could do it in my sleep. I didn't know what was next, and I was anxious to move up the ladder. I couldn't advance my career in the Congressman's office because there was nowhere to go. I resisted the pull to work for a trade association or lobbying shop on K Street, the well-worn path that Hill staffers take. I also wasn't enamored with the House GOP leadership at the time—they just weren't my style. My options felt narrow.

On the personal side of things, I hadn't had a boyfriend in years. I had many friends that I hung out with a lot, but the dating scene in D.C. was pathetic. (It still is, right, ladies?) I remember thinking that there just weren't that many men I was interested in around Washington. Most of the guys didn't look like they'd ever worked outside a day in their lives—soft hands, limp handshakes, pale skin, and pudgy middles. The good-looking ones were either already hitched or married to their political ambition with little senses of humor. It was slim pickings for a single woman. And so, facing career limitations and no romantic possibilities, I felt stuck.

I didn't realize that I had company. Believe it or not, it's common that young women around age twenty-five (which now seems so young!) go through the kind of crisis that men go through later in life, when they realize that the dreams of their youth aren't coming true and that those dreams may not have been so great in the first place. She hasn't been swept off her feet nor is she on her way to having two kids with a loving husband, a second home in the mountains or at the beach, and a growing retirement account. A few years out of college, she's already received a couple of promotions at work but then feels like she's treading water and can't reach the sides. The college scene is way behind her but she doesn't feel grown up. She's not sure she even *wants* to grow up—it looks boring and hard. But the clock ticks. She puts more pressure on herself and worries that her best years are behind her.

Right before my twenty-fifth birthday, I took a personal inventory (I love lists). I felt I was falling short in several categories. It looked something like this:

- Dating: Need to try to get out more. Stop going to "hang outs" with the gang. Cast a wider net. Don't lower expectations!
- Career: Next stop—work for leadership? No. Campaign in 2000? No experience. Chief of staff role? Maybe but not qualified—have to fund-raise. Trade association? Ugh. Lobbying? Yuck. Leave D.C.? Yes/no... but where?
- Personal growth: Travel—seen nothing of the world. Need to get out more. Take some classes? Get another degree? Read the *Iliad*!
- DIET!

How overwrought it all seems now—What should I do? Where should I live? What should I study? How do I keep from being tied down? How can I keep myself from getting stuck in a rut? Where could I meet a strong, solid, handsome guy? What if I've made too many mistakes to turn things around? What if I fail?

I needed to chill out. But at least I wasn't alone in thinking things over. Chewing over big life decisions is what young people in America have the freedom to do—we can redefine our goals and change course, move away, and try something new. Far from being stuck, I was perfectly positioned to succeed.

I itched to travel overseas, something I didn't have a chance to do as a kid beyond a beach vacation in Mexico and a trip to England with my godmother when I was sixteen. When we took vacations, it meant the ranch, which suited me just fine. But as an adult, I started reading a lot of travelogues and wanted to be in the writers' shoes—I can still remember passages from *Blue Highways, Under the Tuscan*

Sun, Notes from a Small Island, and also *A Year in Provence*. I started to realize how sheltered I'd been from the world. But was I too old to change that?

After years of structure, I suddenly longed to be spontaneous. I wanted to be able to leave town at a moment's notice, so I stopped accumulating stuff. I only had one cup, glass, plate, bowl, and a single set of silverware. To cook things, I had a pot for oatmeal in the morning and soup in the evening. I also had a fajita skillet that was given to me by my landlords (it was a wedding present they never used). I didn't use it to make fajitas—I made toast on it.

I wasn't quite a grown-up but I didn't want to conform to my previously held visions of adult life. Looking back, I felt as if I'd done all of my maturing in junior high and high school when I put every effort into being able to succeed. After all that hard charging to achieve "success," I was now resisting conformity. I didn't want to get stuck, so I tried to ignore my instincts to have my life planned out. I wanted to be a free spirit and not so consumed with what I was going to do next.

The quarter-life crisis rumbled beneath the surface in secret, but I did talk about it at one of my favorite places in Washington—Reformation Lutheran Church on Third and East Capitol Streets, a stone building that blended twentieth-century Washington architecture with medieval Christian features. It was right behind the Supreme Court and next to the Folger Shakespeare Library. It was mostly a politics-free zone, and I spent a lot of time there.

I was part of a singles group that got together a few times a month (there was one marriage that came out of that group). On Tuesdays, we tutored kids from southeast D.C. in Anacostia who really needed our help with reading, math, and general guidance on life. I worked with a nine-year-old girl who struggled to read.

When her frustration got to be too much, I let her draw pictures or braid my hair. She made a portrait of me that I hung in my office for years—the biggest feature being my backside (I took that as a compliment). Once a year we pitched in to help one of our friends who organized a major home renovation and repair. It reminded me of going out to help resettle refugees with my mom. Volunteering always gave me what I call Perspective (with a capital P). During all of that personal turmoil, the church helped me feel grounded.

We also took time for ourselves. On Wednesdays, we had a Bible study in the church's basement and went potluck for dinner. Every other weekend, we did an activity like taking long bike rides or hiking in the Shenandoah Valley. Our group functioned like an extended family for many of us who had moved to D.C. from somewhere else. It was at one of those sessions that a woman I admired noticed my restlessness. She asked me what was bothering me and I was open regarding my worries about my age (though she was about forty-five, she didn't laugh at me) and my changing views about what my life would be like. She gave me great advice that I've since passed on—she said to remember that God told us not to fear. "Fear not. Say that to yourself—'Fear not.'" She suggested I write it down and carry it in my back pocket so that it was always there if I needed it. I did that and it kind of helped. Eventually, after my twenty-fifth birthday, I stopped worrying all the time. I'd pulled through it. But just as I settled down, God shook things up again.

Taking Off!

On August 17, 1997, I was booked on a midmorning flight back to D.C. after a round of editorial boards I'd done with Congressman

Schaefer at the *Rocky Mountain News* and *The Denver Post*. My sister drove me to the brand-new Denver International Airport, and she and I misjudged how long it would take to get there from downtown. I kept glancing at my watch but I didn't say anything because I didn't want to make her any more nervous than she already was. I made it just in time to board before the flight closed. I handed my ticket to the agent and noticed just one person behind me in line. A year later that man became my husband.

No seriously, that really happened. How? Well, since everyone prefers his version of the story, here's Peter McMahon's take on when we met (and I suggest reading this in a proper English accent):

Sunday, 17th August 1997. I had been in Denver on business and was flying to Chicago, about a two-and-a-half-hour flight. Having been at a party the night before, I arrived at the airport rather late and was the last person to board.

Walking down the jetway, I saw a cute young blonde in front of me, her ponytail swinging as she walked and I thought to myself "I hope I sit beside her." And then I saw Dana. I'm kidding! As she showed her boarding card to the attendant, I smiled because we were indeed seated next to each other.

As Dana was getting her bags organized, I asked her, "Would you like me to put your bag up above?" She declined with a smile, and so I settled in my seat. In the same way as a dog who finally catches the car and doesn't know what to do with it, now that I was sitting beside Dana, I didn't know what to say, so I quietly opened my book and started reading.

Dana then asked me a question about the book, John le Carré's The Tailor of Panama, *and we started talking. Conversation came very easily, and before we knew it, we were almost telling our life stories. She was clearly much younger than me, so pretty that I considered her out of my league, and lived in America. In addition, I was coming out of a marriage and was in no way seeking any kind of relationship. So I did not hit on this cute girl in any way, yet I found her incredibly attractive and found myself unexpectedly captivated and intrigued by this extremely smart, very pretty girl.*

The flight came to an end all too quickly and we exchanged details. Dana had no business cards left, so on the back of one of mine she wrote, "Dana Perino, home number, office number, fax number, e-mail address." So I was excited by the thought that Dana was apparently interested, or was she just being very friendly? I insecurely bounced back and forward between those thoughts for days.

We parted at the airport, and when I rounded the corner away from her, I did something I had never done—I jumped up and clicked my heels. For the next few days I was working in various U.S. cities but could not stop thinking about her. Upon my return to the U.K. on Thursday the 21st, I told only two friends about this incredible girl I had met, one of whom, my assistant Lynn Bradley, said, "She was just being friendly, you daft bugger." Lynn was trying to protect me.

The next day, on the premise that I had nothing to lose, I wrote an e-mail explaining how I felt—how I couldn't stop picturing her there in the seat beside me, those eyes constantly smiling, her laugh enchanting, and how I really wanted to see her again.

That was Friday the 22nd and the following week I was on vacation, a motorcycle tour. I didn't remember until later but Lynn said that I told her, "If something happens to me on this trip, will you please let Dana know?"

On the Tuesday I called the office from Wales, and Lynn said I had a postcard from America. I excitedly listened as she read it over the phone, Dana telling me how much she enjoyed meeting me and hoped to see me on my next trip to the U.S. Then Lynn broke the news that my e-mail had bounced back; in those early days of e-mail we were in the middle of changing providers. Dana had sent the postcard but had not heard from me!

Devastated by this news, the next day I canceled the remainder of my vacation travels and headed back towards the office, arriving at 5:30. It was closed, but I let myself in and hurriedly resent the e-mail with an explanation as to its tardiness.

Now, back to Dana...

As I sat down on the flight, he asked if he could put my bag up above, and I immediately noticed his British accent. (American women fall for it every time.) I did a quick scan and saw no wedding band. (I'd later find out that he'd only decided two months before to stop wearing it, just before his divorce was almost final. I probably would not have talked with him if he'd had a ring.)

I thought he was quite handsome, and I loved his blue eyes. Like most travelers, I just like to be left alone on a plane. I was reading Toni Morrison's *Beloved* and wanted to finish it on the flight, but he seemed friendly and I wanted to be a nice American to keep up our reputation as a welcoming nation, so I asked him about the book he'd put in the seat pocket. Two hours later we were still talking. From books we'd moved on to talk about his recent travels, European and American politics, and where we grew up. He loved the free market and a strong national defense (so did I), and wasn't a fan of President Bill Clinton (neither was I at the time—we met in the middle of the Monica Lewinsky scandal). We realized we were on safe terrain to discuss our political beliefs.

Peter was so easy to talk to. We just kept chatting, going from one subject to another. I loved his laugh. I could see he had great legs through his jeans. And his hands were strong and tanned. I learned a lot about him in a short period of time. (I was a good interviewer.) His dad was an air traffic controller in the Royal Air Force and he'd moved around a lot as a kid. His mom died from a massive heart attack when he was only eighteen years old. For a couple of summers he worked on a farm. He grew up with dogs and wanted one of his own (good sign!). He liked to ride motorcycles and scuba. He'd traveled all around the world, to so many of the places I wanted to see. He was well read and educated at a Scottish boarding school, kind of like Harry Potter. He had two kids from his first marriage—they weren't much younger than me. He'd lived in Germany and Saudi Arabia for work in the medical device industry, and near championship golf courses in Scotland but he didn't play the sport (another good sign). Norwich was his favorite football team—he supported them out of loyalty even though they rarely won a match. I admired that about him—he was a solid, steady, and dependable man of character and charm. What wasn't to like? And for as much information I got out of him during the flight, he was also interested in me and knew a lot about me before we landed. There's something about being on an airplane that makes you say things more openly than you would if you ever thought you were going to see that person again. Little could I imagine (well, I was already starting to)....

At one point I had to tear my eyes away and look out the window because I realized I was falling in love with an older guy from Britain who happened to be assigned to sit next to me on a plane. I felt myself losing control of my emotions and thought how silly and immature I must seem to him. As he was talking, I privately said a little prayer, "God, I know I asked you to help me find somebody, but this can't be right. He's much older than me, he lives in England, he'd been married twice before, he could be an axe murderer, and did I mention he lives in ENGLAND? How could I fall in love with him on a plane? Come on. This can't be for real."

But the rush of feelings didn't stop. This was very new to me— I hadn't had a date in quite a while, let alone someone who I was attracted to as much as I was to Peter during the trip. For much of that flight I felt giddy. When I'm asked the secret to our marriage, I agree with couples that have been married a long time—he's always made me laugh. Even that day on the plane he told me silly jokes that still make me giggle, like, "Did you know that Mahatma Gandhi had a brother who worked in a coat check in England? His name was Ma-HAT-ma Coat." He can't believe I keep laughing at that one, but to me, it never gets old.

There was just one little thing, however. Peter had brought a McDonald's Filet-O-Fish on the airplane. That's disgusting. He later explained it was because he had a hangover from the big conference party the night before and it was the healthiest thing he could find on the menu at the time, but still, that's gross. No one should bring fish on a plane. He hasn't since.

As we were landing, I felt a mix of panic and dread. I didn't want the flight to end, and we had an awkward moment about whether to share contact information. I didn't want to look too forward and offer my number, but thankfully he brought it up. I was out of business cards from the media tour, so he gave me one of his (the card stock quality was excellent) and I wrote down every which way he could get a hold of me. Admittedly, I went overboard when I gave him my fax number.

Then I didn't hear from him.

*   *   *

I went back to work on the Hill the day after I met him. We were still in August recess so the Capitol was a ghost town. I decided to get my files in order, and when I opened my desk drawer, I saw a postcard of Georgetown in spring with lots of tulips that I'd picked up with the intention of sending it to someone. Peter and I had talked about my favorite flower, tulips, and how much he would like to see Georgetown one day. Serendipity? I figured I had nothing to lose by sending it to him, so I wrote an innocent little "so nice to meet you" note and mailed it.

And then…silence. No reply. I was a wreck. I couldn't sleep, eat, or concentrate. I needed to get my act together. The Congressman was coming back for the start of the fall session, and I had to refocus.

I hadn't told many people about Peter—just Helen Morrell, our office mom, and my best friend and landlord, Desiree Sayle. I was afraid to tell the other guys in my office because teasing was their sport and I wasn't ready to have my romantic dreams killed just yet.

Since it was the last day of recess, I decided to spend my lunch hour reading a new book I'd borrowed from the Congressional Library about the life of Michelangelo, *The Agony and the Ecstasy* by Irving Stone. I vowed that when I got back to the office, I would never ever think of Peter again.

I picked a spot in the courtyard of the Rayburn House Office Building that had a fountain. It was hot and humid, and sweat beaded behind my knees and on the back of my neck, but I didn't get up and go back inside. I made myself sit through the hour and tried to forget about Peter and think about Michelangelo. Finally, when my insides started to melt, I stood up, stretched, and snapped my book shut. I was over him. Until I got back to my desk, that is. I had mail.

While I was trying to forget I'd ever met Peter McMahon, he was rushing to his office to resend the original e-mail that had bounced back. And so I sat down at my desk and fired up my computer (it was 1997, remember), and the first e-mail in my in-box was from Peter. In his note, he didn't hold anything back—he figured he'd never see me again and so he just said what he felt in a few paragraphs. I read it a few times, tuning out the office chatter.

So I hadn't been crazy after all—he'd felt the same way about me as I did about him. I printed the note and put it in my wallet. I sensed my life was about to change dramatically. Despite the odds, and a flight I almost missed, I'd finally met my match.

We followed up with more e-mails and soon were talking by telephone a few times a week and then multiple times a day. He'd call me during his long commute home from work, which was my lunchtime, and I'd whisper into the phone so that my colleagues couldn't eavesdrop. The calls cost a fortune, but he said not to worry about that (and his boss, a real friend and a bit of a romantic, told him he'd cover the personal calls even though it was a company phone). Peter also sent me handwritten letters (they were kinda sappy but lovely), and I responded twice a week. It was a traditional, long-distance, whirlwind romance—like something from one of the books I'd read.

Now if you could name the last thing you'd think Dana Perino would do, it might be flying off after work one Friday to meet up with somewhat of a stranger in New Orleans for a weekend, but that's what I did. I'd told myself during my quarter life crisis that I wanted to be more spontaneous, to live more in the moment, and to travel to places so that I could experience some things—and there was Peter offering me the chance to do it. I trusted him enough to go with the flow.

I didn't accept his offer to meet up in the Big Easy right away.

(I wasn't *that* easy!) I said I'd just see him the following weekend in Washington when he was scheduled to visit. But the day before his trip, I changed my mind. I said I'd go to New Orleans. He was thrilled but panicked. I'd waited so long to say yes that he had trouble getting me a plane ticket and finding me a hotel room. (Such a gentleman!) But he didn't tell me it was a hassle. All I had to worry about was what I was going to pack (and whether to tell my parents—I didn't).

My flight to New Orleans felt like the longest I'd ever taken. My nerves were on fire and I thought they'd either be pushing me off the plane or I'd be climbing over the seats to get to the front of the line. This was before Facebook and Skype—Peter and I actually had met on a plane two months before—and I worried we may not recognize each other.

But he was there waiting for me as soon as I exited the gate. It was kind of awkward, but not in a bad way—our excitement and nerves pushed us to the cab, where we kissed a lot on the drive into the city. I felt sorry for the driver, but as we were in New Orleans, I'm sure he'd seen worse.

"Nawlins" makes for a good weekend of partying and sightseeing. Peter had plans to take me to famous restaurants, like Felix's, where he ordered the red fish (that's when he found out I don't like fish—that hadn't come up on our hour-long phone calls). I was a bit too anxious to eat, so I drank instead, thinking that would help me relax. I even threw back some Jell-O shots (this is not like me). I must have been really nervous because the alcohol didn't affect me at all. Peter, on the other hand, had never had a Jell-O shot and after several drinks felt very drunk. We tried to rally on Bourbon Street but we threw in the towel and called it a night.

The next morning we met up for beignets and coffee at Café du Monde, walked through Jackson Square, and then went to the

Aquarium of the Americas to watch an IMAX film about killer whales. I thought it was sweet that Peter fell asleep during the movie and snorted himself awake (the difference between just meeting and being married seventeen years: I no longer think that's cute—well, maybe a little). We topped off that night with dinner at the Court of Two Sisters. By this time our hands were locked and we were comfortable with each other.

Saying good-bye was tough. He took me to the airport. I got that panic that people in long-distance relationships get when you know the loneliness is about to overwhelm you. Thankfully, that was offset since I'd see him the next weekend in Washington. There was something he felt he needed to say before I left, and it wasn't easy for him to tell me. Before I went through security, he told me that after his son was born, he'd had a vasectomy and wasn't able or planning to have more children. He thought I would balk at that, or even be mad at him for starting a relationship without that fact being revealed. I was eighteen years younger, after all, and he didn't know that I'd gradually come to realize I didn't want to have children of my own. He was relieved when I said, "Oh, thank God!" Talking family planning after meeting on a plane and seeing each other two months later is a sure sign that the relationship is going somewhere.

It sounds impossible, but we knew we would be together as a couple from that weekend on. It was when I felt like I was becoming the person I wanted to be—one that was a little less cautious and rigid and more willing to be unconventional (and loved).

The next weekend in Washington, I got to take Peter through the Capitol and he liked it when I flashed my badge and we bypassed the tourist line. I introduced him to my friends and they fell for him, too. I took him to my favorite place, the National Cathedral.

In the courtyard by the roses, Peter suddenly asked me to marry him. Whoa. I knew that we would get married but I said, "Hold that thought." I was drunk with love, but I was sober enough to hold back.

Two months later, I was planning a move to England. My quarter life crisis had cleared the way for a lifetime commitment.

Little Person, Big Move

We were a couple in a hurry. Over the next nine months, Peter flew to the U.S. ten times and brought me to the U.K. twice. Nine months after we met, I moved to England. To give me some control over my circumstances, Peter bought me an open-ended return ticket. I thought that was very thoughtful—he knew that I was concerned about being financially dependent on him, and he didn't want me to feel trapped. Knowing that I had a way out of England gave me some personal security and showed me he had the confidence and maturity I'd been looking for in a man.

I moved to the U.K. in May 1998, right in the middle of all the sordid details and tedious hearings about the intern and the President. I had mixed feelings—I couldn't wait to get out of D.C. but I really wanted to be around for whatever was going to happen.

It took me a while to get used to saying that I was quitting my great job on the Hill and moving to England. It sounded so unlike me. My friends were shocked but pleased, perhaps a little envious of my chance for an adventure. Even my parents were happy—I worried about telling them I was going to live with Peter (imagine!), but I got their full support. Although I kept expecting someone to say I was making a mistake, I never heard that. I decided to stop trying to talk myself into thinking that our love story was too good to be true.

We lived in a northern village called Lytham St. Annes, near Peter's parents and a thirty-minute drive from his office in Blackburn. Lytham is about twenty miles as the crow flies from Liverpool and an hour south of the Lake District. Any meteorologist could tell you that it's one of the dreariest places on earth (a weatherman in the U.K. has the easiest job—it's *always* going to rain). When I landed in London, the sun was shining and the countryside looked so pretty on our drive. But the sun in England is a big tease. The summer of 1998 in the U.K. was the wettest and coldest in twenty years. It really put a damper on things.

I had nothing to do—no responsibilities, obligations, meetings, dinners, or events. Wasn't that exactly what I thought I wanted—total freedom and flexibility? I thought so, and for a few months it was great. I didn't really have to get up early in the morning, but I rose to have tea with Peter and see him off before he left for work. It helped me feel somewhat productive, too, even though my to-do list was very short. I'm a morning person (most optimistic people are—maybe it's in our DNA, some code from a long time ago that says, "Get up! There's so much to do!"), but that meant that I had really long days with nothing planned, so it's not surprising that I got a bit...restless.

I learned to cook a few vegetarian meals from the *Moosewood Cookbook*. (Blue Cheese Heaven—what's not to love?) I got a library card and read lots of historical novels, including my favorite, *The Autobiography of King Henry VIII* by Margaret George. I joined the fitness club and took step aerobics classes and race-walked on an old-fashioned treadmill. I took swimming lessons and learned to dive without holding my nose. I watched the World Cup on TV, cheering for Uzbekistan because I liked their uniforms better than the other team. I even started volunteering to help a mom in the village who had a little boy who had never walked—his legs didn't work and he had to crawl along the floor to get around. She needed my help to watch him while she ran errands. I'd play board games with him and let him teach me how to speak with an English accent—"May I have a *glass* of water, please?" we'd say back and forth, practicing for Peter, who was determined that I'd get at least that phrase right. Volunteering helped me feel a connection to my mom—it was the most fulfilling way I spent my days.

I tried to keep busy and do all the things I'd envisioned during my quarter life crisis. I watched documentaries, read the entire *Telegraph* and *Times* newspapers every day, and then counted the hours until Peter would get home. I tried riding my bike and headed down to the village green on a mildly sunny afternoon, but when I turned south to head along the waterfront, the wind stopped me dead in my tracks. I had to get off and walk. Humiliated, I went home, put the bike in the garage, and never rode it again.

I rocked the pub quiz on Wednesday nights. Well, not really, but it was my favorite activity. We cobbled together a pretty good team from Lytham, and I was better at English history than anyone there. For example, I was the only one who knew the answer to which queen had served for just nine days (Lady Jane Grey). Unfortunately, I blurted it out. "Thank you, madam!" someone at the next table shouted. I learned to whisper after that.

On weekends, Peter would take me to visit places I'd read about in books: Hampton Court outside London, Durham Cathedral in the North, Beatrix Potter's house in the Lake District, and Robin Hood's Bay on the east coast. Once he even took me to several countries in Europe when he had to go on a business trip. We took our SUV on the overnight ferry and drove through Belgium, Holland, Italy, Germany, and Switzerland. I had never traveled like that and learned a lot on that trip and saw some beautiful scenery, like Lake Como in northern Italy. When we passed by Torino, I thought of my great-grandparents who'd come from that region. It must have been difficult to leave there without knowing what they'd find in America, but I think I'd have done the same if I were in their shoes. One side of the mountain was beautiful, and the other was dusty and without hope. Considering the Perino and sons' ranch, they certainly made the right choice.

I didn't think I stuck out like an American tourist with Peter by my side, though in a bar in Zurich I got a lesson in European political correctness. We were having a drink and watching one of the World Cup games—Iran versus the United States. I cheered a couple of times for the Americans (as one should) and got some strange looks from others at the bar. I thought it was because I'd been too loud so I dialed it down a notch; to the contrary, when Iran took a shot at the goal and almost scored against the Americans, the rest of the bar cheered. I was shocked. I couldn't imagine supporting the Iranians over the Americans, but they did. They thought *we* were the enemy? Europe seemed like a continent with a short memory.

The best thing we did right away was get a Vizsla puppy from a breeder in Scotland. He had a smooth red coat, long ears, and blue eyes. I held him the entire ride home to Lytham. We named him Henry, after the king. He became the second love of my life (and lived in two countries and three cities, visited twenty-six states, and briefed the White House press corps with me in Kennebunkport, Maine).

Since I wasn't working, Henry was my project. I taught him everything you can think of—all the regular stuff like sit, stay, come, lie down, and some unconventional things like barking once for please and twice for thank you, and barking a lot when I asked him if he thought Bill Clinton should be in jail. (It was a joke, folks!) Henry and I were inseparable, and after our walks on the dunes at the beach (a place we dog owners affectionately called The Dog Sh*t

Park), he would sit on my lap and rest his chin on my forearm while I sat at the computer refreshing the *Drudge Report* for hours to see if there was anything new on the Lewinsky front. I didn't know that the local telecom company charged *by the minute* for Internet access. Whoops.

I got a bit stir-crazy, so we decided I needed a vehicle so that I could explore a little on my own and at least go to the grocery store. Peter wasn't entirely confident of my driving, especially when I would veer to the wrong side of the road. In order to pay for a used car, Peter sacrificed one of his treasures—a Yamaha motorcycle. I didn't fully appreciate at the time what a bummer it was for him to part with it. Before he handed the bike over to the buyer, he took me on a ride and claims we went 140 mph at one stretch on the highway. I loved it, which seems strange to him now that I'm such a nervous passenger. Recently he replaced the bike with a new toy—a Harley with a sidecar (you can bet the sidecar wasn't for me but for our current dog, Jasper).

After a while, it was time to get hitched. On the anniversary of our meeting, I was finally ready to accept his marriage proposal. He'd given me the time and space I'd asked for, and I didn't know how to get him to bring it up again.

So I did the best I could and wrote him a letter. I sat nervously while he read it and wondered if it wasn't clear when he didn't respond right away. But he says he read it twice, taking it all in. He was thrilled...and I still can't believe I almost missed that flight.

We eloped a few weeks later at the registry office (nicknamed in Britain as the Office of Hatches, Matches, and Dispatches) and spent two weeks as a secret married couple in Santorini, Greece. We zipped around on a motorcycle, fed the stray dogs, drank champagne while we watched the sunset, and listened to opera in a restaurant carved into the walls of a cave.

When we passed by a shop window, I'd catch of glimpse of myself and think, "Is this really me?" My values and heart seemed intact, but the adventurous part of me was new. It may have been the first time I felt like a grown-up, and I liked it.

My parents came to England for a visit a couple of weeks after our honeymoon, and Peter spilled the beans at a dinner we arranged to have with his parents. We held up our ringed fingers—I was wearing my great-grandmother Rosi's gold wedding band. Everyone seemed happy but my mom didn't seem surprised. I later learned that before she'd left for London, she told my sister that she suspected we'd gotten married. I couldn't get anything past her, even if I was thousands of miles away.

But honeymoons end. After many months of not being employed, I started to get bored. I could feel my brain shrinking. I was afraid that all the gains I'd made in Washington were for naught and that I'd have to start over somewhere. I thought about what kind of work I could do in the U.K. There wasn't much need for a Republican press secretary, and there really wasn't anything else I truly wanted to do.

And then there was the weather. Every day showers from the Irish Sea washed away the English charm. To mess with my brain, the sun usually only came out about thirty minutes before sundown, right about when Peter came home, making it look like I didn't have much to complain about weather-wise. The sun gave me false hope for the next day, and we'd take a drive and go walk on the beach or go up to the McDonald's drive-thru and get shakes (vanilla for me, chocolate for him). The next morning it'd rain again. My sunny disposition clouded over.

Peter and I always thought we'd move back to the States—and in our newly found spontaneity, we brought forward our plans to just after the New Year in 1999. There wasn't much for us to miss in England and a lot for us to look forward to in America. We chose San Diego. Why? Because we could. I wanted palm trees and sunshine. Just how impulsive was that?

I started to purge—the opposite of nesting. I couldn't wait to leave. I gave away furniture, kitchenware, and clothes. What we couldn't give away and didn't absolutely need to move to the States, we sold at a car boot sale (like a garage sale but a gathering of people in a field selling stuff out of the back of their cars). In a bitter memory for Peter, I basically gave away most of his CDs for about ten cents apiece while he was arguing with a woman over what she wanted to offer for an old Chinese tea set he'd brought back from one of his business trips. I didn't want any of his music. I sold albums by Pink Floyd, the Beatles, and Paul Weller. Though Peter was upset, a friend of ours agreed with my decision and said that, except for the Beatles, it was all overpriced.

While I was excited to be going home, I realized that Peter was about to leave his, and probably forever. I thought he'd be sad, but he didn't have a hard time leaving. His dad encouraged him to go— he knew it was a great opportunity and an adventure. Peter said he'd really only miss the beer and the football. He missed his kids, but they were out of college and on their own by that time. Years later I'd have reason to return to visit—Peter's daughter Kelly and son-in-law Warren had twins in 2006, Sebastian and Rachel, and they call me Grandma America (I love that).

We flew by the seat of our pants. We didn't have jobs, transportation, or anywhere to live. We had a six-month-old puppy and some dreams. Looking back on it now, I can't believe we didn't plan anything. I don't know if I could ever do that again. We had to borrow a bit of money from Peter's boss to help start his business and put down a deposit on a one-bedroom apartment off the I-5 next to the Mormon Temple in San Diego.

This is one of my mom's favorite pictures. It was taken in Evanston, Wyoming, when I was fifteen months old.

Grandpa and Grandma Perino, my dad, and the best present I ever got—a pony named Sally.

I was taught that our country was special and to respect our flag. I posed on our milkman's delivery box holding a cowbell for a picture on the Bicentennial.

An eight-year-old version of "The Look" in my backyard in Denver, Colorado. Joco, my dog, and the balance beam my dad made for me are in the background.

In 1979, when I was seven years old, we visited the White House, where my mom's friend worked on Air Force One manifests. I told my parents that one day I'd work in the White House, but none of us really believed that.

My great-grandmother Rosi Perino paved the way for my sister and me. She walked into one side of the American dream, and we walked out of the other.

I always loved to read. My favorite book was a personalized account of Snow White and the Seven Dwarfs. It was magic to me to be named in a book.

Who rides her grandpa's gray horse, Mito, in a fake Izod polo shirt? Er, me at age eleven. Sometimes I was too wrapped up in the day's fashions.

Feeding the calves was one of my favorite chores—and Angie "helped" me. I was sporting a new orange Denver Broncos coat that my grandparents bought for all of the grandkids.

Every summer we took a photograph of "the whole fam damily" before Angie and I went back to Colorado for school. My late uncle Tom is the first on the left, next to his wife Janet and my dad. My grandpa died in 2001, my grandma a decade later. My uncle Matt, far right, still runs the ranch with his wife Donna and their sons, Wade and Preston. My mom took the picture.

An early success of marketing feminism. My parents bought the T-shirt I wore for years, "Anything boys can do, girls can do better." Love the tube socks.

Working on the school paper and yearbook during high school. Thank goodness my mom made me take a typing class, but I should have listened to her about my posture. (*Courtesy of Ponderosa High School*)

I graduated from college in 1994, and my niece, Jessica Wilkerson, stole the show. My dad is standing behind us.

Peter and I return to the U.K. now and then to visit family and friends. Edinburgh, pictured here in 2007, is one of my favorite cities.

The only snapshot of our wedding day on September 30, 1998. We eloped and got married at the registry office in Blackpool, England. Henry, our first Vizlsa, was our first "baby" and pictured here at four months old.

Our first family photograph taken by a professional at Del Mar Beach in San Diego, California, with the standard uniform of jeans and white T-shirts, in 1999. We thought we'd live there forever. Little did we know....

We bought an old Ford Explorer and I used some loose connections to land a job at City Hall. It was tough to swallow after working on Capitol Hill. Let's just say the deputy mayor wasn't exactly the same caliber as the congressmen I'd worked for, and I lasted in that job only two months (I don't even list it on my résumé). That said, I think city government is the toughest—that's where dollars and cents really matter and where people typically don't go into public service to make a living. They actually have to make a difference.

When we didn't have much income, I worried about money a lot. Eventually I turned our finances over to Peter and trusted him to handle that. I love that he still makes sure I always have cash for a taxi and that he's in charge of balancing the checkbook. That's one of the ways I learned to let go and not control everything. Turning over the money matters to Peter has eased a lot of stress in my life (except when he waits to pay the bills until the last moment—that drives me crazy. I like to pay bills a month ahead of time).

Job stability was not my middle name. Over two years, I worked at three different public relations firms—but every move was an upward climb. The public relations companies ranged from small to medium to international. I tried to put a good spin on it, but I didn't like my experience at any of them. I love communications strategy and being a spokesperson, but the structure of most public relations companies doesn't fit my style.

I had one chance to escape—the problem was it didn't pay anything. In March 2000, an old friend I'd stayed in touch with from Capitol Hill, Mindy Tucker, called me from the Bush campaign. They wondered if I could help out as a spokesperson in California until the election. I was so glad they still remembered me and thought I was good enough to speak on the governor's behalf, even though I knew they didn't think he'd win California. It was a great opportunity, but I was the only one in our family who had a salaried job with benefits, and we needed my income to make ends meet. I had to turn her down. I felt awful and dreaded hanging up the phone, cutting off the connection. I cried and said, "Now I'll never get to work for George Bush."

It was time to get real. Poor Peter, no matter what job I had, I seemed bored (my mom told him this was not a new problem). I was happy with him and liked our lifestyle of dog beach visits on weekend mornings and Mexican food restaurants on weekend nights. (Peter had a hard time differentiating between enchiladas, tostadas, and burritos. I finally told him it's all the same ingredients in a different wrapper.) Peter got a surf board and a wetsuit. We were trying to fit into the southern California lifestyle, but I couldn't get comfortable.

I kept up with politics in Washington and longed to be a part of the action. I naturally put a D.C. angle into my public relations tactics, even helping one medical device company get invited to testify at a Congressional hearing on a new set of Department of Transportation rules (about how many hours a truck driver needed to sleep before he could haul a load on the highway). The CEO of that company loved it because it was a different way to get the word out about his invention, a CPAP machine for people with sleep apnea. Happy clients, happy bosses. But I still was unsatisfied.

The White Board Incident

Peter knew I was restless. He'd spent most of his career with Johnson & Johnson and that set him up to have a successful start-up business of his own later in life. He didn't want to hold me back from what I really wanted to do just so that we could stay in San Diego.

He finally told me to sit down while he stood in the living room with a white board and a dry-erase marker. He told me to list everything I wanted to do in a job (speak on the record for a major political player, advise a politician on how to talk to the media to advance a policy or cause, and work on more exciting clients dealing with bigger issues than how to get more venture capital money). Then I had to list all the things I didn't want to do in a job (send pitches to reporters who were too busy to care about some .com business, be at the beck and call of senior vice presidents who always overpromised results to a client, and have the pressure of finding new clients when there was no time to work on the clients we already had). The PR business was a pyramid scheme to me, and I didn't see how you got to the top unless you broke out of it. Even then, I didn't think I wanted to be at the top.

I gave him my lists and then he made me assign a value to each thing. The final score? Anything in D.C. was better than what I would do anywhere else.

"I think this is pretty clear. We need to move to Washington," Peter said.

Peter doubled as a career counselor. He helped me get out of my rut. Forcing me to put my goals down in black and white, leaving aside any lifestyle questions, showed a stark contrast. He made me realize that we shouldn't be afraid to move. We'd already proven we could do that and survive.

I didn't want to be so impulsive, though. I had hundreds of "buts"—we had just bought a house, he loved San Diego, I should try harder, I should give it more time, I was scared of going back to East Coast winters, etc. But he was right—I wasn't going to be happy unless I gave it another shot in Washington. And because I had his support, I had the freedom and the financial security I needed to take a chance.

That was August 2001. I wasted no time and e-mailed my friend Mindy, the same person who called me about volunteering on the campaign in 2000. She was now at the Justice Department running communications. I told her and some other former colleagues that I'd booked a flight for the week of September 17 to come look for a job. Several of them said they'd love to see me, so I felt that I was set up to at least get back in the mix for any good jobs that might open up.

But a week before I was to make the trip, terrorists attacked America.

On 9/11, Peter woke me at 5:30 a.m. as usual and set my English Breakfast tea on my nightstand and left to take Henry for his morning walk. The weather was warm, so I went into the living room and opened the windows. I turned on the morning news and the first thing I saw was Charlie Gibson on *Good Morning America* reporting about a fire at the World Trade Center. I looked up and the very next thing I saw was the second plane hit the second tower. I screamed and ran outside to get Peter, yelling, "They're attacking the World Trade Center with planes!" He thought I meant with small planes and light weaponry. We rushed back and stood in our living room in front of the news while our tea got cold.

We had friends in Washington and sat nervously watching the news with all of the false reports of planes hitting the Capitol and the Treasury Building. Then the plane hit the Pentagon and Flight 93 went down in Pennsylvania, and it felt like the beginning of the war my dad warned me about as a kid. Good versus evil. I wasn't sure at that moment that we could win such a war.

But it was President Bush's reassurance, his steady demeanor, sense of purpose, and leadership that made me feel safe. After 9/11, I was more determined than ever to go back to Washington and serve in the administration, in whatever capacity they could use me. Years later in my office at the White House, I kept my favorite quote from him on the wall: "We will not tire, we will not falter, we will not fail. Peace and freedom will prevail."

A couple of days after 9/11, Mindy e-mailed me saying she needed another spokesperson on her team at the Justice Department because the amount of work for the public affairs team was overwhelming. The Justice Department bore all of the responsibility from the FBI to immigration services and prosecuting the terrorists. She asked if I would be willing to come back, and I started packing that night. I hated the circumstances that were propelling our move, but I was ready to go and thankful for the opportunity to contribute.

Returning to Where I Once Belonged

I flew to Washington in October 2001, leaving behind the palm trees of southern California in time to see the leaves of the Mid-Atlantic change color before winter. I moved into the same place I'd left—my old English basement apartment at Desiree and Stephen Sayle's house on Capitol Hill had been converted into their family room and a guest bedroom. They had two little girls, Isabela (two) and Vivienne (four months).

While I waited for my security clearance to start at the Justice Department, I worked with Desiree at the White House correspondence office. She was the director, and her office was swamped with letters of condolence and support after the terrorist attacks. She often had to work late, so I hurried home to help look after the girls. We watched *Toy Story 2* over and over again. I hadn't been around young children in years, and I caught several colds during the three months I lived there. By December that year, I started my job at DOJ and after the New Year, Peter arrived in D.C. with Henry. We rented a house of our own not far away from the Sayles in the Lincoln Park neighborhood.

It didn't take me long to readjust to being a government spokesperson and I immediately fit in with the public affairs team. Right away, I handled some of the non-terrorism-related Justice Department issues: Environment and Natural Resources, Anti-Trust, Tax, and personal feature stories about Department of Justice officials. We took a lot of calls at DOJ—it wasn't unusual to get eighty messages a day from reporters asking for comment on different cases. After a few weeks of learning the ropes, I could write a book, *101 Ways to Say No Comment*. Because so many of the press calls involved active litigation, it wasn't possible to say anything beyond "Yes, the government plans to appeal," and "We've received a copy of the filing and will respond in due course." We had to be careful with what we said so that we didn't compromise any of the cases. But in a repeated theme of my life, it didn't take long for me to get bored again—not with the content, but with the mundane tactics of the job.

I handled some of the major cases at the time, including the government's suits against major U.S. businesses, coal-fired power plants, cities out of compliance with the Clean Water Act, and companies that were accused of violating the Endangered Species Act. My favorite case was a Russian immigrant who got busted by an undercover Fish and Wildlife Service agent trying to pass off the roe of endangered Mississippi Mud Fish as Black Sea caviar. That crook did some time, and I worked on a story that landed on the front page of *The New York Times*'s Dining Out section. That's PR gold.

Working on environmental issues is how I came to know Jim Connaughton, the appointee running the White House Council on Environmental Quality (CEQ), an office of the White House that was set up by President Nixon to coordinate environmental, energy, and conservation policies across all of the federal agencies. Trust me—in times of terror threat and war, the last place a Republican staffer wants to work is on the environmental issues. It wasn't the main attraction, but I learned early on to take the jobs that no one else wants, in a place where you can shine. If you take the toughest and least glamorous assignments and don't totally screw them up, you're going to stand out as competent and reliable.

That's how I ended up going from the Justice Department to the White House. Moving over to be the director of communications for the CEQ was a step up for me and it linked me even closer to the White House press office. CEQ had offices across from the White House on Jackson Place, a row of old town homes that line Lafayette Square. I felt energized—I had a lot to learn and a lot more responsibility.

I hooked up with the White House communications team right away and was invited to the morning meeting where the agenda for the day was set and any questions were put forth to the group and its head, Dan Bartlett. I tried to be helpful but didn't seek the limelight. I knew that the environment division needed to be managed and that the best way for me to help was to take those press calls off their plates and to alert them when I thought a media ambush was coming their way. I had known Ari Fleischer, the press secretary, from our days on the Hill (though he doesn't remember ever knowing me then!), and I got to know Scott McClellan, his deputy assigned to energy issues and who later became the White House press secretary when Ari left the role. I became a go-to person for Scott, because I was ready and able to handle all of the press calls about the environment—and believe me, there were plenty of them. The Bush White House was constantly under attack by environmentalists determined to extract blood from the administration, and they ignored many of the good policies he advanced on wildlife, wetlands, air pollution, and oceans.

I learned early on that working in the White House can cause severe head swelling and that the only cure is a dose of humility. My mom gave me that after my first week at CEQ when she called on Friday night and asked how I was doing. In one breath I told her all about what I had been assigned, how I saw President Bush get off Marine One on the South Lawn, and the call I got from Karl Rove about a Presidential statement I was drafting. I told her how Karl was so nice and approachable and how he really improved my document and on and on. When I finally stopped talking, my mom asked, "Who the hell is Karl Rove?" (Eventually, I became Karl's spokesperson, and he loves that story, too.)

I was at CEQ for over two years, including during the 2004 election. My mom worried about what would happen if President Bush lost to Senator John Kerry. I told her that we'd all have to find new jobs. She called back a few days later, now more worried about my employment future.

"Maybe John Kerry would want to keep you?" she asked, hoping I'd put her mind at ease.

I laughed. "No, Mom, it doesn't work that way," I said.

I wasn't worried about finding a new job if it came to that. I'd gained so much experience working at the White House level, and Peter and I were really happy in D.C. By that point, I had enough money saved to get by for a few months if it took that long to find a job. The only thing I worried about was the election, and there wasn't much I could do about that. Thankfully, the President won and we looked forward to a second term. I just had that itch again—I'd outgrown the job at CEQ.

It turned out I didn't have to wait too long for a new opportunity. I didn't want to stay at CEQ for another four years, so I interviewed for a new role at the Treasury Department for the upcoming

Social Security reform effort. But on the day I was going to accept that job, I got an offer that changed my plans.

The White House press secretary, Scott McClellan, asked me to stay in his office after the morning meeting. I immediately thought I might be in trouble. I didn't expect him to ask if I would be interested in the deputy press secretary job. Um, yes please! The deputy press secretary position was my dream job—it meant getting to contribute in a more meaningful way, taking on much more responsibility and additional issues, and being able to help across the policy front, not just on the environment. I would be working with the national press corps and supporting the press secretary so that he would have all he needed to be successful at the briefings. I'd get to know the President more as one of two deputies who alternated working holidays and weekends (this is worth it—I always recommend that young people take the deputy job—no matter what industry or organization. Being the second in command is where you learn how to be the leader, and it's when you establish a good relationship with the boss).

I was so excited for that opportunity. I thought it was the only job I'd ever really want. Scott called Treasury and told them about my change of plans. Two weeks later, on Inauguration Day of the President's second term, I started work in the White House press office. I would be there until the President's last day, but I'd have a different role by then.

~~~~~~~~

CHAPTER 3

Stepping Up to the Podium

Scratch That

The day I learned about becoming the next White House press secretary was the day I planned to resign from the White House.

It was the summer of 2007; I had been the deputy press secretary for two-and-a-half years and with the Bush Administration since right after 9/11. I'd gotten up every weekday just after 4 a.m. and worked until I passed out around 10 p.m. On weekends I went to bed earlier than most children. Often I'd wake up in the middle of the night and could not fall back asleep.

I was consumed by work, but not unhappily so. I knew the hours, pace, and pressure were taking a toll on my well-being and my marriage, yet I thought I could handle them. My husband was tired, too, though he rarely complained—it's just one of those things that a wife can sense. To avoid disgruntled looks and arguments from Peter, I started making excuses to run upstairs so I could check my e-mails in secret. I was the fastest BlackBerry typist in the Western World, especially when I was hiding.

Around that time, the White House chief of staff, Josh Bolten, suggested that if any of us felt that we couldn't make it to the end of the administration, then we should think about moving on because the President intended to "sprint to the finish" and he needed a strong and energized team around him. By leaving early, the White House could replace us with people fresh off the bench.

I was very torn. My loyalty and dedication to the President and the country grew daily, no matter how battered we got in the press. The more hits he took, the more strongly I felt about being there to defend him and his decisions. Professionally, I was still enjoying the job and felt challenged (that's an understatement). I was learning more with every news cycle, and I never felt like I knew enough. I used to volunteer to be the press office representative at all of the policy meetings, no matter how obscure, so that I could listen and learn.

On the occasional slow news day, I'd invite one of the policy managers to lunch to pick their brain. Once in a while I asked career civil servants to come over to the White House and give me a more in-depth look at a major geopolitical hotspot. When the State Department's expert on Pakistan walked me through a brief history of the country and the various challenges we faced there, I summed up what I'd heard, "So we're totally screwed?" She agreed with my assessment.

Another reason I was reluctant to leave my White House job was the bond with my team. After all of the time we spent together, we could read each other's minds and finish each other's jokes. I knew that kind of teamwork was a once-in-a-lifetime experience (and it took many of us a long time to realize it could never be replicated).

Out of pride, I didn't want to admit that I was tired, that I might not physically be able to make it. And I couldn't imagine how I'd say good-bye to the President.

I talked to Peter about it a lot. I stayed up at night fantasizing about my choices. Being able to browse at Target became more attractive as the e-mails from reporters came in asking about everything under the sun.

I asked Peter to walk me through our financial situation, and he said we could make it just fine for a few months with me not working. There was a little financial pressure, but nothing we couldn't manage by tightening our belts.

Then in August 2007, with all of this on my mind, we took a short vacation to Oregon. Peter was in an overnight relay race through the mountains—Hood to Coast. I joined up with Susan Whitson, a former colleague at the Justice Department and the White House, while Peter and Susan's husband, Keir, ran the race. We spent some girl time together, even going for manicures and pedicures.

Susan had recently left the White House, where she had been Mrs. Bush's press secretary. She got married during the administration and then wanted to start a family. When she announced her resignation from the East Wing, the press asked her why she was leaving and she said, "BlackBerrys don't make babies." Not long after that, she and Keir moved full-time to Washington, Virginia, near the Shenandoah Valley, and now they have two children.

Over that long weekend in the Northwest, I envied Susan's serenity and her easy laugh. I noticed she didn't have the permanent scowl that marred the space between my eyebrows. I went over the pros and cons of staying at the White House, and she listened but didn't have an answer—she knew it was a tough decision both personally and career-wise.

That night I decided to try a trick that had worked for me when I couldn't make up my mind about moving to Washington originally—slipping my indecision into the gap between wakefulness and sleep to help settle on a solution. The next morning, after the runners crossed the finish line and were playing touch football on the beach after the race, I looked at Peter and said, "It's time." I told him I'd decided to leave the White House. He asked me if I was sure, looking at me sideways as if he didn't quite believe me. I said I was. His fist pumped the air and he yelled, "Yes!" Hugging me close, Peter made an announcement, "Hey, everyone, I'm going to get my wife back!" They cheered and slapped him on the back. (As some of these onlookers were strangers, I'm not sure what they thought he meant.)

We flew back to Washington on Labor Day. We held hands on the flight and talked about all the things we wanted to do when I wasn't working all the time. I decided I'd sleep until 6 a.m. (instead of 4:15 a.m.) and make breakfast twice a week. We'd walk Henry together in the mornings and read the entire paper—even the Style section. We'd visit his family in the U.K. and then take a road trip to the ranch in Wyoming. We had big plans to do small things.

With every mile closer to D.C., I became more comfortable with my decision and was gathering my courage to break the news. My stomach fluttered when I thought about telling my press office team. I felt that in a way I was letting them down, but I knew they'd understand. I set aside all thoughts about telling the President. I figured the best approach was to rip off the Band-Aid; it would only hurt for a second.

The next morning started as any other—a senior staff meeting at 7:30 a.m. in the Roosevelt Room across from the Oval Office followed by the communications meeting in Ed Gillespie's office upstairs in the West Wing. I pulled Ed aside before senior staff and asked if I could see him after his meeting. He said yes because he needed to talk to me, too, but I didn't know what it was about. I'd made the first step toward telling them I was resigning. There was no going back. Or so I thought.

At the communications meeting, staff filed out and Ed said,

"Dana, can you stay for a minute?" signaling to others we needed to be left alone. Ed's a happy Irish-American guy, and even the way he says his name on his voicemail message cracks me up. But he didn't look like he was in a joking mood.

I stayed seated in the chair across from his desk. As the door shut behind the last person to leave the room, I took a deep breath and started to speak when he stopped me and said, "Mind if I go first?"

"Sure," I said and sat back in my seat, afraid I'd chicken out.

"We would like to name you as the press secretary by next week," Ed said.

"You what?" I was stunned. The blood drained out of my body and a mix of dread and delight ran from my heart to my toes. I thought of Peter's joy on the Oregon beach—he wasn't going to believe this. Our plans just went poof. I'd mentally checked out and in my head was already making breakfast and taking the dog out. In an instant I had to summon back all of my work energy.

Ed had knocked me on my heels and I stammered in a rare moment of speechlessness. It was an overwhelming honor, and I realized the significance of crossing the threshold from deputy to press secretary (I'd been a bridesmaid for so long). I believed that after all of those years I was finally up to the task. I'd have an even bigger role in influencing White House communications, and I had ideas on how to improve some practices in the briefing room. Plus, I'd be only the second woman to serve as the press secretary (and the first Republican woman). Immediately, I knew that by accepting the opportunity, my future career prospects would change dramatically.

The moment was bittersweet, however. As Ed explained, Tony Snow was going to be leaving the White House to focus on his health and take care of his family. Tony had been a trouper at the briefings during his colon cancer treatment, which had started in 2005, a year before he came to the White House. He was diligent about following doctor's orders, and from where I sat watching him every day, I thought he was doing well enough in 2007 that he was going to stay as the press secretary until the end of the administration. But to keep healthy, Tony needed to reduce the pace and pressure of his job and he wanted to spend more time with his wife, Jill, and their three kids. And who could blame him?

Tony Snow

It's time I told you about Tony Snow. So many people remember him fondly, and for good reason. Tony was one of a kind, a man of great character and wit. He might have had the smallest ego of anyone in Washington. Whereas most people in D.C. decorated their office with photographs of themselves with "Very Important People," Tony had three 8-by-10 photographs of his kids in frames on his desk, which left little room for paperwork. He kept a messy desk, but it was part of his charm.

When Jill turned fifty, he wanted to give her fifty presents to open. The press office pitched in to get the gifts—her favorite candy, tickets to a play, a new CD. He threw a party for her at their home and they pushed the furniture against the walls and "danced like teenagers until three in the morning."

Tony never missed his kids' events at school, and he didn't apologize for it. He trusted me to run the press office while he was away, and he didn't worry if he missed a meeting. In the afternoons, we'd book him on lots of talk radio and cable news programs and he sparred with the hosts and represented the President's position beautifully. While he sounded great, he had a terrible tie collection, which he kept on the back of his door. On several occasions I made him change before going in front of the cameras.

At home, Jill and Tony shared their love for each other with several rescue animals, including a dog that once decided to chew through his White House–issued BlackBerry. Tony could seem scatterbrained, including once losing another government smartphone, which turned up a month later in his winter boots—even though it was July.

Because of his chemotherapy treatment, Tony needed to keep his weight up, so he ordered a lot of food from the White House Mess. His favorite breakfast was three pancakes with sausages stuffed in the middle with maple syrup smothered over the top and dripping on his desk. He drank three large vanilla lattes a day. At lunch he'd eat whatever the special was—in particular he liked Tuesday's pecan-crusted chicken salad. Despite all of those calories, he didn't gain weight.

Tony studied philosophy and math in college, not journalism. His passion for debating served him well in his jobs before he was the White House press secretary—daily editorial writer, Presidential speechwriter for George H. W. Bush, talk radio host, and Sunday show anchor. He worked at Fox News for years and remains a legend. And you know who liked Tony the most? The crew guys and gals—and that's how you really know that he was as good a person as everyone thought.

On his last day at the White House we took a press office group picture, and looking back, I'm shocked to see how thin he'd become. His hair had been salt-and-pepper when he started, but just a little over a year later it was starkly white. He was affectionate and emotional saying good-bye to us. Everyone at the White House lined up outside to cheer him on and wish him well as he drove away, and he cried openly. As did many of us.

Less than a year later, Tony collapsed while traveling to a speaking event in Spokane, Washington. He spent the next several weeks in the hospital. Jill told me that he'd watch the press briefings from his bed and get so frustrated with the reporters' questions that he'd throw his plastic cup on the floor and raise his fists at them in solidarity with me. He could always spot media bias when it cropped up, but it didn't make him bitter, and I tried to adopt his attitude. It was the best way to approach the job and to keep from getting depressed or mean.

Tony put up a valiant fight against cancer, but ultimately he did not win it. He died on July 12, 2008, the morning after the President and his staff arrived back from the G8 meeting in Japan.

I was woken up by a phone call from Ed Henry, who was the White House correspondent for CNN. I pretended I'd been up for hours even though the jet lag felt like a lead blanket.

"What's up?" I asked, trying to sound alert.

"I'm sorry to call so early, but could I get reaction to the news?" Ed said.

He sounded so sad (Ed is one of the most sentimental guys you'll ever meet). My instincts kicked in and I guessed the reason for the call. I didn't want CNN to be able to say that it was the news network that had informed the White House about Tony's death, so I said I'd call him back. I scrolled through my e-mails. And there it was, a little after 4 a.m. Jill had sent me a note to say Tony had just passed away.

The White House helped Jill make arrangements for the funeral at the National Shrine of the Immaculate Conception because the outpouring of support was overwhelming and she had three kids to take care of. The advance team ensured every detail of the service was perfect. There was a full Mass and President Bush, though he'd been to many funerals, gave his first eulogy for a friend. He was concerned he wouldn't get through it, but of course he did and it was a fitting tribute to a remarkable man. We were fortunate to know Tony Snow.

Taking Over at the Podium

Meanwhile, in Ed Gillespie's office, I still hadn't responded to his news. He raised his eyebrows and asked, "So?"

I didn't immediately accept because something was bothering me about how this was happening. You'd think when you're named the press secretary that the clouds will part, the sun will shine, and beautiful music will start playing in the background. But this wasn't a fairy tale.

"What does the President think about all of this?" I asked.

Ed looked surprised and he said, "Well, he just assumed you would."

"Oh, he did, did he?" I teased.

I told Ed that I was honored to accept, but I was a bit concerned about how I was picked. Tony had been a very outside-the-box selection, and even his hiring was a message in itself that said the White House was stepping up its game, choosing a big-time media personality who wasn't biased by White House-itis, a disease you can get if you work there too long. Naming Tony Snow sent the public a very strong message at the time, and it helped us get the storyline of an insular White House turned around. This helped us with media coverage and Congressional relations.

I was not that kind of pick—I was safe. It crossed my mind that I had been an obvious choice and that perhaps they thought it was easier just to have me take over officially since there wasn't that much time left in the administration. Was I just the convenient choice, the most obvious option, or did the President really have confidence in me to do the job well?

Ed assured me it was the latter, but I had a few nagging doubts. He and I agreed to keep the conversation between us until they could work out a smooth transition plan and announcement. Press secretaries change infrequently at the White House, and this was going to be a big story, especially when it came to speculation about Tony's health.

I walked down the stairs and thought about what I'd say to Peter. He expected me to say that I'd resigned. But here was another example of how just when I'd make a plan, God had another idea in mind.

I called Peter and whispered into the phone from my office so that no one could overhear the news. He was stunned, and a bit overwhelmed with pride at the same time (Peter is not my most objective critic). He rallied and said, "Whatever you need me to do to help, consider it done."

A few hours later I went to the Oval Office for a previously scheduled policy meeting. I walked in and saw the President. I raised an eyebrow that said, "So you just assumed, huh?" And he winked at me and nodded his head, with a look that said, "Well, well, look at you—the new press secretary." His facial expression said it all. It reassured me that I was a deliberate choice, that I wasn't just the next in line. I decided not to fight it with self-doubt and just spend a rare moment feeling good about something. I took my seat for the meeting and tried to focus on the topic, but I started writing a list in the margin of my briefing paper. We had a lot to do.

The morning of the announcement, the press still had no idea that big news was coming. Only a few people inside the White House were aware that I'd be taking over for Tony. It was August 31 and hot outside. I decided to wear a lavender dress with a matching jacket and paid a little extra attention to my hair and makeup. I was distracted because the very next day the President was leaving on a secret trip to Iraq, and I was in charge of the planning for the press office while also getting myself packed and ready to go. No one could know about the trip, so I could delegate only certain tasks.

I went to the senior staff and communications meetings as if it were a regular day, while Tony Fratto, my good friend and the new principal deputy press secretary, stepped up to help make sure everything went smoothly. He even wrote some remarks the President could use about me since Ed and I had forgotten to do that. Then Tony Snow and I gathered the press staff and gave them the news. A few of them bit their lips to keep from crying—they feared the worst about his health, too, despite Tony's insistence that he was fine.

One of the press assistants made an overhead announcement to the reporters in their offices in the West Wing that the President would be coming to the briefing room to make a statement about a change in personnel. The press office phones started ringing off the hook. The press isn't patient, asking "Who? What? When? Tell me!" they pleaded. We held firm and said they'd know soon enough.

Just before the big announcement, the President walked down to the press office and we made small talk before taking the stage. By now, word had leaked to the press what the change was going to be, and the photographers were in place to capture the moment.

When it was time, Tony and I followed President Bush into the briefing room and I felt really short as I stood there next to them. I looked around and saw Peter dressed in a suit. He gave me a big smile and a subtle thumbs-up. "Can you believe this?" we said with our eyes.

The President thanked Tony for his service and complimented his many talents. He did not mention Tony's cancer directly, but he spoke admiringly of how Tony had managed the competing pressures he was under with class, dignity, and good humor. Tony's remarks were equally gracious.

After that, the President turned to his written remarks about me. But that felt too formal to him and about halfway through he put down his notes and said what I needed to hear.

"Look, I chose Dana because I know she can handle you all."

That sealed it. With his impromptu remark, he signaled to everyone, including me, that I had his full confidence. It said that he knew I had the ability, management style, and commitment to serve as his press secretary and assured the reporters that I was going to have the access I needed to be able to do my job. He immediately boosted my credibility and made the transition smoother for everyone.

A few weeks later, the President saw Peter and said, "I owe you an apology. I made a mistake when we announced Dana as the press secretary. I didn't see you there and I should have recognized you."

Peter was blown away that he remembered that. It was another example of the thoughtfulness of President Bush, who made sure our significant others felt a part of the White House experience. Peter even had a Presidential nickname, "The Englishman," and was presented a cake by the Commander in Chief at Camp David one June. Having "Happy Birthday" sung to him by the President and Condoleeza Rice is one of Peter's favorite bragging rights.

Visits to Camp David are unforgettable experiences. But it was what I learned about leadership while serving under President Bush that left the biggest impression on me.

I know that my personal take on the Bush presidency won't necessarily affect how historians write about him—they'll continue to rank his decisions, accomplishments, and failures for the rest of time. President Bush didn't worry about that. When asked about his legacy, he'd say, "Last year I read three books about George Washington. So if they're still analyzing the first President, then the forty-third doesn't have a lot to worry about." He did not mean that he had confidence in being viewed favorably, just that there was nothing we could do about the future. He taught me not to dwell too much on his legacy, which helped me keep things in perspective.

But I hope that my memories can help fill in the gaps of the story of him as a President—the shorthand of history hasn't gotten it right yet. So with that in mind, I compiled some of my strongest impressions from my years with President Bush. I call it leadership from a follower's perspective, and it starts with my big lesson in humility.

The White Ho

One of the most professional young men that worked in the press office was Carlton Carroll of Tallahassee. He was there to help me manage being the acting press secretary while Tony Snow had some exploratory surgery that kept him away from the office for three weeks.

On the Friday night before I was to take over at the podium for that interim period, Carlton knocked on my office door and said, "Ma'am, I'm sorry to bother you, but do you think they should build you a new podium over the weekend?"

He asked because the White House Communications Agency had built a podium for Tony in the temporary space on Jackson Place that we were using as a briefing room until the renovations of the James S. Brady Briefing Room were completed. Now, Tony was six-feet-five and I am an even five feet tall. I could barely see over his podium without my heels.

"Oh, goodness no, I don't want to waste any time or money. Just get me one of those apple boxes and I'll stand on that. It'll be fine."

"Yes, ma'am."

We got through that first week without triggering any major national or international catastrophes, so I was feeling pretty good. Then Carlton came back.

"Ma'am, I'm really sorry to bother you with this again, but I think that we should have them make you a new podium," he said.

"Don't be silly. We got through this week and next week we are traveling two days—before you know it, Tony will be back," I said, barely looking up from my computer.

Carlton looked at the floor and didn't leave. He was gathering some courage to tell me something I never expected to hear.

"Well, actually, NBC News showed me the camera shot from the back of the room. And when you're at Tony's podium standing on that apple box, the seal above your head is partly blocked by your head—so it doesn't say, 'The White House'... it says, 'The White Ho.'"

I stared at him for a minute. We started giggling. The cameraman, Rodney Batten, had been kind to me and shot the briefings wide all week to spare me any embarrassment.

I gave Carlton the go-ahead, and by Monday, I had a new podium.

I was grateful for Rodney and Carlton's protection. Staying connected to the staff and crew was really important to me, and it paid off. I didn't want to get a big "senior staff head" and was grateful for the reminder of where I came from—in Wyoming, being cocky was a sure way to fall off your high horse.

Strength When No One Is Watching

In January 2008, President Bush went to the Middle East. He traveled to the region several times, though this was his first visit to Israel as president. As always, the stakes were high.

The Bush Administration had just hosted the Middle East countries at the U.S. Naval Academy in Annapolis, Maryland, the previous November. It was the first time that all of the Arab nations had joined such a meeting, and there was some hope that Israeli Prime

Minister Olmert and Palestinian President Abbas would be able to take the next steps toward a peace agreement (I know—but bear with me). The President's first stop was Israel.

When Air Force One landed, it taxied to the hangar where the Israelis were gathered to greet us. Since President Bush didn't waste any time, we were up and ready to go, standing by the door as the plane came to a stop. The President had just put on his suit jacket and was straightening his tie. I loved when he said to his personal aide and his advance man, "Look alive, boys! America has arrived."

As we walked down the steps of the plane, the Israeli national band played "The Star-Spangled Banner." It was an inspiring start to the trip. Our delegation lined up just outside Air Force One, and President Bush then introduced us one by one to Olmert. It was a wonderful bit of formality, except for President Bush's personal touch of using our nicknames, which showed he was very friendly with the Israelis. When he got to me, he said, "This is Sweet Dana, Dana Perino, my press secretary." I nodded, stifled a laugh, and shook the Prime Minister's hand.

In the morning, President Bush had meetings with President Simon Peres, and in the afternoon, we took the choppers over to Ramallah, where he met with Abbas. It was shuttle diplomacy by chopper.

That night, our delegation dined at Olmert's residence. The dining room table was very long and narrow with a full formal dinner setting for about twenty people. The walls were painted a pale yellow and decorated with Israeli art. The Prime Minister served wines from the region and the conversation was very easy and comfortable.

I sat next to Raffi Eitan, who at the time was the Minister of Pensioners Affairs. He'd dedicated his life to Israel, serving in many different government positions. In his youth, he had been in charge of the Mossad operation that led to the kidnapping of Adolf Eichmann. In his eighties when I met him, Minister Eitan was a bit hard of hearing and at dinner kept raising his glass to me and in a loud voice saying, "Bon appétit!" At one point, President Bush shot me a look of "What the heck is going on down there?" I just smiled, shrugged, and toasted Eitan back.

As we finished the main course, Olmert took a moment to thank President Bush for coming to Israel, and he described how much it meant to them to have the special relationship with the United States. On the Israeli side of the table, there was at least one person who was very much against the idea of the peace agreement as it had been loosely defined. Olmert's coalition wasn't strong, and any change in the cabinet would have triggered elections under the Israeli system. So keeping everyone on the same page was key to preventing a breakdown in the discussions.

After Olmert wound down, President Bush took charge of the dinner. I'd never seen him quite like this before, and I'd been in most of the foreign leader meetings for the previous couple of years.

The President said, "Thank you, Mr. Prime Minister. We are honored to be here. The relationship between Israel and the United States has never been stronger. And we have an opportunity here to ensure security for your citizens through decisions we have before us," he said and then paused as he looked around the room. "But I'm telling you right now—if there's anyone sitting at this table that is waiting in the tall grass with plans to attack this good man"—pointing at Olmert—"as soon as he makes a tough decision, please tell me now. Because I am the President of the United States of America, and I will not waste my country's capital on you if you aren't serious."

Silence. I was stunned and teared up. It showed such strength and demonstrated clearly President Bush's commitment to helping the Israelis and the Palestinians come to an agreement. No cameras were there to capture the moment, but we saw him stand up for America when no one was watching.

The Israelis started shifting in their seats after the President's remarks and they murmured, "Oh no, no, no, there are no problems here, nothing to see, let's move along."

But President Bush didn't let them off the hook so easily. "Tell you what—I'd like to hear more about all of you. Who here was born in Israel?" Only one cabinet official raised her hand.

The President then asked, "Well, what are your stories—how did your families come here? Let's start with you," pointing to Olmert's chief of staff at the opposite end of the table from where I was sitting.

There was a short hesitation and then he said, "Well, Mr. President, my family came here from Iraq . . ." And then—Ukraine, Poland, Russia, Hungary, and elsewhere. As they told their stories, some ministers leaned forward and said, "Wait, your dad was in Poland in 1928? So was my dad!" There were several small world exchanges like that, and they kept saying that they'd never known this or that about one another.

President Bush let the discussion last awhile. Then, when the conversation started dying down and there was a renewed sense of camaraderie and shared purpose among the Israelis, he said, "I had a feeling you all may have forgotten why you were here in the first place. Thank you for having us. Good night."

And with that, he pushed back his chair and everyone stood up. Dinner was over. Afterward, the President and Olmert went into the Prime Minister's private study to smoke a cigar and discuss the day's events. The delegation waited in the lobby and chatted with our counterparts. The Prime Minister's spokesman and I worked on a description of the dinner that could be shared with reporters who were waiting outside.

The next morning the U.S. delegation left Israel for Kuwait.

While on the flight, I needed President Bush to sign off on something before I did the press gaggle. I went up to his office on Air Force One, and he invited me to have a seat. I didn't want to bother him, but I loved any time I had a chance to talk with him more casually. When I sat down, I said, "So about last night..."

He looked at me and winked. "Pretty cool, huh?"

"Yes, sir. Pretty cool."

I asked him how he knew to get the conversation going among Olmert's cabinet. He said that based on his observations and his gut instinct, he believed they'd become so wrapped up in the daily politics that they'd lost sight of the overall goal of signing a peace agreement that would secure Israel in a hostile neighborhood. He had a feeling that they'd just stopped talking to one another, so he decided to take a chance to get them to start seeing themselves as allies for a common cause, rather than as individuals fighting their own political battles.

My experience with the President was that he was able to look beyond the briefing papers, to cut through to the point right away. He kept a broader perspective in mind, focused on a goal, and figured out what was needed from everyone to reach it. He never admonished or lectured other leaders, but he was firm and encouraged them to do better by their people. Moments like these didn't happen in front of reporters, but I'm glad I was there to let Americans know how he conducted himself overseas on their behalf.

"I Think He Wants the President"

News of America's military men and women were wounded and killed in Iraq and Afghanistan almost overwhelmed me on some days. I may have sounded strong when I was talking to the press, but sometimes I had to push my feelings way down in order to get any words out of my mouth to make statements and answer questions.

The hardest days were when President Bush went to visit the wounded or families of the fallen. If it was tough for me, you can only imagine what it was like for the families and for a President who knew that his decisions led his troops into battles where they fought valiantly but were severely injured or lost their lives. He regularly visited patients at Walter Reed military hospital near the White House. These stops were unannounced because of security concerns and hassles for the hospital staff that come with a full-blown Presidential visit.

One morning in 2005, Scott McClellan sent me in his place to visit the wounded warriors. It was my first time for that particular assignment, and I was nervous about how the visits would go. The President was scheduled to see twenty-five patients at Walter Reed. Many of them had traumatic brain injuries and were in very serious, sometimes critical, condition. Despite getting the best treatment available in the world, we knew that some would not survive.

We started in the intensive care unit. The Chief of Naval Operations (CNO) briefed the President on our way into the hospital about the first patient we'd see. He was a young Marine who had been injured when his Humvee was hit by a roadside bomb. After his rescue, he was flown to Landstuhl U.S. Air Force Base in Kaiserslautern, Germany. At his bedside were his parents, wife, and five-year-old son.

"What's his prognosis?" the President asked.

"Well, we don't know sir, because he's not opened his eyes since he arrived, so we haven't been able to communicate with him. But no matter what, Mr. President, he has a long road ahead of him," said the CNO.

We had to wear masks because of the risk of infection to the patient. I watched carefully to see how the family would react to President Bush, and I was worried that they might be mad at him and blame him for their loved one's situation. But I was wrong. The family was so excited the President had come. They gave him big hugs and thanked him over and over. Then they wanted to get a photo. So he gathered them all in front of Eric Draper, the White House photographer. President Bush asked, "Is everybody smiling?" But they all had ICU masks on. A light chuckle ran through the room as everyone got the joke.

The marine was intubated. The President talked quietly with the family at the foot of the patient's bed. I looked up at the ceiling so that I could hold back tears.

After he visited with them for a bit, the President turned to the military aide and said, "Okay, let's do the presentation." The wounded warrior was being awarded the Purple Heart, given to troops that suffer wounds in combat.

Everyone stood silently while the military aide in a low and steady voice presented the award. At the end of it, the Marine's little boy tugged on the President's jacket and asked, "What's a Purple Heart?"

The President got down on one knee and pulled the little boy closer to him. He said, "It's an award for your dad, because he is very brave and courageous, and because he loves his country so much. And I hope you know how much he loves you and your mom, too."

As he hugged the boy, there was a commotion from the medical staff as they moved toward the bed.

The Marine had just opened his eyes. I could see him from where I stood.

The CNO held the medical team back and said, "Hold on, guys. I think he wants the President."

The President jumped up and rushed over to the side of the bed. He cupped the Marine's face in his hands. They locked eyes, and after a couple of moments the President, without breaking eye contact, said to the military aide, "Read it again."

So we stood silently as the military aide presented the Marine with the award for a second time. The President had tears dripping from his eyes onto the Marine's face. As the presentation ended, the President rested his forehead on the Marine's for a moment. Now everyone was crying, and for so many reasons: the sacrifice; the pain and suffering; the love of country; the belief in the mission; and the witnessing of a relationship between a soldier and his Commander in Chief that the rest of us could never fully grasp. (In writing this book, I contacted several military aides who helped me track down the name of the Marine. I hoped for news that he had survived. He did not. He died during surgery six days after the President's visit. He is buried at Arlington Cemetary and is survived by his wife and their three children.)

And that was just the first patient we saw. For the rest of the visit to the hospital that day, almost every family had the same reaction of joy when they saw the President. But there were exceptions. One mom and dad of a dying soldier from the Caribbean were devastated, the mom beside herself with grief. She yelled at the President, wanting to know why it was her child and not his who lay in that hospital bed. Her husband tried to calm her and I noticed the President wasn't in a hurry to leave—he tried offering comfort but then just stood and took it, like he expected and needed to hear the anguish, to try to soak up some of her suffering if he could.

Later as we rode back on Marine One to the White House, no one spoke.

But as the helicopter took off, the President looked at me and said, "That mama sure was mad at me." Then he turned to look out the window of the helicopter. "And I don't blame her a bit."

One tear slipped out the side of his eye and down his face. He didn't wipe it away, and we flew back to the White House.

Oh, Vlad...

The responsibilities of a deputy press secretary are to gather intelligence on what the press is going to ask at the briefings or of the President, answer the questions they can, and facilitate interviews and prepare talking points for them. That meant hanging out with the reporters on the road and dropping by their cramped offices in the West Wing to shoot the breeze, gossip, and get the lay of the land. One of the deputies always went with the press corps on the chartered plane before a Presidential trip—usually reporters leave a half a day before the President for a domestic trip, and a full twenty-four hours before Air Force One for foreign travel.

I had only been working in the White House press office a few weeks in 2005 when I was assigned to go with the press to Europe, where the President was having several meetings, including a one-on-one with Russian President Vladimir Putin. After that meeting, they were scheduled to hold a press conference where they would take two questions each.

By this time, the President and Putin knew each other fairly well and had a rather complicated relationship. I came along well after Bush had said that he looked into Putin's eyes and gotten a sense of his soul (years later Bush explained that the leaders had just met and had spoken about Putin's mother and the cross she'd had blessed in Jerusalem that she had given to her son—that was the context for the comment). Putin and Bush cooperated well on some things, such as sharing intelligence to prevent more terrorist attacks, but were in strong disagreement about other things, including the war in Iraq and Iran's intentions for a nuclear weapon.

In the ultimate dig at the President a year earlier, Putin showed how competitive and petty he was when he insulted Barney, the

President's beloved Scottish terrier. While the President was in Russia, Putin took President Bush outside to see his dog. The hound was loose and running around. Putin crossed his arms over his chest and said, "See? Bigger, faster, and stronger than Barney." You have to imagine he wasn't really talking about his dog.

I had specific instructions that I should listen for what reporters were interested in that day and gather any intelligence about the kinds of questions that the leaders could expect at the press conference. The communications director, Dan Bartlett, reminded me to include in my briefing for President Bush and President Putin that the American press corps was likely to ask about press freedoms in Russia (this was a regular topic that was asked anytime our press had a chance to question Putin, and I silently cheered them on).

I had never briefed a foreign leader before, and up to then had only had limited interaction with President Bush. I was waiting in the holding area so that I'd be in place for the briefing. I'd been diligent about getting a sense of the questions that would come up, and I knew that I needed to be thorough and concise. The last thing I wanted was to have them blindsided by one of the reporters.

President Bush came in first and he said, "Okay, what do you have?" Putin stood near him, expressionless except for his steel blue eyes. He's a cool customer.

I told the leaders the topics and questions that I thought would be asked, and then I added the bit about a question on media freedom in Russia. I was looking at President Bush but I gathered my courage and finished my sentence looking directly at Putin.

President Bush looked at Putin and asked, "You all set?" wanting to be sure that Putin had understood everything I'd said.

"Why would I answer any questions about press freedoms in my country, when you just fired that newsman," Putin said.

"Excuse me?" Bush asked.

"You know, you fired that newsman."

The President looked puzzled but then he realized what was going on. He said, "Vladimir, are you talking about Dan Rather?"

"Yes, the man you fired."

"No, Vladimir, that's not how it works. A private company employed Dan Rather, and they made the decision to let him go. I had nothing to do with it," the President explained. "I'm telling you as your friend, don't go out there and say that. It isn't correct." He was trying to educate Putin about the free press and to spare the Russian leader embarrassment on the world stage.

But Putin wasn't buying it. It was an interesting look into how a former KGB officer viewed the United States. And sure enough, a reporter asked a question about press freedoms in Moscow and Putin gave the answer he had planned to give. The reporters looked confused until they figured out what was going on. They tried not to snicker, and I suppressed an instinct to feel embarrassed for Putin. No one should ever feel sorry for him.

Can I Throw Him Under the Bus First?

The very most important lesson I learned from the President was about forgiveness.

In May 2008, during the middle of the Presidential primary campaign, a former White House colleague released a book that received a lot of news coverage. In general, the book was considered quite negative about the President, and of course the media thought it was extra juicy because the author was former White House press secretary Scott McClellan.

Scott and I had been friends since my first days at the Justice Department when I was his contact for all of the energy and environmental lawsuits. We bonded further when I was at the White House Council on Environmental Quality. Our spouses got along well, too, and we'd get invited to their house, where Scott's wife, Jill, would make homemade popovers, short ribs, and molten chocolate cake. In January 2005, Scott hired me to replace one of his deputies, Claire Buchan Parker, who was moving up to be chief of staff at the Commerce Department. He took great care to show me the ropes, even drawing a diagram of Marine One's seats for me so that I wouldn't worry about where to sit when on my first trip with the President.

Despite Scott's hard work and determination, his briefings were unnecessarily heated and often ineffective. That wasn't entirely his fault as there were many circumstances that fed into the chaos, including the initial implementation of Medicare Part D, the response to Hurricane Katrina, the Supreme Court nominations, and the ongoing investigation of Scooter Libby and Karl Rove over the Valerie Plame issue (there are many more—we had more than enough on our plates in the press office). Scott failed to gain a foothold and lost the confidence of many reporters and some senior staff in the White House. The President, however, did not blame him for the bad press coverage and remained loyal to him.

But eventually it became clear that in order to change the dynamics of the White House communications, there needed to be a change of press secretary. When the new chief of staff, Joshua Bolten, took over in 2006, one of the decisions he made was to replace Scott with media star, master communicator, and former Presidential speechwriter, Tony Snow. Though we knew internally that Scott was being fired, we managed to maintain in the press that after six years of being on the campaign and in the White House, Scott was going to move on to the next great opportunity in front of him. Even if the press suspected the change was because of an inability to effectively deliver a message, they didn't throw Scott to the wolves. He was personally well liked by many of the reporters.

Fast-forward. The night before Thanksgiving in 2007, I was the press secretary and was up at Camp David with the President and Mrs. Bush for their interview with Charlie Gibson of *Good Morning America*. My BlackBerry was buzzing me constantly, so I checked my messages one last time before I left for home.

The e-mails were from reporters asking for comment about a report that Scott's memoir was due out in May 2008 and that it was described in a prepublication sales pitch as one that would reveal information that would reflect badly on President Bush.

I knew Scott was writing a book, but that was not how he'd described it to me. These reports seemed out of character and I assumed it was the publisher's marketing people trying to make the book sound juicier than it was going to be.

Ed Gillespie, counselor to the President, was with me.

"Ed, don't you think you should tell the President about this before we go?" I asked.

"Yes, I think you should," he said, pushing me in front of him.

All of us had become skilled in delivering bad news, but no one relished it—especially not on the night before Thanksgiving.

The President walked us to our vehicles to say good-bye.

I hated to sour the mood, but I had to. I said, "Sir, before we go, there's just one little thing that you may see in the news over the weekend." I described the messages to him.

"Scott wouldn't do that to me, would he?" the President asked.

"No, sir, I don't think he would," I said, though I was worried. Rarely is anything that wrong by the time it hits the press.

"Let's call him," he said.

"Right now?" I asked.

"Yeah. Let's call and ask him."

They had known each other for many years. I imagine that Scott had once felt as close to the President as I did, so the President thought nothing of just calling him up to ask what was going on.

I met eyes with Jared Weinstein, the President's aide. He was shaking his head no. I think he didn't want to completely disrupt the President's holiday.

As luck would have it, I didn't have Scott's new phone number. I told the President I would track him down. My plan was to use the White House switchboard, where dedicated staff was able to connect us to anyone in the world at any time. I said I'd call back to Camp David after I'd straightened things out (though I had a sinking feeling I wasn't going to succeed).

It took me a while to reach Scott, but when we were finally connected, the tone was chilly. At first, he said that the publisher's description was over the top. I suggested he try to get a correction and he said he'd rather just let it ride. I advised him that that was unwise. I knew that this little blurb for a sales pitch to bookstores would brand Scott as a traitor among his friends and a hero (for a while) to the Left. I made gentle suggestions, and then the more he talked, the more alarmed I became for him personally—with this move, he would find it very hard to have any future employer trust him. I knew this was going to hurt the President, because of the sheer disloyalty it displayed. And the press would have a field day.

I told Scott I'd call him back. I phoned the White House and asked my deputies, Tony Fratto, Scott Stanzel, and Gordon Johndroe, to stay until I got back. I didn't want to detain them the night before Thanksgiving, but I needed their support. They didn't mind—we all could see the coming train wreck.

I got back to the West Wing, gathered my staff in my office, and called Scott once more (but I didn't put it on speaker). I told him I thought there was still time for him to fix this. I saw the personal public relations disaster that was about to rain down on him and the President. While I knew the President could weather it, I wasn't so sure about Scott. I told him I worried about what this would do to his and Jill's future. Well, that did it. He blew his top.

"Where the f*ck was the White House's concern for my future when it hung me out to dry?" I knew he didn't mean me personally, because I was just the messenger. I realized he was too angry for me to smooth anything over, so I just let him vent. Though we'd all played like he left the White House voluntarily, Scott must have felt stung and he wanted to get his version out there. Once he wrote the book, however, it was clear to everyone he'd not left on his terms. I wish that had always remained a mystery, but if it was going to be confirmed, it was better that he did it himself.

My team sat with me in the office while I was on the call. It was a rare moment when none of us could think of anything to say, and it was one of the only times I cried in front of anyone at the White House. We'd all worked with Scott and liked him personally. "Such a sweet guy," you'd hear from everyone, including reporters. But that night we knew we'd just lost a friend. I told them that Scott's life would never be the same and that his potential for a great post–White House career in communications was ruined. The worst part was that I knew the President would feel betrayed and any slight against him was one that I felt as well.

We got through that news cycle and I forgot about Scott's book for several months. Before its release, the White House counsel's office had a copy for several weeks (to do a check for any security or classified information concerns) but didn't reveal anything to me until the night before it was released in May 2008. And that's when I knew how bad it was.

As predicted, the media ate it up—"former staffer tears into President Bush" and all that. It was another way for the press to say that President Bush was unpopular and that he'd even lost the confidence of a former loyal staffer. The press loves that kind of stuff.

While I'm usually pretty calm, at least on the surface, this book was tearing me apart. I fretted over how I'd answer every question. I was an uncharacteristic wreck.

One morning that week I skipped my 6:30 a.m. meeting with Steve Hadley, the National Security Advisor, and told my deputy to go without me and explain that I needed every second to prepare for the briefing since I knew it would be about the book.

A few minutes later, Hadley knocked on my door. Tall and thin with round glasses, he's the gentlest and politest person in Washington. He said, "May I come in?"

"Of course."

"I understand that you're concerned about Scott's book," he said, taking a seat across from me.

"Yes, I am, because the coverage is so bad and it's not going to end for a long time and—" I said.

"I know it seems bad," he interrupted. "But I have to tell you that I've worked for three presidents—Reagan, Bush 41, and this President. And a President never knows who it's going to be that writes something like this while they're in office, but it's always going to be somebody. So a President can't worry about it. He just has to do his best and make decisions without regard to who might want to write a book in the middle of his administration."

I thanked him for putting it in perspective, but after he left, I went right back to reading all of the negative stories and taking notes on the questions I thought the press would ask that day.

At 6:40 a.m., my phone rang. The display said, "Oval Office." It was unusual to get a call from there that early in the morning.

I answered and Karen Keller, the President's executive assistant, said that the President wanted to see me. I put on my jacket and walked the thirty steps to the Oval. As I entered the outer Oval, Hadley was walking out. He smiled at me sheepishly, and I realized he'd told the President I needed shoring up over Scott's book.

President Bush was writing personal correspondence to families of the fallen and getting prepared for his daily intelligence briefing. It made my issues seem very petty. He had his reading glasses on the end of his nose, and as I walked in, he put down his pen. He looked at me over his glasses.

"So I hear you're upset about this book," he said.

"Yes, sir, I am," I said, adding that I wanted to make sure he knew how bad the coverage was and how I was concerned it would last.

His answer surprised me. "I'd like you to try to forgive him," he said.

"But I—" I started.

"No buts. I don't want you to live bitterly like he is. Nobody will remember this book three weeks from now. And we can't let a book like this take us away from the important work we have to do here on behalf of the American people."

I glanced down at the letter he was writing and said, "Well, can I throw him under the bus first?"

"No," he said with a smile.

"Okay, thank you, sir." I turned around to leave the office. As I crossed the threshold, he called after me. I stopped and turned around and he said, "Hey—by the way, I don't think you'd ever do this to me."

And that's when I realized that sometimes the President knew me better than I knew myself. I'd been worried that the close personal relationship that we shared would be shattered by the violation of trust by someone we used to work with. He realized I needed to hear that he knew that I'd never be disloyal to him. I was hugely relieved.

I got back to my desk and scooped up all of those newspapers and threw them in the recycling bin. I was done with that book and all the negativity that came with it.

The President's suggestion of forgiveness freed me, like a weight being lifted off my shoulders. It's a lesson I try to remember for all sorts of situations in life when I feel slighted and disappointed by others. And it was a blessing to have the President of the United States be the one to remind me to let it go.

Family Ties

Working for the President is amazing not just for the staffers but also for their families. My mom, sister, brother-in-law, aunt, and uncle all got to meet President Bush in chance-of-a-lifetime encounters they'll never forget. The President had an amazing talent to recall stories about our families, because he was very interested in the people who worked for him. And it was because of his interest that he helped repair a relationship in my own family that was very important to me.

I'd personally come to know the President very well because of the travel we did together. As the deputy press secretary, I handled a lot of the evening, weekend, and holiday trips, and that was when we'd talk more casually. The other deputies and I called ourselves the "B team" though he assured us we were his favorites.

One of my first trips was on Marine One when we traveled to an event in rural Virginia for the Boy Scouts Jamboree. Bad weather had kept the President from attending for two days, but on the third night, he insisted he was going and the Secret Service acquiesced and said he could depart.

On the way home, he wanted to share his peanut butter and honey sandwiches with the chief of staff, Andy Card, and me. I declined, not wanting to eat his dinner. But the President said, "Oh come on—have a sandwich." So I took half and a handful of Sun Chips (no cheddar—he doesn't like those) and we munched during the ride. The sun began to set as we left to return to the White House, and we talked just like friends. I loosened up and started chatting. I remember every moment of that ride—including the orange and pink sunset that lasted the entire flight.

The President liked hearing about my family's Western ranching roots and asked me about my mom, my dad, and my sister. Being an animal lover, he even asked about my family pets, especially my dog, Henry. He was the kind of person you could open up to, dropping any formalities even though he was the Commander in Chief.

Eventually over those first months of traveling together, the President heard my story that my parents had divorced in 2000 and that I took it very hard. Even though I was an adult when they split, I still felt somewhat abandoned and alone.

My dad and I had always been very close and had shared a love of political discussion and news consumption, but over the years after I'd moved away and he and my mom broke up, I didn't see him very often. And at the end of the eight years in the White House, he still had not been to D.C. to visit or seen me brief the press. He'd missed out on the White House magic. I had one last chance to change that.

In the middle of the financial crisis on Columbus Day in 2008, Prime Minister Berlusconi of Italy was coming for a dinner at the White House. Mrs. Bush planned a small event and invited me—I was grateful to be included as the Italian-Americans would be there in force. I almost always took my husband to those events—he loved everything about the White House and would get emotionally patriotic, but this time I had another idea. I decided to invite my dad to the dinner, but I prepared myself that he might not accept. To my surprise, he did, so Peter arranged the flights and rented him a tux. It would be my dad's first black-tie event.

I didn't tell the President that my dad was coming. He had so much on his mind that small talk and dinner parties were not something I wanted to bring up. But he'd noticed that my dad was on the guest list when he and Mrs. Bush were looking over it one morning before we headed out for an event.

I was already seated on Marine One when the President came out of the Diplomatic Reception Room. There were lots of people cheering for him as he walked across the lawn and boarded the chopper. As he sat down, he looked out the window and waved at the crowd.

Without looking at me, he said, "So I see you've invited your dad to the White House."

"Yes, sir, I did."

"That's a big deal," he said, still waving to the crowd.

"Yes, sir. It's a pretty big deal," I said quietly. We sat in silence for a few moments.

Marine One had lifted off the ground, and then, just as we were passing the Washington Monument, the President looked me right in the eye and said, "And I am so proud of you."

He could really capture a moment, and he didn't try to rush emotions. He let them sit. I was touched the President knew what it meant to me and that, despite all he had going on, he knew that telling me he was proud was the most valuable thing I could hear. That would have been enough for me, but the best part was yet to come.

The night of the dinner arrived. I was trying to contain my excitement to show my dad everything all at once, so I played it cool—like it was perfectly normal to roam the halls of the White House.

The first person we saw was Mayor Rudy Giuliani. He gave me

a huge hug. Then there were Supreme Court Justices Antonin Scalia and Sam Alito. General Peter Pace, Chairman of the Joint Chiefs, was also there. They were giving me all sorts of praise in front of my dad, and I think it was a bit overwhelming for him. I know it was for me.

We joined the line to be announced to the President and Mrs. Bush, Secretary Rice, and Prime Minister Berlusconi. Before the military escort could announce us, however, President Bush said, "Oh, I know who this is! LEO PERINO! We have been looking forward to your visit for years! Have you met Condi...."

And then the President took my dad off my hands and started showing him around. My dad and I weren't seated together for the dinner, so I just trusted he was fine. Thoughtfully, Mrs. Bush had seated him next to other Wyomingites, the Cheneys. The White House chef, working closely with Anita McBride, the First Lady's chief of staff, served squash soup, artichoke ravioli, and lamb with crispy eggplant and chard. The dessert was special: a chocolate napoleon called the Santa Maria.

At the end of the evening as we walked out of the White House, I tried to gauge my dad's reaction. I couldn't tell what he was thinking.

"It's pretty amazing, isn't it?" I said.

"It sure is..." replied my dad, a bit of wonder in his voice as we drove away. The White House magic had worked its spell once more.

President Bush knew what he was doing that night, but I'm not sure he understood how much it meant to me. I had started reading the papers with my dad when I was in third grade, when the White House seemed so far away. And yet there we were, dressed in formal attire at an intimate evening in the State Dining Room as guests of the President and First Lady of the United States. That night President Bush gave me back my relationship with my dad, an invaluable gift for which I am very grateful.

Feeling Every Blow

In the fall of 2008, the nation was gearing up for a Presidential election, but at the White House, we were trying to manage a major financial crisis while solidifying the gains made in Iraq because of the surge. We followed the election closely, of course, but President Bush wasn't on the ballot so the main media attention was appropriately focused on the candidates, Senators Barack Obama and John McCain.

For any President who has served two terms, the next election means becoming the target for all things old and washed up and wrong with Washington. This was especially true for President Bush. In 2008, America wanted something new and different, so everyone was distancing themselves from him. After a consequential and often tumultuous two terms, his approval numbers were very low and he was the easiest person to attack.

I still cringe at some of the things that were said about him during that campaign. We had been instructed to ignore the attacks and not get in the middle of any political fights. President Bush knew that McCain had to throw some punches his way if he had a hope of winning the election. He shrugged them off while I felt every blow.

One day I couldn't take it anymore and I pushed back against a ridiculous charge that Hillary Clinton made about President Bush during a campaign stop in her failed bid to win the Democratic nomination. It was something along the lines of how the President didn't care about the elderly and wanted them to live in poverty eating cat food (a classic Democratic attack against Republicans). It might have been something I'd have ignored on most days, but I must have had vinegar for breakfast. When I was asked during the briefing about Senator Clinton's swipe at President Bush, I launched a counterattack using facts and figures that I had memorized. The press wasn't expecting that kind of response from me, and it was a slow news day, so it made some news.

Within about two hours, the Clinton campaign was using my words as part of an e-mail fund-raising appeal against McCain, and the press was leading with headlines about Bush getting defensive during the campaign. The press loves a fight; it helps ratings and sells papers.

I knew that I'd gone too far. And sure enough that afternoon, the President called me.

"I appreciate what you're trying to do, but it's better for McCain if we don't take the bait. I know you're trying to protect me, but trust me, I'll be fine," he said.

It took me a few years to realize he was right about that, but I sometimes still wonder if it wouldn't have been better to have fought back more fiercely against all the misperceptions. I guess history will have to decide that—I can't go back and change anything that happened.

Yet there's one thing that sticks with me—and that was the night of the GOP Convention in September 2008 when President Bush was scheduled to give a speech to the crowd in Minnesota. However, we never left Washington; Mother Nature decided that was a fine time to send Hurricane Gustav to the shores of the United States. And after Hurricane Katrina, concern about hurricanes was higher than ever.

While the weather wasn't good, we could have flown to Minneapolis for the speech. We decided to leave it up to the McCain-Palin campaign on whether President Bush should make the trip. After a while, we sensed that the campaign was stalling to make a decision until it was too late for us to leave in time. Deep down I believe they must have thought it would be better for them if President Bush didn't come to the convention.

So instead of addressing the GOP that night, the President gave a short statement on hurricane preparedness from the Cross Hall of the East Wing. At the end of it, the President noticed the monitor showing the live shot of the convention floor.

He quietly asked, "Do you think they know they're insulting me?"

I waited a beat, looking at the screen with him.

"Yes, sir. I believe they do."

We met eyes and I remember feeling angry on his behalf and yet so close to him that I gave up caring about the campaign at all anymore. We just focused on what we needed to do at the White House and stayed out of the campaign's way.

I learned from President Bush when to let things slide. One time I asked him why we always had to turn the other cheek when our opponents did not. He joked, "It's our burden to bear." But it's not such a heavy load when you think of it like he did.

While these are some of my favorite stories about how President Bush gave me the best career opportunity of my life, even more important, he inspired me constantly to try to improve myself. Around him, I was more positive, attentive, and gracious. He lives by a code—duty and honor to his country and commitment to and unconditional love for his family. You won't read it in the media, but that's who he was. And I tried—and try—to be more like him whenever I can.

CHAPTER 4

~~~~~

The Five

A Big Shrimp

The day we celebrated the launch of *The Five*, Bob Beckel choked on
a shrimp and almost died. If Eric Bolling hadn't been there to save
his life, our next event would have been Bob's funeral. It was that
serious.

Roger Ailes, the CEO of Fox News, had invited us to lunch at
Del Frisco's, a popular and upscale steakhouse near the studio. All
of the co-hosts and the top executives and producers were there. Bob
sat next to Roger at the head of the table, and Eric was across from
him. The rest of us filled in the seats, and I remember that all the
men were wearing ties—except for Greg Gutfeld. Always the indi-
vidualist, he wore a magenta wool sweater with a little alien creature
on the front. Something of a self-portrait.

Roger had been kicking around the idea of an ensemble cast for
a while. He wanted a group of people with different backgrounds
who could have an hour-long discussion about the news of the day,
much like families would have over dinner. Roger got his chance to
give it a try when Glenn Beck left the network and opened up the

5 p.m. hour. Beck's show was a rare success in that time slot. Most programs didn't last too long in that hour, when families aren't quite home from work yet and, if they are, they've traditionally liked to watch their local news programming. To give *The Five* some breathing room, Roger made it a temporary show, to run from July to Labor Day. (Describing it as temporary kept the media critics at bay.) Expectations were low, and Roger threw us into the deep end.

We didn't sink. *The Five* surprised everyone, including us. We had an instant following and got good ratings, holding on to most of the audience that had been devoted to Beck and adding new viewers, many of them younger people. We flew by the seat of our pants, but that was part of the appeal. We also laughed more than any other show on cable news. People tuned in because they wanted to see just what we were going to say next.

Once again, Roger outwitted his naysayers in the media. He decided to make the show permanent, and he called us together to raise a toast. Lunch hadn't even been served before Bob starting turning purple.

Del Frisco's serves some of the biggest shrimp in town, and Roger had ordered some for the table to share as appetizers before our meals arrived. When the starters came out, Bob tucked his linen napkin under his collar and started eating.

Bob and Roger go way back—they met during the Kentucky U.S. Senate race in 1984 when they worked for the opposing candidates, and they were swapping campaign war stories. For political junkies like us, it was very entertaining.

Just a week before this, Bob had played a trick on me in Atlanta, where he pretended to be having a heart attack on air during a special anniversary show for Sean Hannity. It was very hot and humid and Bob had complained all day about the heat. He sweated through his makeup and there wasn't enough powder in Georgia to keep the shine off his forehead. I worried about him but figured we'd do our hit and then I'd get him back into the car to cool down.

During our segment, I started off, and while I was talking, Bob's head slumped forward and his hand went to his heart. I didn't want to make a scene on live TV, so I frantically tried to get the stage manager's attention without disrupting Sean. Bob let his little prank go on for just one beat too long, and I started to panic. He finally popped his head up, laughing at how he'd tricked me. I didn't think it was funny.

So that day at Del Frisco's when I saw Bob turning red and not talking, I rolled my eyes and thought he was joking, looking for attention. Roger asked Bob if he was okay and Bob just stared straight ahead. I still wasn't sure if Bob was pulling a gag, but in a second I realized he was in real danger. I wasn't the only one. Roger jumped up and got behind Bob and tried to put his arms around him to do the Heimlich, but Bob was too big around, and Roger couldn't hit the right spot. Bob's face started turning purple.

Eric to the rescue. He literally vaulted across the table, wrapped his arms around Bob, and in one swift move pulled hard right under Bob's diaphragm. The piece of shrimp came back up and Eric held him for a couple more seconds to make sure he was breathing again. Then Bob sat down and tried to catch his breath.

No one else at Del Frisco's noticed. With our table in the back, the rest of the dining room went about eating their lunch. We tried to play it cool and change the subject from Bob's near demise to anything else, but it was difficult to eat. I took my meal to go.

That night right before we went live, Bob told us he didn't want to mention it on the show. He was embarrassed and still shaken up. Gutfeld insisted that we had to talk about it, since we wouldn't be able to do the show if we tried to pretend nothing had happened. So Bob led the show with the story and he thanked his good friend

Eric for saving his life. Eric was modest about it, but he really was a hero that day. Kimberly and I tried not to cry and Gutfeld let the emotion hang for a couple of seconds before he moved on to the A block.

I think of that day as the real first day of the show. It was when we finally gelled and knew we'd be together for a while. And to think, we almost lost Bob before 5 p.m.

The Five saved my life, too—in a way. Before the show, I was burning out in my post–White House life. I wasn't less stressed or working fewer hours, and I still hadn't browsed at Target. I had my own business and felt more uptight than ever. I had clients all over the country and two employees in Washington whom I rarely saw, paid speaking gigs, a new nonprofit called Minute Mentoring, and a Presidential appointment by the Obama Administration to the Broadcasting Board of Governors (BBG) that oversaw the Voice of America and other entities. I also was a Fox News contributor, which was my favorite thing on my to-do list.

I never complained when Fox called to ask if I could be on, and it reminds me of what Marlin Fitzwater, the press secretary to Presidents Reagan and George H. W. Bush, told me as I was figuring out what to do after I left the White House. He said I should simply try to find something that was fun to do and that I was good at—that was his mix for happiness and success.

I had not figured out that formula, and I said yes to every request, thinking that every phone call might be the last one. I was overly blessed with opportunities, but it was way too much. I barely saw Peter because of my travel schedule, and when I was home, I worked all the time. I had to keep spinning the plates faster to keep them all going. You'd think that the last thing I needed was the pressure of a new TV show in New York City, but it was actually the best thing that happened. It broke the cycle that I'd created for myself.

I got the call about *The Five* when I was at baggage claim in Washington. I'd just returned from a trip to Africa with my BBG colleagues and good friends Susan McCue and Michael Meehan. We'd traveled to Ethiopia, South Sudan, and Nigeria to see where we could improve and expand American broadcasting. Africa remains a passion of mine, and I was glad I went, even if the trip was dangerous and they forgot to have security for us (I slept with the lights on in Juba). While I was away, my work had piled up.

John Finley, an executive producer, had the secret assignment to create the show Roger had in mind. When I answered the phone, I thought it would be about my weekly appearance on Hannity's show. When he told me they'd like to have me up for the rest of the summer to be on a temporary show called *The Five*, I didn't think I'd heard him correctly. "You what?" I asked.

Finley said he knew it was a big request. And he was right—my first concern was about logistics.

"But I don't live in New York," I said.

They had that all worked out—I'd stay in a hotel near the studio to make it easier. And the hotel allowed dogs, so I could bring Henry if I wanted. I said I worried about Peter's reaction, since I was already away from home a lot. Finley said they'd pay for him to come up once in a while, too. He'd thought of everything. There was nothing left to do but accept the offer.

I called Peter in Seoul, South Korea, where he was traveling for business. His initial reaction was different from mine.

"Congratulations—this is what you've always wanted to do!" he said.

He knew me so well, and he promised we'd make it work (and

that he'd take care of Henry). I was closer to finding Fitzwater's formula.

My transition from White House press secretary to Fox News contributor wasn't as smooth as I thought it would be. I'd been President Bush's spokesperson for so long that both the anchors and I would fall back into the habit of speaking for the former President. But I liked being in that role—at least there were a few of us still in Washington who were publicly advocating for his positions.

Nevertheless, I pulled my punches when asked about the Obama Administration. I didn't want to throw jabs at the new administration on behalf of the previous one. I avoided direct criticism of President Obama and used my experiences to provide context and keep things positive. That was my style, but I also thought viewers would tune me out if I took a sledgehammer to everything the White House said. I rounded my edges to keep people from changing the channel—and tried to bring a new fact or perspective to every hit to keep them watching.

It took a while for me to come out from behind my press secretary shell. When I was on camera initially, I'd move my hands a lot and fiddle with my rings. Even my mom noticed I was uncomfortable and called often to ask me what was wrong.

I had a difficult time letting people get to know me as Dana. It was new to me—I'd never actually spoken for myself until then. I'd always spoken on behalf of someone else.

I held tight to my shield until *The Five* required that I set it down. After the first few shows, I was totally exposed: Dana Perino starring as herself. Our viewers started to get to know me better, and Bob— my weekly commuting partner to D.C.—said that I was the most straitlaced person he'd ever known. I took that as a compliment.

Greg once described *Special Report* as a smooth trip on a G7 and *The Five* as a bumpy motocross ride. It can be a wild show. When I finally stopped being so cautious, I started to let myself laugh, get mad, and make fun of myself. I even pushed the limits of my self-imposed propriety, like when I had to spell out H-E-L-L and S-E-X. But things changed—in year three, I was the first woman ever to get bleeped on the show (I told Bob to stop "bitching"). I even shocked myself.

One day when Brian Kilmeade filled in for Greg and in a commercial break said to me, "You know, all of those years at the White House I never knew you were funny."

I knew what he meant. It wasn't my job to be funny at the White House. And maybe people don't think I'm all that funny—all I know is that I've never laughed so hard in a job. I love it.

Behind the Scenes

We like to mix it up on *The Five*. We talk a lot about politics, culture, and even sports. Everyone pitches ideas for segments, and our producer, Porter Berry, gets the final say on the topics. The rundown comes out around 10:30 a.m., and then each of us starts preparing for the show. We don't talk during the day before we see each other in the greenroom, and even then we rarely talk about what's on the show. Instead, we chat casually about our families, what we watched on TV the night before, or any chatter we've picked up throughout the day.

I like to overprepare (if I'm the Lisa Simpson of *The Five*, Greg is the Bart). I keep in contact with friends in Washington and they help me understand what's going on inside the Beltway and out on the campaign trail. I read a lot of articles and send them out as "FYI" to the show, most of which they probably delete. For cultural topics, I'll choose a few friends to ask their opinions, especially when it comes to parenting issues. I live vicariously through them.

I can't stand talking points and the kind of argument that comes out of conventional wisdom from the political parties. To avoid using them, I let all I've read and talked about sink in, and then when I walk to the office, I usually think of some original way to get my argument across. Sometimes I pull over to the edge of the sidewalk to type myself a reminder. Our comments need to be short since we don't have that much time to make points. When you do the math—an average of seven minutes per segment with five people to comment on the subject—there's not a lot of time to pontificate.

When we sit down to put on our mics and get our final makeup touches, we still have no idea what's going to happen. That's part of what makes it so fun. We just roll with it. The producers cue up the videos and the music that bumps in and out of our segments—country for me, acid or punk rock for Greg, classic rock for Eric, pop hits for Kimberly, and whatever's leftover for Bob.

Sometimes our debates get heated, and I've had to get comfortable with the yelling. My instincts still pull me toward trying to get group consensus and to smooth things over, but I've learned from my co-hosts that it's okay if we don't agree. They seem to like the emotional roller coaster of the show, but it still takes me a while to calm down afterward. I use my walk home to shed the excess energy that builds up on live TV—sometimes I call my mom or my sister and they "walk me home" through Central Park. By the time I get to the apartment, Peter has dinner started and we eat while we watch my lifelong standbys—*Wheel of Fortune* and *Jeopardy!*—happy shows where no one yells or gets mad.

* * *

The best part of *The Five* isn't always seen by the viewers. The commercial breaks can be intense and hilarious. At times the arguments spill into the breaks, but usually we ask Bob if he "really believes that" or tell him why he might have to apologize in "One More Thing." And since I don't get much of the innuendo, my co-hosts have to explain it to me when we're not on camera.

Sometimes we vent our frustration with one another in those few short minutes when we're off air. In fact, the only time I've ever lost my temper at work was during commercial breaks on *The Five*. It's happened twice. I erupted and didn't stop until about thirty seconds before we were back on camera. But we played it off well—no one at home knew what happened either time. Bob's the best during those outbursts—he knows to just nod his head and agree with me no matter what I'm saying. His imitation of me is priceless.

All of us have been victims of being "Beckeled" at some point. That's where you reveal something in the commercial break that you would never say on TV. But when the cameras are rolling, Bob lets out the secret and you're busted. The charming thing is that he doesn't mean to do it—at least I don't think he does. It's a good thing he's so likable, or we'd have killed him by now. We may yet.

A Perfect Mix

The Five is made up of several people with diverse backgrounds and lots of personality. We are an unlikely crew—that's why the show works. Here are a few things you may not know about them:

KIMBERLY GUILFOYLE

Kimberly Guilfoyle is a former teacher, prosecutor, and Victoria's Secret model. Eat your hearts out, guys! On TV, Kimberly knows when to bring the heat and when to have some fun. Sometimes you don't know when she's going to bring down the hammer, which makes it really entertaining when she does.

When there's a legal topic, everyone listens to what she has to say. She is blessed with patience, so she's really good at dealing with Bob.

Bob never tires of making fun of Kimberly by suggesting she has five ex-husbands (that's not true—she only has two but we're working on finding her the perfect guy for round three). Despite Bob and Kimberly's play fighting on the show, they're very funny together. I'll never forget when she laid a kiss on Bob on the live New Year's Eve special in Times Square in 2014—everyone was shocked but maybe no one more so than Bob himself. It was the "Kiss Seen Around the World."

Kimberly has great television skills, especially during breaking news. One time there was a manhunt for a cop killer in California that we covered live on *The Five*. She led the entire show, and it wasn't until halfway through that I realized she was doing it without a teleprompter.

Her mom died when she was very young and she helped raise her little brother. Then, Kimberly's father died when her son, Ronan, was only two years old. As a single mom, she shoulders a lot of responsibility, and she still makes sure Ronan has a lot of joy. She lets him drag her to the costume store near their apartment so they can dress up and play different characters at home. She has a cooperative relationship with her ex-husband, and the way they work things out is a model for other families sharing custody.

When Kimberly's on the show, our viewers love how she jumps

when Bob surprises her by yelling "'ONE MORE THING'...is up next," and then she pretends to kick him with her pointy shoes. And that brings up one of the questions I'm often asked about Kimberly—can she really walk in those high heels? Yes, she can.

ANDREA TANTAROS

Andrea Tantaros spent the first three years of the show with us. Now she's a permanent co-host of another popular Fox News show, *Outnumbered*, and we still get to see her on *The Five* now and then. She grew up working hard waiting tables in her family's restaurants and diners. Her dad emigrated from Greece and found true love in America—with his wife and his country. He raised four children and built several successful family businesses. By the time he died from cancer a few years ago, he'd overshot the American dream. Andrea says her mom and dad taught her that if she took personal responsibility and was self-reliant, she'd be able to do anything. She took their advice and lives confidently and without fear.

Believe it or not, Andrea was an intern on CNN's *Crossfire* when Bob co-hosted that show. She used to get his coffee, and he doesn't even remember her. (How rude!) Andrea loved politics, writing, and policy discussions. She worked on Capitol Hill and on several campaigns. She's taken a lot of risks and worked for a couple of candidates who weren't sure bets, and some that were downright abusive toward her. She persevered and it paid off.

Andrea worked in public relations and became a columnist for the *New York Daily News*. She's a great writer and brings an edge to her commentary that makes people pay attention.

Not only does Andrea have a knack for explaining politics from her point of view, but she knows a heck of a lot about popular culture and entertainment. And when Peter and I moved to Manhattan, she helped us with everything from doctors to day trips to restaurants.

She wanted us to love living in the city and she tried to make things easier for us. We relied on her advice.

JUAN WILLIAMS

Juan Williams is a journalist that I have followed for years. He's had a varied career as a writer and columnist, and his books, especially the ones on race and education, have challenged policymakers to do better.

When I was at the White House, Juan wrote for *The Washington Post* and did commentary on NPR and Fox News. On occasion, we had a reason to work together. In fact, one of the times that Juan got in trouble with NPR was when I offered him an interview of President Bush on race relations. The public radio network accepted my invitation to do the interview, but to my surprise, the show's brass told me that Juan was being kicked aside and replaced with another anchor. I pushed back—the President had agreed to do an interview with Juan, and I wasn't going to go back and tell him that NPR was calling the shots for his interviews. NPR held firm. So did I.

I called Juan and asked if Fox News could run it instead of NPR. Juan appreciated my loyalty to him, and Fox gave the go-ahead. NPR was mad. I'd beaten them at their own game.

With the knives out, NPR was looking for a reason to cut Juan, and a little while later they got their chance. Their loss was Fox's gain, and when Bob takes a rare day off, Juan fills in for him.

Juan and his wife have three children and two grandchildren. Two of his sons are Republicans, so I tease him that he must have done something right along the way. Actually, it shows that he was an excellent parent that gave his children the critical thinking skills and confidence to choose for themselves what ideology would guide them. We could use more parents like that in the world—and more children!

ERIC BOLLING

Eric Bolling and I had met a couple of times before *The Five*. For a while, Eric had a show on Fox Business called *Follow the Money*. I appeared on it once and it felt like being on a Tilt-A-Whirl with no seat belts. It was so raucous that I just sat there all shaken up. He took pity on me and understood when I said I didn't think I could do the show again. We still laugh about it.

Eric started his working life as a professional baseball player, but an injury scuttled his chances for the big leagues. As a result, he had to take the first job available. He pumped gas for a few weeks, and then he got a call from a friend who'd heard about a job opening in finance in Boston. He packed that night.

Eric grew up in Chicago with very modest means and was taught the value of education and hard work. That foundation helped him later on when his business sense and tolerance for risk in the oil and gas business helped him achieve financial security for his family. Sadly, he witnessed both World Trade Center attacks and lost many friends on September 11, and he speaks passionately about matters of national security and freedom.

Eric married Adrienne, a bright light wherever she goes. She's beautiful—in fact, Bob tried to hit on her one night before he knew she was Eric's wife (he didn't get too far). They have a teenage son and he's given them several minor heart attacks, as teenagers do. Eric is an attentive father—his son will do well.

When Eric's mom went through chemotherapy treatment, she had to fast on Tuesdays and so he did, too. Even after she died, he continued the tradition to remember her.

Eric's a solid, dependable guy. Of all the people I've met in New York, he's the first person I'd call if I ever needed help (then if I needed a lawyer, I'd call Kimberly).

GREG GUTFELD

Where to start? He's the brother I never wanted. We'd never talked before we sat down to tape the pilot of *The Five* and we hit it off immediately.

Greg is a comic genius—he's got a lot going on up there in his brain. I get his sense of humor, and his jokes send me into fits of giggles. Sometimes I start laughing before he's finished a sentence because I can see where he's headed. Every now and then I'll suggest he say something that I would never say out loud—unlike me, Greg is not afraid, and that's why he has so many fans.

Greg is astounded by my innocence and thinks I'm goofy. I love his phony grumpiness and have learned to read his moods. Our conversations are my favorite part of the day. We crack ourselves up.

He met his Russian wife, Elena, when he was in Portugal at a conference. They both worked in the magazine business—he was an editor and she was a photo stylist. He told his friends, "I'm going to marry that woman." They thought he was crazy, but he proved them wrong.

Greg's been fired from every job he's ever held, so we worry that it's just a matter of time before it happens again. But Fox appreciates his talent and humor. They give him a lot of room to run—and thankfully, they're not watching *Red Eye* at 3 a.m.

Greg lost his mom, Jackie, to cancer in 2014. She was eighty-nine. He wasn't afraid to write in her eulogy that he was a "momma's boy" and proud of it. When Greg was a kid, his mom recognized his unique sense of humor and encouraged it. She'd buy him *MAD* magazines and *National Lampoon*, which fed his imagination. Later Greg's mom appeared as a guest on *Red Eye* and would spend all day preparing for the segment. She was one of the most recognized faces on Fox News.

Another thing I like about Greg is that he makes us work harder by forcing us to abandon the jargon he hates (his banned phrases are famous). His commentary is so good and so different that sometimes it takes a few seconds for it to sink in. He uses humor to get us to think about issues differently. It was a little unconventional to have him on air at 5 p.m. on cable news, but that's why he's built a loyal following of viewers that adore him. So do I.

BOB BECKEL

If you watch *The Five*, you know that Bob is one of life's great characters. There's not enough room to tell his whole story (after all, he covered Abraham Lincoln's inaugural).

Bob is like a cat on its ninth life. He's a recovering addict, and he says he's living on borrowed time. While some guys his age think about retiring, taking it down a notch, Bob thrives on work. *The Five* gave him a new lease on life, and he's become a Fox favorite.

Our viewers have a love-hate relationship with Bob—they hate a lot of what he says, but they love him for who he is. They know that as the only liberal on the show, he's working against the odds. Bob says it's four against one, but anyone who's watched Bob spar with us knows it's more one against four.

Sometimes our audience thinks that Bob is a secret conservative and that he's coming around to thinking like they do. The truth is Bob is a true liberal, with an open mind, and he calls balls and strikes in politics just like an umpire would. He's just about seen it all, and our show is better because he can share his real-life experiences.

Bob is a good sport who puts up with a lot from the rest of us on *The Five*. That includes me. As he says, "She may look sweet but watch out when she gets mad." One night I hit him below the belt with a shot about his age, and I felt bad about it for three days. He handled it perfectly by making fun of me for not being such a nice person after all. He let me off the hook (and reminded me what President Bush had taught me—forgiveness is the key to being happy in work and life. Bob does that naturally).

It wasn't the first time I relied on his good nature. On election night in November 2012, the Republican Party lost big time. A lot of us had false hope that Mitt Romney could beat President Obama. For a couple of weeks before the election, Bob warned us it didn't look good for the GOP. He wasn't playing mind games—he was right.

Bob and I got paired up to give reaction throughout the night on Fox. Megyn Kelly and Bret Baier were anchoring the network's coverage and occasionally they'd call on us for commentary. We had a lot of downtime, so we just sat and watched the returns. It was depressing.

"Bob, this is terrible," I said.

And instead of pouncing on my disappointment, Bob didn't rub it in.

He said, "Yeah, kid, it's bad. Now, let's keep it in perspective— it's not like losing forty-nine states kind of bad—now *that* was embarrassing." He was referring to the 1984 Presidential race when he managed Walter Mondale's campaign against Reagan. Mondale lost in a landslide.

Fox wanted us to stick around that night until the returns in California came in, but I desperately wanted out of there. I tried to leave and a producer stopped me. But Bob whispered, "Go—I'll cover for you." So I thanked him and snuck out the studio door. I walked home to our Hell's Kitchen apartment, took a shower and an Ambien, and was asleep by midnight.

Bob's become our favorite houseguest on weekends. We invite him over to watch football on Sundays, and he pretends to hate Jasper but he lets him sit on his lap while he eats his pot roast (he'll walk a mile for a meal made in a Crock-Pot). One time we took him to a comedy show downtown, and I laughed harder at Bob's reactions than I did at the comedians.

At Peter's sixtieth birthday party, Bob gave one of the toasts and stole the show. Watching everyone hang on his every word that night, I realized that this really is Bob's world—we're just living in it.

The Magic Formula

When I accepted the offer to be on *The Five* and move to New York City, I felt that familiar worry about taking a different direction from what I'd planned. I was concerned that moving to New York for *The Five* would cut me off from other interests, or prevent me from being able to return to public relations—I'd just spent two years building a business and knew how hard it was to start over. In D.C., I was on a couple of charitable boards—one matched wounded warriors with rescue animals and the other encouraged more support for better maternal health and early childhood development in Africa—and had just been appointed to the Broadcasting Board of Governors.

But far from limiting my involvement, Fox News has helped me expand upon it. In August 2013, my husband and I went to Congo and spent a week with Mercy Ships, a charitable surgical ship that serves the forgotten poor around the world, but mostly in West Africa. Peter and I went on our own accord, but Fox sent us with some audio equipment and Peter shot amateur video that the young producers at Fox turned into a three-minute package. That Mercy

Ships segment aired multiple times on the network and reached millions of people. That was my first experience after leaving the White House where I finally found the best way to make a difference when it came to issues I cared about.

Somewhat to my surprise, I've come to find being on TV very professionally fulfilling. I say that because I wasn't sure at first. I'd just left a job where I spoke for the President of the United States, managed a team of twelve people, and started my own consulting business. I wasn't sure that being on a roundtable for an hour a day would be enough to keep me busy. I was wrong. I take the show preparation seriously, and I really love that part of my job.

I also wasn't sure if I'd consider being on the show enough of a contribution to national debates. But that concern was crossed off my list when we started hearing from our fans. They loved the show and said that it kept them informed and laughing. One fan stopped me at a Broadway play to say I'd helped her win arguments with her neighbors by presenting ideas in a fact-based and more persuasive way.

I'm regularly impressed by how many people can recall specific moments from the show, even from years ago. They remember that I dunked Bob on the Fourth of July in 2011, and that Kimberly beat him in the chicken wing eating contest. They love Greg's banned phrases, Bob's swear jar, Eric's Constitution, Jasper's appearances, "One More Thing," and more. My career change came at just the right time and now sharing my thoughts with our fans every night is the best part of my day.

What's the secret to *The Five*'s success? It has to be the chemistry of the co-hosts. Chemistry is something that can't be manufactured—you either have it or you don't. And since we do, we just have to stay unpredictable, authentic, and smarter than our competition. That's our recipe for success.

Oh, wait—there's just one little thing we have to do—remind Bob to take smaller bites. We're counting on him to be around for a long time.

Bob's Unlikely Nemesis

Five fans know a few personal things about us by now—such as how much I love my dog, Jasper, and that Jasper drives Bob crazy. And that makes fans happy—they like to see Bob's head nearly explode whenever I mention him. Bob's turned making fun of Jasper into a daily rant. "That damned dog!" he yells. He's just kidding— I think.

Before Jasper, there was Henry—and Fox fans knew him, too. Those who followed me at the White House heard about Henry occasionally, and when I started with *The Five*, I talked about him a lot. I bonded with other dog lovers that watched the show.

Henry was a Hungarian Vizsla, handsome and loving. Peter and I were extremely close to him. He was nearly fourteen and in failing health when we moved to New York City, and I knew it would be a tough move for him.

Henry was my only companion during the days in England, and I taught him to behave better than the other dogs and to do all sorts of tricks. Political jokes were his specialty. In 2004 I asked him to show us what he really thought about John Kerry, and he'd fetch my flip-flop. His last trick was to play dead if I asked him about Obamacare.

Henry grounded me during the White House years. He was the

only one in Washington that wasn't impressed with my job. He disliked the BlackBerry and would sulk when I checked e-mails. He was one of the only reasons I ever set my phone down.

When Peter and I argued, we'd lower our voices when Henry was around because he hated fighting of any kind. Once we had to tell a friend she couldn't say the "F" word in front of him because he'd get too upset.

I worried about moving to New York because I didn't think he'd survive the stress of relocating to Manhattan, where it's so noisy and hard to find a blade of grass. Everything that was familiar to him would be left behind in Washington.

Henry slept most of the day by then, and was almost completely white in the face. Sadly I was right, and after the move, Henry's health went downhill. We hired a young pre-med student named Kyra from Columbia University to take care of him when we went out to dinner because he needed constant care. I knew the end was near, and I wanted to give him one last trip to his favorite place—the ocean.

I looked online for a dog beach. It was slim pickings in New York, but we found one that was about an hour's drive away. It was a long walk from the parking lot to the water, and the March wind was really cold. But when we got to the ocean, it was worth it. Henry put his nose up to sniff the sea air. He had pep in his step and even pranced a bit in the water. My chest was tight because I felt like I was walking with twenty-pound weights on my ankles. I knew it was the last time Henry would be on a beach.

On the way back to the car, Henry fell and Peter carried him for a while. It took us three times as long to get back to the car. I held Henry's face in my hands and we drove in silence back to the city. At home we gave him a painkiller, and when that didn't seem to work, the vet said we could give him another. But the second pill made Henry seem like he was drunk. Finally, at midnight, Peter took him to the all-night emergency vet to get him stabilized. I kissed Henry's head as Peter carried him to the elevator. It was a rough night.

At 10 a.m., we got a call asking us to come back to the hospital. It wasn't to bring him home but to say good-bye.

I felt bad for the taxi driver that picked us up—he must have thought the world was ending since we could barely speak through our distress. Somehow we managed to give him the address and he got us there safely. There were many different animals in the emergency room, as if on that Saturday night in New York City, every puppy, bunny, kitten, parrot, and ferret got sick and went to the doctor. Thankfully, Henry was away from the chaos in the intensive care unit.

The young veterinarian led us to Henry. He lay on his side with an oxygen mask over his nose. He was barely conscious. We took turns getting on the floor and kissing him good-bye. We thanked him for being such an important part of our lives, and I tried not to cause a scene. I remember what my grandfather said about not letting any creatures suffer, and I gathered myself and took charge.

"We're ready," I said.

I pulled Peter toward the door and we waited in a room for the doctor to bring Henry in to give him the final shot. My hands shook and Peter was collapsing inside.

The vet walked in, but he was empty-handed. He said he wouldn't have to give Henry a shot because he'd died as soon as we walked away. Ever a noble dog, Henry seemed to have waited for us to say our last words before he left.

We thanked the doctor and slowly walked home. Our doormen were waiting for us and they expected good news. But when we shrugged and looked upward, they were crushed. We'd been in New York for only six months, but they loved Henry, too.

To get the news out all at once, I tweeted a "Rest in Peace" note and was flooded with sympathy (even from Bob). The outpouring shored me up, and the next day *The Five* gave Henry a fitting send-off on the show.

I still think of Henry every day. He was the kind of dog that made me a better person.

Jasper

The night Henry died, I got a call from Greta Van Susteren. She and her husband, John, knew Henry from trips we'd taken to visit them in Annapolis. She had some advice.

"I know this is the last thing you want to do right now, but take it from me, the best thing you can do is to get another dog immediately," she said.

I told her I didn't know if I could handle a dog in Midtown Manhattan. She said that I could and that I must.

She was right.

We called a Vizsla breeder we knew in Maryland who used to take care of Henry when we were out of town. She'd heard about Henry on *The Five* and was expecting our call. She had a litter coming and could reserve us a male puppy. We named him Jasper before he was even born. It sounded like a good name—like a gentlemanly rascal.

The day before we were to pick him up, I took off from *The Five* and Peter drove us to Washington, D.C., to go to the Queen's Jubilee celebration at the British Embassy. It was a proper English garden party and we ate mini ice cream cones and drank a British version of a mimosa called Bucks Fizz (it was just like being at Buckingham Palace—the only thing missing was the rain). A lot of our friends were going out on the town afterward, but we declined. We had an important pickup in the morning.

As we pulled into the driveway at the breeder's house, I was opening the car door before we'd come to a full stop. I had to see him.

The puppies were penned in the living room. Newspapers lined the floor, and a few toys were strewn inside the gate. The breeder reached down, grabbed a pup, and handed him to me.

"Here he is—Jasper. He's the sweetest one of the litter."

He had fuzzy red-brown fur, blue eyes, a fat little belly, and pink paws.

"It's nice to meet you, Sir Jasper," I said.

I snuggled him but he wouldn't settle right away; he kept pushing his legs against my chest trying to get a good look at my face. I kissed his head and tucked him into my arm. Then I gave him to Peter so that he could meet him, too.

On our way home, we went through a drive-thru for Diet Cokes and showed him off to the cashier. It wasn't until about an hour into a journey that Jasper finally gave up and relaxed into me. We both breathed a little easier and I started to stroke his head.

That's when I noticed that he had an odd-shaped ear. It was much shorter than the other one and it looked to have been cut somehow. We don't know what happened to it, but we didn't care either. Jasper was such a gorgeous puppy, and his little ear makes him even more endearing. He has no idea how cute that marking is. It kills me.

Potty training in a high-rise apartment from forty-six floors up was a challenge—that's a long way for a puppy to hold a pee. To keep his mind off having to go before we got downstairs, we'd race him down the long corridor to the elevator. Then we'd rush him through the lobby and finally outside to a very busy Forty-Second Street. That was a lot to ask of a nine-week-old pup.

Jasper was very much like Henry, especially in looks and size, but immediately I could tell he was more of a baby than Henry ever was. He was super-sensitive, with every emotion emphasized—joy, fear, love—all of it. I was very protective of him, which is why Peter didn't tell me right away about what happened while I was working over Labor Day weekend.

During the Republican Convention in Tampa in September 2012, Peter took Jasper on a mini-vacation down to Annapolis and Washington, D.C., to visit old friends. They went down to City Dock Coffee and Peter tied the leash around one of the metal tables outside, just like he used to with Henry. But Jasper wasn't Henry and was confused about being left outside. He strained the leash so that he could see Peter inside the shop.

The metal table slid along the sidewalk, making quite a noise and startling him. Jasper got spooked and started running with the table still attached behind him, the clanging noise getting louder as the metal scraped and banged on the cobblestones—which only made Jasper run faster.

Someone in the shop said, "Dude, is that your dog?"

Peter looked up and then ran outside calling, "JASPER! BABY! COME BACK! IT'S OKAY!"

Jasper doubled back and started running back across the street with the table still clanging behind him. He was headed straight for the expensive vehicles parked diagonally along the street. With Peter running after him seeing dollar signs in his eyes from the possible damage to the cars, Jasper cleared the vehicles and then kept running around the town square. All the while, Peter was yelling and running after him, "JASSSPPPEEERRRR!"

Finally, Jasper tried going around a truck that had fresh fruit and vegetables at the market, and the table got lodged beneath the tailgate. Peter reached down and picked Jasper up and calmed him down. Eventually he untangled the leash from the table and headed back to the coffee shop dragging the table with him. The table scraped the stones and Jasper started freaking out from the noise and tried to get out of Peter's arms. So Peter had to pick up the table in his other arm and carry it across the street. This time he tied Jasper to the parking meter and went in to get his mocha.

"I don't suppose anyone got that on video?" he asked, embarrassed.

I wish I'd have been there to see that, though Peter was wise to keep it from me until I was back in New York and everyone was safe. For weeks after that, Jasper would jump a foot in the air if he heard any metal scraping on concrete. We had to pick up and move chairs so that we didn't startle him. A fan sent me a note about it and said, "Somewhere Henry is shaking his head and smiling."

On his second day home, Jasper got to be on *The Five*, and a star was born. He's been back to the show a couple of times, and he always steals the spotlight (and is uncharacteristically poorly behaved under the bright lights). A lot of fans want him to come back more often so they can see Bob get irritated.

Within a few months, Jasper became a social media A-lister and gained fans all over the country. I posted pictures of him from our walks in Central Park and on our road trips up and down the East Coast. We made up lyrics about Jasper to "Take It Easy" and "Desperado" by the Eagles and posed him for big events, including my most popular post ever, Jasper and all of his "friends" (toys) getting ready to watch the Presidential debate, complete with snacks. I was fortunate that Peter indulged the fun I was having with Jasper—he didn't think I was crazy. A couple of my co-hosts, however, certainly did. And maybe I am—in a good way.

Like Henry, Jasper doesn't care if his mom is on television or occasionally gets to speak to the former leader of the free world. He doesn't know that President Bush 43 painted his portrait and that it's his mom's most treasured possession.

Jasper gives me a joy that I'd hate to have missed in life. Because of him, I have connected to more people than I ever would have with politics alone. I love my dog friends, and I have no idea if they are Republicans, Democrats, Libertarians, or Martians. Pets are a great equalizer. It doesn't matter what your politics are. If you're a dog person, you're all right by me. And if you're not, give me five minutes alone with you and Jasper.

On *Red Eye* in 2013, one of the topics was about a Hollywood actress who wanted the paparazzi to stop taking pictures of her little dog. Always kidding, Gutfeld said that I was known to fly into a rage if people took pictures of Jasper. I said, "I don't believe in keeping my dog from people. I share my dog with everyone. Jasper is America's Dog...." And we've called him that ever since. He's worthy of the title.

It's not lost on me who the real TV star of the family is—and I wouldn't have it any other way.

CHAPTER 5

~~~~~~

Take It from Me—Please

On my first official morning as the White House press secretary, I got a call from the Secretary of Education, Margaret Spellings. Margaret had been with President Bush since he was the Governor of Texas and led the White House Domestic Policy Council during his first term. After his re-election in 2004, President Bush nominated her to serve in the Cabinet.

I considered Margaret a mentor, colleague, and friend. She has a terrific laugh and a delightful Southern drawl. She was plenty busy, so it was thoughtful of her to call me before my first briefing. She must have sensed my anxiety. I was the first woman press secretary in a Republican administration, the President was unpopular in the polls, and the White House was managing several simultaneous crises. Plus I had Tony Snow's very big shoes to fill. My "new job honeymoon" wouldn't last long.

"How ya doin'?" she asked.

"Well, actually, I'm pretty nervous," I said.

"Well, you're gonna have to put your big girl panties on and deal with it!"

*   *   *

So that's what I did—I snapped out of my worry-induced funk. That wasn't the first time that I'd been given advice just when I needed it. As you've read so far in this book, I've been blessed to have many people who have helped me succeed in my career. I benefited from suggestions to shine at a smaller college rather than to party at a big one, to go for the job opening as a press secretary on Capitol Hill even if the timing was off, and not to let negative press get under my skin—all advice that has made a huge difference to me.

A person I used to admire from afar but is now a friend and mentor is former Congresswoman Susan Molinari, who now runs public policy for Google. I like her mix of grace, smarts, and spunk. When I thanked her for her help in making a career decision, she told me that the only thing mentors ask in return for their advice is that it be passed on to others. I agreed and have tried to hold up my end of the bargain.

Susan, along with my friends Dee Martin and Jamie Zuieback, helped me turn an idea I had into a reality. To keep up with requests for advice from young women and their parents about the keys to achieving their life and career goals, I came up with a version of speed dating, but with mentoring instead of romance. We called it Minute Mentoring and focused on helping young women starting their careers. Susan and Dee worked for the law firm of Bracewell-Guiliani, and the firm was our main sponsor.

We invited women leaders from all sorts of professions to meet with small groups of mentees, share their top three pieces of advice, and take questions for the allotted time. Then, that group would get up and move to the next mentor. The mentees usually got to see six mentors, and then we hosted a cocktail reception where the young women could practice their networking skills.

Somewhat to my surprise, the advice was neither gender nor age specific. We got requests from young men asking for opportunities to participate (some of them volunteered at the events, hoping to learn something and maybe get some of the young ladies' phone numbers). The idea of speed mentoring caught on and we had requests to host events all across the country. Our little group wasn't able to fulfill demand, so we came up with instructions on how we put together our events so that they could host their own.

I like to help young professionals think through what they need to improve their careers. I enjoyed being a mentor at our events, and I also learned a few new tips that I started using myself—especially about how to better manage my schedule.

When I had the idea to write this book, I realized that passing some of these lessons on remained a major motivation. So the following are some of my favorite pieces of advice, broken into three categories: Quick Fixes, Good Habits, and Big Picture. I hope you can benefit by them.

This is not a comprehensive list, and many of the usual tips about what to wear to the office and having a good attitude I didn't include here. Those are standard pieces of good advice. I don't really need to tell people that dressing like a slob won't get you promoted or that a positive person is more likely to get a raise than a negative one—that should be well understood by now. But if you already know those basics and have incorporated them into your life, what follows can help you take your career to the next level.

But before I get to the practical advice, my first big overarching lesson, which I've relied on over and over, had to do with butterflies....

Making Butterflies Fly in Formation

Shawnalee Whitney was my college speech team coach. Shawnalee had long sandy brown hair, beautiful skin, and blue eyes. She was also talented, clever, and cheerful. Shawnalee drove our small team all around the West, racking up miles on her minivan.

On those road trips across the mountain ranges over to Utah and back to Pueblo, Colorado, we got to know each other very well. We learned about each other's families, favorite books, pets, hopes, and dreams. We also used to come up with fantastic insults for the university, which seemed to give all of its money to sports while we scrimped by, even though we used to win our tournaments and make good grades.

While we had a measly budget, Shawnalee worked it out so that we could go to competitions in Austin, San Francisco, Tucson, Seattle, and New Jersey. We had a great time in Monmouth, New Jersey, when we realized the staircase at the main hall was the scene for the movie version of *Annie*, the musical (it was also the summer retreat of President Woodrow Wilson during the campaign season in 1916). We climbed up the curving marble steps a few times just so we could pretend to be singing orphans. Our university looked nothing like many of the schools we went to visit (the story was that many of our buildings had been designed by the same architect that built the state prison, if that gives you an indication of how far that was from leafy green quads and the hallowed halls of New England's campuses).

At one tournament when I was a freshman, I completed my rounds and changed into jeans while I waited for everyone else to finish. One of my teammates rushed around to find me—I'd made it to the finals and had fifteen minutes to get back to the classroom. It never crossed my mind that I'd make the cut, so I hadn't bothered to look at the list. Shocked that I was still in the competition, I changed back into my suit in a little bathroom stall and ran to where the judges were waiting.

Shawnalee was there and took me aside to offer some encouragement. She could sense I was nervous, so she gave me what ended up being one of the best pieces of advice I'd ever heard.

"It's okay to have butterflies in your stomach, as long as you make them fly in formation," she said.

In my imagination I could see it—butterflies flying like the Blue Angels, obeying my instructions. After that, I could channel my nerves into a more positive energy that came across as enthusiasm rather than anxiety. I started to learn how to ride the waves of fear of speaking in front of judges. And lo and behold, I actually won the tournament.

I still get nerves before a speech or a TV show, but I've learned that adrenaline is essential for a good appearance. The anxiety alerts my brain that I need to be ready to perform. Without nerves, my delivery would be flat and no one would watch. So now I get nervous if I'm not nervous (Peter says if I'm not worried about something, I worry that I forgot something to worry about).

I'm not always able to manage my anxiety, though. Once I was almost crippled by my nerves. It was when I got a chance to compete for a charity on *Celebrity Jeopardy!* Alex Trebek has been in my living room since I was a kid, and I still watch the show every night with Peter. I shout out answers without concern that I'll embarrass myself if my answers are wrong (Peter, on the other hand, gets almost all of them right). But on stage that day, outside of the comfort of my home, I was completely exposed. My butterflies were all over the place, from my toes to my throat.

The *Jeopardy!* team could not have been kinder, and they tried to put us more at ease in the greenroom. We took pictures as a group— they put me, five feet tall, next to Kareem Abdul-Jabbar, seven-feet-two. Even though I wore five-inch heels and was standing on a box, he towered over me. It made for a funny picture.

In the audience, I had a great group of supporters there to cheer me on—including Bob Beckel, who wore a suit for the occasion.

I won the practice round, so I felt pretty good (and maybe a little too confident). My pulse slowed down. In the actual show, I was leading going into the first commercial break. But after that, I fell apart. I swung and missed at one clue about a stringed instrument, and then I never recovered. In "Final Jeopardy," I could have caught the leader but could not come up with the "Guggenheim" art museum. I knew it started with a "G" but I could only think of Getty. David Faber of CNBC won the match, but I still raised $10,000 for Companions for Heroes (matching rescue animals with war veterans diagnosed with posttraumatic stress syndrome). So my appearance was definitely worth the embarrassment (and now I sympathize more with other *Jeopardy!* losers).

I wish I'd remembered Shawnalee's advice and made my butterflies fly in formation that day. My voice was caught in my throat most of the time I was on stage, and I couldn't click the buzzer at the right time. I let my anxiety get the best of me, and I didn't get to enjoy the experience as much as I'd have liked.

Still, having competed in speaking events helped me get in front of groups and cameras and not totally fall apart. I encourage parents who are looking for activities for their sons and daughters to urge their kids to join the speech team. The number one fear in America is public speaking, which can hold people back from future career opportunities.

On the speech team, students learn skills and techniques that help shore up their confidence. Just look at what it did for me—I learned how to think critically, spot flaws in someone's argument, and persuade people to agree with me. (Right, Bob?)

Of all the things I did to prepare for a career in communications and journalism, by far the speech team was the most important contributor to my success. It's where I learned to herd butterflies.

Quick Fixes

FIND YOUR STRONG VOICE

How people present themselves is directly proportional to their success. One of the biggest weaknesses of young people today is talking like a Valley Girl, where the end of every sentence goes up making every statement sound like a question. It's called up-talking. I think you'll know what I mean? If you started reading this out loud? You've heard this before I'm sure? It's like super-annoying?

Up-talking starts when kids become teenagers. It used to be confined to girls, but I've noticed more young men doing it, too. People try to assimilate to make social situations easier, and up-talking helps them fit in with their friends. Group-think turns into group-talk. They think it sounds cute or sophisticated, and they use it as a shield to protect themselves from a disagreement or confrontation. It masks a lack of confidence in their comments and opinions—if everything is a question, then they can't be accused of being opinionated (or wrong). Young people used to grow out of this habit, but for some reason they're holding on to this verbal tic well after college (maybe another sign of America's protracted adolescence).

Up-talking makes most adults cringe. It suggests immaturity and a lack of seriousness. It grows tiresome, especially for employers. I'm convinced that one of the reasons young people have a hard time moving up in companies is because they can't stop up-talking after they graduate. What boss would want to have someone who talks like that visit an important client?

Thankfully, up-talking can be addressed fairly easily. First, the adults have to intervene to help someone break the habit, or these youngsters will be hobbled in their careers. If you have a child or an employee who up-talks, you have an obligation to discourage it. As uncomfortable as it can be to point out someone's shortcomings, it's for their own good. You can do it in a way that doesn't embarrass them. I suggest taking the person aside and gently saying that you want them to succeed and that you've noticed something that's holding them back. Tell them that they need to find their strong voice.

Usually a young person will not have any idea what you're talking about, so you might have to do an imitation so that they can actually hear what it sounds like. Try saying the same sentence like they do and then saying it again with a strong, steady, and confident voice. Then they can hear the difference.

Another way to explain how to find their strong voice is to show them that there is a physical aspect to it. I think of it this way: Right behind your chest bone at the top of your diaphragm is a little power center. If you put your finger right there, you can feel it. You turn the power center on by taking a breath and then tightening your core as if someone was about to punch you in the upper abdominal area. And then there—that spot right in the center, the strongest part of your upper abs is where it is. Hold your finger there while you breathe and you can feel it. Now try speaking from there. It works for me. It helps me stand up straighter, opens up my lungs, and makes whatever I'm saying sound convincing.

BAN THE EXCLAMATION POINT

Another part of finding your strong voice means cutting out emotion in e-mails and texts. Exclamation points should be used sparingly, not for things like "I need to schedule a conference call for next week!!" In professional communication at the office or when applying for a new job, resist exclamation points and any other sort of unnecessary melodrama. Your colleagues and bosses want to see steadiness, and superfluous exclamation points suggest the opposite. You don't want your e-mails to come across as angry or overexcited. This is especially true in the subject line of e-mails—raise your threshold for "URGENT!!" so that you don't risk giving your boss a heart attack. You want to be taken seriously if you ever really do have an emergency that needs immediate attention.

The same goes for emojis and emoticons—don't send them to the boss. She doesn't need to be prompted to be happy that her employee finished a project on time. Just finish the project and don't ask for praise—that way you're more likely to get it.

Writing better business communication, which is now almost exclusively via e-mail, can really set a person apart from their colleagues. Most people end up working for people who are a generation older than they are for most of their careers. That can change as people age, but a boss is probably closer to a young person's parents' age than to theirs. That means that they think and communicate differently from the friends they hang out with. So the trick is to start thinking like the boss and write better e-mails.

Let me give an example. Young people often make the mistake of introducing new topics in response to previous e-mails. This drives the boss nuts. An employee needs to stick to the subject or risk confusion and miscommunication. Rule of thumb: new topic, new e-mail chain, and new subject head. This can help people easily find previous messages if they're needed.

Another good practice is to keep e-mails rare, spare, and specific. Your subject lines need to be simple and descriptive of your message. An effective thing is to title an e-mail "Three Things" or "Friday's Delivery Issue: Solved" to help keep things straight. Responses from the boss are more likely to be answered quickly if they're set up like that.

Also, use bullet points or numbers to keep the format clean for someone reading quickly, and include a request for a response and by a certain date or time, if needed. Anticipate their questions and include answers in the original e-mail. You'll soon get compliments like "That's a great e-mail." A little effort here goes a long way.

NO UGG BOOTS AT THE OFFICE

You have to dress for the job you *want*, not just the job you have, because you never know when you might get a lucky break. When that happens, you don't want to be wearing jeans.

A friend started her legal career like many others, but one day she got picked to argue her first case in the Southern District of New York only because she was the most senior person on the case who had a suit on hand to change into when they had an emergency application at the courthouse. Without that suit, she wouldn't have had that chance to shine.

I won't belabor the dress for success point, but I have to tell you the one thing I think you should not wear around the office: UGG boots.

Now I like UGG boots and I wear them to walk Jasper. They're warm and great for colder weather. So by all means, wear UGG boots to commute back and forth to the office, but bring a pair of appropriate shoes to change into once you arrive. I see so many young women wearing their UGGs all day long, and it makes them look like they're shuffling, not picking up their feet. Shuffle, shuffle, shuffle—to the copy machine and back. To the kitchen and back. To the restroom and back. Shuffling makes it look like you're not really interested. I think that it leaves a bad impression, and it's something really easy to fix.

SPIT IT OUT (YOUR GUM, THAT IS)

Gum is a very dangerous thing—and not because you risk swallowing it. Gum chewing could actually hold you back at work. This might sound ridiculous, but believe me, the boss doesn't want to see or hear anyone chewing gum. No matter how discreet you think your gum chewing may be, it isn't worth someone being distracted by it. I'm all for fresh breath, but I suggest choosing mints over gum at the office. Never go into a client meeting chewing gum, even if you don't have a speaking role. It's a little thing but this is a quick fix that everyone can do immediately.

ALWAYS TAKE YOUR HUSBAND'S PHONE CALLS

This is not a relationship advice book, though your work life does affect your love life. Stressful jobs mean that sometimes our loved ones have to take a backseat. But they can't stay there forever.

I learned a good lesson from the White House Communications Director Nicolle Wallace. We were in a meeting and she saw me hurriedly press a button on my phone to ignore an incoming call. She said, "Do you want to take it?" And I said, "No, it's just Peter. I'll call him back."

She gave me some advice that turned into my New Year's Resolution that year: "Always take your husband's calls." She helped me reset my priorities, and I became more understanding of people needing to manage work and home while they're at the office.

One Christmas, I had a chance to show my staff that together we could manage our work and family obligations. I'd noticed they were a bit agitated, but they hadn't said anything to me directly. So I finally asked them what was wrong. It turned out they were stressed because they were running out of time to buy presents for their families. They hadn't wanted to complain because I was working just as hard as they were.

I said we could fix the problem, and we came up with a rotating scheduling where each of them could get an afternoon off to go shopping—they just had to cover for each other during those hours. They were so relieved. As a manager, you have to show them it's okay to put their families first and help them figure out how to do so if they're stuck. They'll be more productive if they know the office's priorities match theirs.

SPEAK UP WHEN IT COUNTS

One of the responsibilities of an employee is to identify problems and help prevent full-blown crises. That doesn't mean becoming Chicken Little and raising every little thing as *the most important issue*—if you do that, people will tune you out. But employers depend on people to sound an alert if they're really worried about something. And good managers make sure it's safe for the employee to do so without repercussions.

The consequences of not speaking up can be serious—whether it's a safety or an ethical issue, or just a problem that needs to be nipped in the bud to protect the brand of the product—it's better to speak up than to regret that you didn't. I learned that the hard way once when I was the deputy press secretary.

Any good press office constantly scans the horizon for trouble ahead and tries to get in front of it, and part of my job was to read a couple of extra newspapers in addition to *The Wall Street Journal*, *The Washington Post*, and *The New York Times*. My boss at the time, Scott McClellan, assigned *The Washington Times* and *USA Today* to me. I would read those before he called me and the principal deputy Trent Duffy to meet with him at 7:15 a.m.

One morning I told Scott that I'd seen a story in *The Washington Times* about a company based in Dubai that wanted to buy a controlling stake in one of our nation's ports. My instincts told me that in a post-9/11 world, if a company from the Middle East wanted to buy and have control over one of our ports, the public was going to worry about possible terrorist threats or connections (even if it was an unfounded concern) and that the backlash could hurt President Bush's chances of expanding trade to keep our economy growing.

Scott didn't think that it was a story we needed to worry about and told me that it would never come up in the briefing, so I deferred to him. After all, I didn't have as much experience as he did, and perhaps he was right.

The next day, there it was again, below the fold but on the front page. I brought it up for a second time because I sensed it was an issue that could explode. Again, Scott told me again that it wasn't going to be a story. Every one of my instincts said that it would. I was thinking beyond the White House briefing room and citizen—not inside the Beltway reporter—reaction. But I dropped the subject.

On the third day, the Dubai ports story was front-page, above the fold with a screaming headline. By 8 a.m. all hell broke loose on Capitol Hill, and it took the entire month of February 2006 to get that issue resolved. It was an unforced error, and I kicked myself over it.

I vowed not to let that happen again—to find a way to get in front of a problem even if the boss didn't want to hear the news I had. I should have asked Scott just to humor me and to bring it up in the senior staff meeting—I think he'd have done that for me, and if I'd pushed the issue, we may have saved us from the firestorm.

If you are truly worried about a problem, it's important to raise it and not to fold if all of your alarm bells are going off. Push back respectfully, so you protect your boss and yourself.

Good Habits

SHARE THE CREDIT

If you want to be a generous employee, colleague, and friend, you have to give heaps of credit to others. What goes around comes around at the office. This means giving everyone else credit before you take any for yourself. This goes for Presidents, too.

I was in the Oval Office talking with President Bush around 4 p.m. in August 2008 when he got a call from the CIA. I got up to leave so that he could have some privacy, but he said, "You can stay."

So I sat silently and listened to his side of the conversation. He said, "How did it go?...Okay...Good...Well done...Tell them when they're ready, I'd love to meet them...When you get back, come see me."

He hung up and I said, "Anything I should know about?" He told me that the American hostages being held by the terrorist group FARC in Colombia had just been rescued, along with Ingrid Betancourt and several others. No one was injured, and they were on their way home to safety.

I knew the news would break shortly, so I asked the President if I could give the reporters some of the colorful details that help tell a story like that. I wanted to be able to say I'd been there when he got the call, and what he said when he heard the news.

But the President stopped me. "I don't want any credit. Make sure that President Uribe gets all the credit—he needs it more than I do."

At the time, he was trying to sign a trade deal between the United States and Colombia, but opponents on the Hill, including then–Speaker of the House Nancy Pelosi, were blocking passage of the agreement. One of their excuses was that Uribe wasn't doing enough to fight terrorism in his country. Since the most well-known hostages were now freed, with help from the Colombian Special Forces, that excuse could presumably be crossed off the list (unfortunately the Democrats found other reasons to block it because of unions and environmentalists objections).

I learned from President Bush that even when you could use a personal boost, it's better to spread the credit if it helps you get closer to your goal. Not to mention, it's just a very decent thing to do.

LOYALTY—A TWO-WAY STREET

In 2010, Mrs. Barbara Bush came to a Minute Mentoring event in Houston. When we invited her to start off the evening with brief remarks, she was surprised. "Why would they ask me? I've never worked a day in my life," she said. True, in a sense—all the work she'd ever done had been in service to her country or for charity.

In her speech she said, "Earlier today I called my son, George, and I asked what it was like to work with Dana. And then I called Dana and asked her what it was like to work for my son. And what I concluded from listening to them describe each other is that loyalty goes both ways. That's what a good partnership is all about."

Mrs. Bush was right—because we knew President Bush was loyal to us, we became more loyal to him. Loyalty was our glue. It meant we had complete trust in each other, could be honest about problems, and ensured we kept focused on productive outcomes.

BE WILLING TO TAKE THE BLAME FOR YOUR TEAM

As a manager, it's so important that your team knows you're on their side. It keeps people from sniping at one another when things don't go as planned.

Take the New Hampshire primary loss in 2000, for example. The Bush campaign was taken by surprise when it got stomped by Senator McCain, and the team was badly rattled. In *Courage and Consequence*, Karl Rove says that Bush had seen plenty of "floundering campaigns" and that something he learned was that you can't "shoot at a wounded staff." So Governor Bush called everyone into his suite and said that he was fully responsible for the loss. He asked them to project confidence and put their game faces on. His loyalty emboldened them and that was how he "got the best out of those around him." That's the hallmark of a good leader.

STICK UP FOR OTHERS—EVEN WHEN
THEY DON'T KNOW IT

I love the feeling I get from sticking up for other people. Once I teamed up with President Bush to defend a young woman reporter— and she didn't know it for many months.

In 2006, I was finishing the President's press conference pre-brief when one of my office assistants rushed in with a new seating chart. ABC News had made a last-minute substitution.

"They big-footed Jessica Yellin for Jake Tapper?" I asked.

"Yes, ma'am."

Well, that was a rotten thing to do. Jessica had been covering the White House for *Good Morning America* for several months but hadn't asked the President a question on camera. Since every network got to ask a question, she was supposed to get a turn that day.

The President looked at me over his glasses and said, "Who's Jake Tapper?"

I described Jake as a well-respected reporter that ABC had recently hired, and I suspected they were trying to raise his profile by having him in the network's chair for the live press conference. I told the President I thought it was wrong that she was being pushed aside for him and that she deserved to be in the seat.

"Well, do we have to call on him?" the President asked, raising his eyebrows.

Catching his drift, I said, "No, sir, I don't think you do."

And so, he did not. For the first time in his administration, he didn't call on one of the networks.

Jake Tapper raised his hand as high as he could through the entire press conference, and the President just kept looking around him and calling on other reporters. I had nothing against Jake himself—he's a fine reporter and a friend. But at that moment, I was proud that we'd sent a message to ABC (even if we didn't tell them why).

Several months later, I caught up with Jessica on a press trip when a few of the women reporters were having dinner. I asked if she remembered that day, and she said Jake had been furious when he got back to the booth and had called Tony Snow to demand an explanation. We laughed because Tony and Jake had no idea that it was the President and I who were in cahoots. It made her feel good that we'd stood up for her, and I learned that standing on principle should sometimes trump tradition. (No hard feelings, right, Jake?)

WHY, THANK YOU VERY MUCH

Writing a thank-you note should not have to be one of these tips, but somewhere along the way young people stopped writing them. A handwritten thank-you note is a must, not an option. And no, an e-mail doesn't cut it.

Not long ago, I helped a young woman who was about twenty-two years old get prepared for a job interview. After the interview, I asked if she'd sent the prospective employer a thank-you note. She said that she'd sent an e-mail. I said no, send an actual thank-you note, on paper, with an envelope, and a stamp.

She said, "Really? Are you sure? Wouldn't that seem too...formal, like I'm trying too hard?"

This isn't the first time I'd heard that kind of response from a young professional who was asking my help to find a job. I assured her that a handwritten thank-you note would not be too formal; rather, it's an essential part of any interviewing or networking.

Imagine how many other people applied for a job or a promotion and how, especially at the entry level, you have basically the same qualifications. You need something to help you stand out, so sending a note on nice stationery will ensure that you at least make a much better impression than those who don't even bother.

Most people in positions of hiring new employees grew up writing thank-you notes, and they appreciate the effort someone takes to follow up properly. I can't tell you how many times someone has called or written to thank me for my thank-you note. It works!

When in doubt, send a thank-you note.

REVERSE MENTORS

Social media has totally changed our lives, especially at work. Instead of snickering about a boss not knowing the difference between Instagram and Snapchat, a young employee can make themselves indispensible by serving as an unofficial reverse mentor on technology.

Helping a boss adapt to new technologies, without judgment, makes for a very valuable employee. When I was running my public relations business after the White House, one of my assistants suggested I join Twitter and Facebook. I rolled my eyes and resisted for months thinking that I had plenty to do without wasting more time online. I couldn't see how social media could help my business, and I was a bit intimidated by the technology. I didn't know how to use it, and I was hesitant to try. I hoped it was a passing fad.

Instead of dropping the subject, my employee set up the accounts for me and showed me a couple of basic things—like how to send a tweet, gain more followers, and post pictures of my dog (this was the best part).

Once she did that, I could experiment a little. It turned out she was right—I liked being able to interact with followers, read other posts, and find out news before anyone else. I enjoyed sharing my thoughts with folks like-minded and otherwise. I don't think I'd ever have had the gumption to try social media without her pushing me.

Something I really liked about her was that she didn't lord over me that she was smarter on the technology than I was—she was just eager to help "build my brand" (a phrase that bugged me but I knew what she meant). After I'd left Washington for New York City and closed down most of my business clients, I offered to be a reference for her. When I got a call from an executive who was considering hiring her, I was enthusiastic about her abilities and relayed this example of her showing initiative, skills, generosity, and a fresh perspective to someone who wasn't as savvy as she was on a particular issue.

ZIP IT

Sometimes the best thing a person can say is nothing at all. Listening is often more valuable, but that's seldom practiced in my profession of politics and media.

Once I watched Vice President Dick Cheney get asked in an interview why he didn't speak very often in meetings. He said he'd learned that leaders need to let people in their organizations speak freely and without judgment. He said that if a staffer thinks that someone higher up the ladder will attack him for his opinions, then he'll be less likely to express his thoughts. When that happens, the bosses don't get to hear what their people are thinking, and they can miss something important.

So that's why the Vice President was so quiet in policy discussions. He never pulled a face or showed any reaction except openness to hearing more, and we all felt like we could say anything in front of him. Only at the end of a meeting would he ask questions or express his opinion. He saw the President regularly, and that's when he'd weigh in on the issues. I thought that was an excellent management approach.

One of my favorite sayings from Cheney was, "You never get in trouble for something you didn't say." Exactly!

LET IT GO

A good memory isn't always a positive. I have an excellent memory (this is a blessing and a curse—just ask Peter) and I can remember anything that's ever hurt or embarrassed me—from childhood taunts to breakups to a misspelling on a PowerPoint presentation that elicited snickers from a client. I even let little mistakes eat at me while others couldn't even remember the event, and it was President Bush who taught me to let those things go.

When I was a deputy press secretary, the communications director, Dan Bartlett, suggested that the President take some time to meet with David Ignatius, a columnist, about Ignatius's recent trip to Iran. Dan was going to have me sit in just to monitor the discussion. But there was a miscommunication between Dan and the President. The President didn't want Ignatius to think that he was getting an interview about Iran because he didn't want to give the impression that he was negotiating with Iran through a newspaper columnist. That made a lot of sense. But Dan and I knew that Ignatius expected to come out of the meeting with something he could use in his columns, so we were stuck.

The President put his foot down—he said he'd listen to what Ignatius had to say about his recent trip to Iran, but he wasn't going to give him something on the record. Addressing Dan, he pointed a finger at me and said, "Therefore, *she* doesn't need to be here." They both looked at me and I slunk out of the Oval Office.

I was mortified. I called Peter and whispered to him what had happened when I'd been told to get out of the Oval. Thankfully, Peter gave me a better way of looking at it. He said, "Just think—for the rest of your life you'll be able to say, 'I've been kicked out of better places than this!'" That helped me laugh about it. But oh, was I embarrassed.

On the President's book tour in 2010, I asked him if he remembered how mad he'd been that day. He had no recollection of it. I said it had worried me for years. He laughed and said, "You're going to have to let that one go."

The President was very good about not letting little things get to him, which meant he could focus on the important things. One of his mottos was, "The President doesn't get do-overs." He'd learn from things that happened and applied those lessons to whatever was ahead, while I wasted valuable energy fretting about trivialities.

It's not always easy to move on from things like that, but when I am able to do it, I find space for more productive thinking.

Big Picture

PASS IT ON

This is one of my favorite tips—everyone should practice good career karma. What goes around definitely comes around at work.

First, you need to build a strong network of allies. Everyone you start working with could one day be in a senior position and you may need their help at some point. Plus, as you get more management responsibility, you have a smaller circle of peers whom you can trust, so it's best to make sure that the relationships you have are solid.

I started on Capitol Hill answering phones, and nearly twenty years later, the friends I made then are still in my network. They're running the shows now, and so we've climbed the ladder together. It's good to have these friendships at work.

Another thing to do is pass on advice to younger staff, especially if they want a mentor. Tell them what you learned that you wish you'd known when you started. Employees learn best from hearing the stories of people they admire, and they're eager to be advised on what they can be doing to succeed. Besides, you never know if one day a kid like that could end up as the boss.

A final point about helping others at the office—if you're a manager, it's really important to encourage your employees to grow so they can be promoted or even move on to another job. Losing an employee can be inconvenient, but it's really a testament to what a good manager you are if they move up and out. If an employee is stuck, ask yourself why...it may not just be their fault.

In addition, young people who have good jobs should help their peers find jobs, too. Networking isn't just about making sure your needs are secure, though favors do get returned. Be willing to open a door, pass on a résumé, or make an introduction. Try not to think of job seekers as competition but as ongoing contacts. Building your network of allies doesn't necessarily yield direct benefits, but that's how karma works. You never know when your good deed will be returned.

TO SCHOOL OR NOT TO SCHOOL?

There's an important ongoing debate right now about whether college is worth it for the majority of American students. I believe it is—every statistic I've seen shows that over a lifetime, a college degree helps a person achieve and earn more than someone who didn't go to college. Even "some college" is beneficial. It is, however, very expensive, especially at some schools, and so student loan debt is a major consideration for most families.

Across the country, there are some good innovations that are disrupting traditional colleges, including some online university course offerings, which give a person more flexibility to take classes when and where they need. And while those are interesting developments, changes there will take time to mature.

In the meantime, many young professionals are also asking the question of whether they should get an advanced degree—in business, law, or another profession. They want to know if it will matter to their future, help them get a better job, and command a better salary after graduation. They ask if they should resign from their jobs and go to school full-time or try to find a part-time program where they can continue to work while they study for their master's degree. Others think they need to go to law school but worry they don't really want to practice law. And almost everyone worries about how they would pay for it.

The answers to all of those questions vary. An advanced degree can certainly help focus the mind, enhance skills, and give you a leg up on your competition. In my case, I became a better journalist, especially when it came to news writing. In my graduate school program we all flunked our first assignments—that was a real wake-up call.

I also fretted about how to pay for it, and I was very hesitant to take out a student loan. I never thought, however, that I wouldn't end up going straight into journalism—and if I had known that, I'm not sure I'd have gone to get my master's degree. But I'm glad I did, because I use what I learned there every day. So for me it worked out, but these are some questions that I ask young people to think about before they make a decision about whether to apply to graduate school:

- Is there something that you really want to study?
- Does your profession respect or even require an advanced degree for promotion?
- Will an advanced degree increase your chances of getting a job that you want?
- Do you have the flexibility in your life to leave work and study full-time?
- Financially, are you able to pay for graduate school, or have you asked whether your employer has any funds that will help pay for additional studies?

- Are you thinking about graduate school because you don't really know what you want to do? Or are you bored in your job and looking for an escape?

My bottom line on graduate school is that you shouldn't go just because you don't have anything else to do. That's an expensive and time-consuming venture if you're not sure what you want to get out of it. But if you can't find a job in your field and know that an advanced degree would help you land one, then by all means it's worth pursuing.

However, there could be other ways to spend that time—I always advocate for young people to try to work in Washington, D.C., on Capitol Hill for at least a couple of years. It's like getting a master's degree—and even if you don't want to work in politics or government, everything you learn on the Hill will be useful in your life. Not to mention the contacts that you'll make that you'll have throughout your career.

I also don't think that parents should pay for their children's graduate or law school. Helping a student with a four-year bachelor's degree is very generous, but an advanced degree should be considered a personal responsibility. That will ensure that the coursework is taken very seriously and makes the young person take ownership of their degree. And when they graduate, it's a shared accomplishment that the whole family can be proud of. But do not encourage graduate school just for graduate school's sake. Work experience is much more valuable if the decision comes down to that.

MOVE OUT TO MOVE UP

At Minute Mentoring events, one of my top three pieces of advice is "don't be afraid to move." A reluctance to move is part of a growing general aversion to risk of all kinds that is taking hold across

(*Jim Watson / Getty Images*)

After I got hit in the face with the mic stand in Baghdad in December 2008, President Bush comforted me in a hold room. He'd seen me crying but didn't know what had happened.

(*Courtesy George W. Bush Presidential Library and Museum*)

An impromptu photograph with the U.S. Marines in Al Anbar Province, Iraq, in September 2007 (I'm the one in the middle).
(*AP Photo / Charles Dharapak*)

This dinner with the Israelis at the Prime Minister's residence was one of the many times I witnessed President Bush stick up for America when no reporters were around. I'm seated at the end of the table with Raffi Eitan, an Israeli war hero.
(*Courtesy George W. Bush Presidential Library and Museum*)

Dinner in the desert in the United Arab Emirates in 2008. The falcon was much heavier than I expected, but I didn't drop him.
(*Courtesy George W. Bush Presidential Library and Museum*)

Before the end of President Bush 43's administration, I convinced father and son to do a joint interview for the historic record. 41 pulled me into the picture, and it became my favorite photo from the White House.
(*Courtesy George W. Bush Presidential Library and Museum*)

This trip to Africa stirred my compassion. Meeting President Ellen Johnson Sirleaf, the first woman elected as President of an African nation, was a highlight of the trip. Peter and I returned to Africa after the White House to get some Perspective (with a capital P) and volunteer at one of the faith-based sites supported by President Bush's program PEP-FAR (President's Emergency Plan for AIDS Relief).
(*Courtesy George W. Bush Presidential Library and Museum*)

Camp David is a special place for the First Family and for White House staff; it had a slightly more relaxed feel than the West Wing.
(*Courtesy George W. Bush Presidential Library and Museum*)

Deputy Chief of Staff, Joe Hagin, pushed me forward to meet Queen Elizabeth during a Presidential visit to Windsor Castle. I tried not to lord it over my British husband too much.
(*Courtesy George W. Bush Presidential Library and Museum*)

Sometimes the President had "One more thing" on his mind, too. Don't worry, I wasn't in any trouble.
(*Courtesy George W. Bush Presidential Library and Museum*)

My dad, Leo Perino (far left), on his first visit to the White House when I was the press secretary. The President and First Lady Laura Bush invited us to the special dinner they hosted for Prime Minister Berlusconi in the State Dining Room. (*Courtesy George W. Bush Presidential Library and Museum*)

Tony Snow's (center, left of me) press office team. We took this photo on his last day at the White House. Sadly, he died nearly a year later in 2008 after a battle with colon cancer. (*Courtesy George W. Bush Presidential Library and Museum*)

There's nothing as professionally satisfying as having the confidence of the President. Here we are in the Center Hall of the White House before taking questions from the press in the Diplomatic Reception Room. (*Courtesy George W. Bush Presidential Library and Museum*)

On Air Force One briefing the press in their rear cabin. This picture reminds me just how short I was compared to everyone else. (*Courtesy George W. Bush Presidential Library and Museum*)

My last briefing as the White House press secretary, capping the most incredible experience of my life. I was asked if I'd ever work for another administration and I said, "You'll have to ask Peter." (*Courtesy George W. Bush Presidential Library and Museum*)

My most cherished possession, shown here for the first time: a portrait of Jasper as a young pup, as painted by the artist known simply as "43." (*Barry Morgenstein, photographer of the original picture of Jasper and of his portrait*)

On Peter's 60th birthday at the 21 Club in Manhattan, we were surrounded by family and friends from all over the world. The cake told our story—complete with the Harley and sidecar that Peter drives with Jasper when we visit South Carolina.

Playing with the kids in Fish Hoek, South Africa, at Living Hope's after-school program. Peter and I volunteered there in February 2009 at the end of the Bush Administration.

Henry at 13 years old still traveled everywhere with us. In the summer of 2011, I let him lick ice cream from a spoon in Kennebunkport, Maine.

When I met Jasper—June 6, 2012. I loved him before I ever laid eyes on him.

Couldn't leave this one on the cutting room floor. Behind the scenes at the cover shoot, it's obvious Jasper is the real star of the family. (*Melanie Dunea / CPi*)

A most unlikely television pairing—Bob Beckel and I together for a special anniversary show of *Hannity* in Atlanta, Georgia, in 2011. (*Chris McKay / Getty Images*)

The Five, plus one special guest—Jasper, on his second birthday. Bob Beckel even got him a cake for the occasion. Eric helped me manage Jasper. Greg Gutfeld looks thrilled. Kimberly cut the cake and the crew ate it.

Celebrity Jeopardy!— the most nervous I've ever been. And Alex Trebek was playing mind games when he placed me next to Kareem Abdul-Jabbar (he's 7'2" and I'm an even 5')—not even a box and five-inch heels could close our height gap. (*Kris Connor / Getty Images*)

The last moment of the administration. Before President Bush boarded the plane with Mrs. Bush, he caught my eye and called me over to say good-bye. Thanks to chief White House photographer Eric Draper for capturing that moment. (*Courtesy George W. Bush Presidential Library and Museum*)

America. Whenever I mention this tip, I get nods of recognition and "I needed to hear that" smiles. In the back of their minds they're worried about being stuck in their careers because there are no additional career opportunities where they live, but staying put can be far worse than leaving. Whether for love, career, or change of pace, relocating can be one of the best things you ever do for yourself.

There are a lot of reasons that people don't want to move—family, climate, lifestyle, and familiarity. Actually, those can be the same reasons for wanting to move!

Today, most people relocate two to three times in their lives, but still there are some young people who feel pressure to stay near to where they grew up because their moms (and sometimes dads) make them feel miserable about leaving. The parent anchor can be heavy.

This happens all over the nation, but is more common in America's smaller towns. Some people worry that if their children leave their small town, they won't come back, and that's true, many of them won't—at least not right away.

Devoted parents might not even realize that they are pressuring their kids to stay nearby, or their children may be too nervous to go out and try something in a new place. If that's the case, then parents ought to encourage their kids to be more adventurous. Kick them out of the nest for a while—they'll return if they have to.

Another thing I've found in Washington, D.C., and New York City is that young people don't want to leave the energy and excitement that a large metropolitan area offers. They love city life and can't imagine being in a "backwater" with nothing to do. I get that. But young people also want to get promoted at work and to earn more money so that they can live one day like their bosses and the owners of the company do.

Sometimes you have to leave one location and get more experience under your belt, so that you can return at a higher-paying level. That means you shouldn't frown when your boss says there's an opportunity in Fort Wayne, Indiana, and they're considering you for the job. Don't turn down an opportunity because it is three thousand miles away from home. Don't mope when you find out the company is moving its headquarters to another state because they want a better tax structure. Don't give up on a new job opportunity just because the office isn't in your preferred location—small and midsize towns are worth a shot when you're working your way up the ladder. Small towns have a lot going for young people—they're trying to lure talent so it's worth taking advantage of that.

Likewise, don't let fear of experiencing something new hold you back from a career opportunity and a mind-opening experience. There are hundreds of ways to keep in touch with family and friends (in some ways there are too many). And if it's a cold climate you worry about, there are these things called coats that work rather well.

Leaving a big city could be exactly what someone needs. Many young singles find it nearly impossible to meet a like-minded life partner in a city—it's strange that the more people that live in one area, the lonelier one can feel. And it's difficult to become fully immersed in a community if you're in high-rises all day. There's something to be said for getting out of the concrete jungle and choosing a place where you can make a difference—where your skills are unique and appreciated. Think of the laws of supply and demand—in a city, there are thousands of people with similar skills and experiences, so the competition for the great new jobs is fierce. Why not go somewhere else and shine?

If I were starting over, I'd head to a place like North Dakota, where there's an energy boom and a 3.5 percent unemployment rate, the lowest in the nation. That doesn't mean you have to be in the energy business—people living and working there need a lot of things and have money to spend. It's a great place to open a restaurant or a fitness club, take a risk on real estate development, or teach school because the state has money to invest more in education than other states.

North Dakota is the Wild West with Wi-Fi. Regulations aren't strangling people there (yet). People have more disposable income there than in other states, which they can save or use to buy something they've always wanted, like a Corvette (automobile dealers are selling a lot of cars up there!). And the schools are thriving—it's a great place for young families to start out. You never know where your career will take you, so why not take a chance on a place where you're more likely to succeed?

And remember this if you're worried about making a move: If everything falls apart, and you just can't stand to be away from your hometown or the exciting city that you love, the good news is that you have a great option—you can always return. As the old saying goes, "Home is where they have to take you back."

IT'S OKAY TO LEAVE A BIG DOG EMPLOYER, TOO

Being willing to move applies to leaving your employer to pursue new opportunities, too. This is especially true of companies or organizations considered the gold standard in their industry, whether in finance, media, technology, publishing, nonprofits, or government. When you work for the best, it's sometimes very difficult to leave it behind because you worry that nowhere will ever measure up.

This was certainly true at the White House. Almost everyone in politics wants to work in the West Wing someday, which means the White House gets the pick of the very top performers. However, for younger or less experienced staff, breaking into the White House was tough and moving up within the White House could take a long time because few people left the top jobs.

My advice to those people was that they consider leaving the

White House to take on more responsibility and gain more experience somewhere else—on Capitol Hill or at one of the federal agencies. That way they could get some experience relevant and useful to the White House and possibly return at a later date.

Emily Schillinger did just that—she started answering phones in Vice President Cheney's office but she had higher aspirations. Jeanie Mamo (a friend who ran the Office of Media Affairs) and I told her she needed to go work on Capitol Hill, where someone young like her could be hired as a House press secretary, get some on-the-record experience, and learn more about the legislative process.

Well, she took our advice, and then two years later, when I needed to hire an assistant press secretary in the White House, Emily came to mind because she had networked and kept in touch with me. All of a sudden, she was working in the White House press office with us and then went on to run communications for a United States Senator. Not too shabby!

GET OUT OF TOWN

Now let's say you don't need to move—you're in a city or town you love, the career opportunities are good, and you're likely to meet a guy or gal and fall in love. If you're not going to move, then you have to get out and travel a bit, to see some of this country, even parts of the world. Nothing opens up the mind like visiting another place. Seeing new things gives you a lot more to talk about, which can also be useful for networking. Stories about your travels can help you break the ice at awkward meetings and make a connection with someone if you can say, "Oh, you're from Flagstaff? I went through there on a road trip once...." That makes for a great conversation starter.

If money is tight, go for a road trip until you're able to fly somewhere. And make it fun—come up with themes for lifetime travel goals, like visiting all of the national parks or Presidential libraries, finding the best BBQ, or going to the hometown of your favorite author.

FEED YOUR BRAIN

When we started Minute Mentoring, almost every mentor would suggest that a young woman should read more. That's pretty bland and standard advice, so we asked them to be specific in their recommendations. What would they suggest a young person read? And why did they think it was important?

For example, Maria Cardona, one of our mentors in D.C., suggested reading the classics because not only did you have perspective reading them as an adult, but it also helped improve writing skills.

In a different vein, when I first started on Capitol Hill, Congressman McInnis suggested I read *The Wall Street Journal* Review and Outlook section every day. I started right then and I've hardly missed a day since. To me, the *WSJ* has the best editorial and op-ed page, and reading it has helped me make better arguments, learn about topics I didn't know much about, and improve my own writing.

I like to read a variety of news and opinion, but I can't always fit everything into my day. So I started a weekend reading folder. During the week if I see something of interest, I e-mail the article to myself and then print the articles to read over the weekend. Brooke Sammon, a young woman who worked for me for a while, used to put my folder together. When she moved on, she started her own weekend reading packet and now she's regarded as the best-read person in her office.

There is power in being the most informed—it gives you a competitive edge. Whenever I prepared for a meeting at the White House and now for *The Five*, I want to have read more than anyone else in a meeting. Having a good and steady flow of information is as important to me as someone with diabetes who needs to keep his sugar at the right level. I just can't live without it. I feel my brain atrophying if I'm not keeping up with the news. Information is my insulin.

Another reason to read is to be able to pass on articles to friends, family, co-workers, and supervisors—it's a great way to keep up your network of allies. One day in the mail I got a clipping from *Sports Illustrated* about how people use sports-related phrases in everyday speech, especially in politics and business ("Congress just couldn't get the ball over the line..." and "That CEO should just take a knee on that issue."). Kevin Sullivan, the communications director when I worked at the White House, sent it to me because he remembered how I used to get my sports all mixed up. (Three-point stance was my favorite—I used it in a briefing but thought I was talking about someone making a basket!) That note prompted me to get in touch with Kevin and we caught up—he watches my show and I refer business to him. We've continued to be good friends and colleagues—win-win.

YOU ARE WHO YOU MEET

I suggest going to at least two networking events a month. That can be something organized through your employer or a mixer put on by the Chamber of Commerce. Have some conversation icebreakers ready so that you can get through those first few minutes of awkwardness.

Try to avoid asking right away, "So, what do you do?" because it's a real turnoff—it's too abrupt and can put someone on the defensive. Instead, find out where people are from, what they like to do on the weekends, and whether they have a dog (you can tell a lot about a person if they don't like dogs). If you have a mutual contact at an event, a safe question is, "So how do you know Jim?" The answer will usually give you a pretty good summary of who they are and what they do.

To build out your personal network, I recommend choosing

five people a month who you want to stay connected to (family or friends, colleagues or former bosses) and then send them a personal, handwritten note. I used to do that naturally, a holdover tradition from my parents, who made us write letters every week to our grandparents and godparents.

Remember, that's one of the reasons I was even on the radar screen when the Bush Administration needed someone to join the Justice Department press office after 9/11—I'd sent postcards and letters to friends throughout the years, including a former colleague who ended up running communications for Attorney General John Ashcroft. She remembered me because I'd made an effort to be memorable (and it's a good excuse to buy nice stationery).

TAKE RESPONSIBILITY FOR THE ONE THING YOU CAN CONTROL—YOUR HEALTH

So much that happens in your life is not in your control, but taking care of your health is not one of them. Every day we make choices about our nutrition, exercise, and sleep, and bad decisions can hurt our careers and personal lives. I found this out the hard way.

When I was at the White House, I worked an insane amount of hours—from 4 a.m. until 10 p.m., and often I'd wake up on full alert, worrying about things I hadn't done or had to do the next day. My brain was able to keep going, but my body had other ideas. Over time, the pace and pressure of the job took a permanent toll on my physical health. I lost control.

The last seven months were the hardest. The President was sprinting to the finish but I was crawling. I couldn't sleep without a pill, my stomach wanted only bland foods, and I often forgot to eat until my assistant made me order something. My go-to was a quarter cup of peanut butter, an apple, and a large hot green tea. I bit Peter's head off if he suggested I eat more.

A lot of my problems were self-induced and could have been resolved with better nutrition. In my worst moment, I got my first migraine during a Presidential trip to Africa. The weather was hot and humid, and I didn't eat or drink enough. I was operating on little sleep and with jet lag, and after four days it caught up to me. In my hotel room by myself I clutched my head and tossed and turned in the fetal position on my bed. I didn't know what was happening.

Finally at 2 a.m., confused and barely able to walk, I crawled along the wall of the hotel to Dr. Tubb's room. After that I got migraines quite a bit, so I carried a prescription with me everywhere I went. I still do, but I don't have to take the medicine very often.

My right arm gave out on me, too. For nearly a month it was numb from my elbow to my fingers—it was definitely a smartphone-related injury. Then I came down with a cold that turned into a sinus infection, which started a ringing in my right ear that was so loud I couldn't think straight. Peter, trying to be empathetic, said the tinnitus was so loud that it even woke him up at night. At a press briefing, I remember the ringing was so bad that I could see the reporter's lips moving but I couldn't hear what was being said. No medicine helped, and it lasted for well over a year.

My back was so uncomfortable under my right shoulder blade that I practically stalked the osteopath on the President's medical team (we called him the Bone Cracker). When I started showing up there three times a week to get adjusted, Dr. Tubb told me not to worry—they'd help me get through to the end of the administration. He thought most of the symptoms would go away once we left the White House.

Dr. Tubb was right, but it took a few months for the worst of it to stop, and I've actually never slept well since. If I ever worked in a White House again, I'd take a much different approach with my health. By not taking care of myself, I hurt myself physically. And just think how much better I'd have been at the job if I'd had proper nutrition and didn't let the stress get to me.

It's not that I didn't try to take better care of myself. I tried cutting out bad habits, like drinking too much soda. In October 2004, just before the election, I realized I'd been drinking Diet Coke all day every day. I'd get a large fountain drink in the morning and again in the afternoon, and then I'd have another with dinner. I decided to quit cold turkey. That was one of the hardest things I ever did but I was proud of myself and felt a little better.

Then in Albania with the President in June 2008, I was in the staff room waiting with my colleagues while the President and Mrs. Bush attended an official luncheon. There was a heat wave and no air-conditioning. The Albanians brought in big platters of fish for us to eat, but I don't like the taste and so I sat there hungry. After a while, I started eyeing the President's Diet Cokes—there were always two cold ones in a bucket for him in case he wanted one. The cans were sweating and looked so good. Finally, I broke down. I took one of the President's Diet Cokes. (Sorry, sir!) Since then, I enjoy my caffeine fix in moderation.

Most jobs aren't as stressful as the White House, but still we all deal with a lot of stress when we're working and keeping up with family and friends at the same time. Stress is relative—how we react to and deal with it is up to us. Good nutrition is a choice we get to make several times a day. We choose whether to take the apple or the candy bar, to walk or sit on the couch, and to drink water or soda (I'm terrible about this one).

And since the only way to really deal with stress is to exercise, we have to make a commitment to that, too. We had an elliptical machine in our spare bedroom on Capitol Hill and every morning at 4:30 a.m. I'd try to read the papers while I climbed fake steps and sent e-mails to White House correspondents—it wasn't the best workout, but it cleared the cobwebs from my brain so I could think more clearly. Then on the weekends we'd do longer walks—"city hikes," I called them. Now that I have more time for myself, I still try to do something every day—in the morning and sometimes in the afternoon too, even if that's just choosing to walk home instead of taking the subway.

While I'm a morning person (which irritates Gutfeld), I always exercise in the morning because a scheduled workout is usually the first thing to be crossed off of a to-do list when something else comes up. If getting up earlier sounds impossible, just try it for a few weeks and you might surprise yourself. Even getting out of bed a half hour earlier every day can make a difference—you'll have better health over the long run (and you'll be in a much better mood).

If you take anything away from this book you can apply to your own life, I hope it's this tip to take charge of your health. It's important to try to get fit while you're relatively young. When you're older, biologically and time-wise, it's so much harder to get into shape. The time you put into being healthy and fit when you're younger is one of the best investments you'll ever make—it's like a 401(k) plan for your body. It'll pay off over the long term.

BALANCE IS IN THE EYE OF THE BEHOLDER

Here's a multimillion-dollar question: How do you find a good work-life balance? If anyone had the answer, they'd never have to work another day.

Many people feel like they're in an unbreakable cycle—hard work leads to working harder and free time gets squeezed out.

How many people do you know that say they just want "to get a life"? When I hear people in their twenties say that, I think they don't really have a right to complain about work-life balance yet. Work *is* your life when you're starting a career. As Gutfeld says, the bottom rungs of the ladder are supposed to be uncomfortable so that you'll strive to get to the next level.

But there are ways to make the cycle more manageable:

Be a Schedule Warrior

One of my pet peeves is hearing people brag about how busy they are. They may think they're venting, but really it's annoying to hear every response to "How are you?" as "I'm so busy, you wouldn't believe it." Actually, I'd believe it, because I feel the same way. But it sounds so pretentious and boring.

I fall into the busy trap over and over. I have many great opportunities to participate in charity fund-raisers, policy debates, speaking events, galas, and award dinners. I like to be busy, but there's a fine line between having a lot to do and being overwhelmed and frantic. My schedule can become my worst enemy (and I don't even have children to look after).

I finally realized that there's only one person who can help me keep a decent schedule—and that's me. I could either let my schedule rule me or I could make it work for me.

I've learned to say no to requests, hold the line when pressed, and not feel so bad about it. I try to keep my mornings free for reading and studying for the show, and I make time for exercise every day, in a class setting where no phones are allowed. That's usually when I free up enough brain space to have a creative thought that I can use later. At Fox, I work an evening or two for one of the prime-time shows, so if I have to do that, I try to schedule requests for mentoring meetings or networking coffees in between shows—that ensures that the meetings can't run long!

Socially, I live in the most remarkable city in the world. In New York, you could go out every night with fascinating people to really terrific restaurants—there is no end to what you can see and do.

That kind of social calendar makes some people feel more alive, but it exhausts me. I finally had to cut back to just one night out a week so that I could handle living there. Instead of worrying that I'm missing out on a great night out, I love being home.

Setting personal scheduling rules can cause worry that your boss or colleagues will resent you or think badly about your performance, wondering if you're really pulling your weight. But I think that being consistent with scheduling boundaries for about three months resets everyone's expectations. Soon enough everyone realizes that you can't stay past 6 p.m. on weeknights but that you'll be able to get your work done on time. At Fox, my colleagues know that I'm at my best before 7 p.m.—after that, I start to fall apart. I can get up before dawn and be firing on all cylinders, but as soon as the day is over, my energy runs out.

As a manager, you can set the tone, too. Your staff follows your example. Karen Hughes, a longtime friend of President Bush's and his communications counselor, remembers that during the first days of the administration, the President told his chief of staff to be reasonable with the schedule and said, "Don't run off all of my young mothers." He knew that he needed a diverse team surrounding him and that moms had to juggle a lot of responsibilities. If it came down to going to a policy meeting or a Little League game, he expected you to be cheering on the sidelines, not sitting at the meeting.

I've got a new way of answering the question of how I'm managing everything in my life. Instead of complaining about how busy I am, I say, "I've found a really good balance." That shocks people! I say it even if I don't feel that way, but it's becoming more believable—even to me.

Lighten Up

If there is something we all do well, it's talk negatively to ourselves all day. With rare exception, no one ever thinks they're good enough at anything—not handsome, pretty, skinny, funny, secure, rich, talented, or smart enough. They fret about not being as good a spouse, parent, sibling, neighbor, and friend as they want to be. We send ourselves negative messages the moment we wake up before we get out of bed, then all day long as we try to pack as much as possible into our days, and then when we try to go to sleep and can't turn off the voices. It takes concentration and effort to overcome those habits. Some of them are impossible to stop—for some, their shortcoming could be their looks while for others it could be their success as compared to friends and colleagues.

I remember feeling quite inferior to the press secretary who held that position before me—Tony Snow. And instead of that making him feel good about himself, he was determined to help me stop thinking that way. On his last day at the White House, he came over to my office and said, "So how are ya feeling?" I said, "Well, not very good. How am I ever going to replace you?"

He then made me stand up and come over to where he was standing. He put his hands on my shoulders and told me to look him in the eye. Since he was well over a foot taller than me, I had to tilt my head all the way back to meet his gaze. He shook me gently and said, "Listen to me. You are better at this than you think you are." I blushed and looked away and started to mumble that I wasn't as good as he was though I was grateful that he was trying to reassure me. But I wasn't totally convinced.

About two weeks later when I was cleaning up my desk on a Friday night, I realized all of a sudden what he meant—that I didn't have to be just like him, that I could just be myself. That sounds like a very obvious and logical conclusion, but it was such a freeing moment. I saw it was safe to step out of his shadow and do the job the way that felt most natural to me.

One of my changes was turning down the temperature in the

briefing room—I was less argumentative and gave shorter briefings. I tried to swallow my sarcasm and bit my tongue when I was
tempted to take a shot at someone. I embraced who I was at that
time in my life—it felt like when I realized I was a conservative and
again when I met Peter. Once I chose just to be myself, everything
fell into place.

Most people will have this experience at some point in their
lives, where they realize that they can't be all things to all people,
especially when it comes to pleasing themselves, and then everything starts to look a little brighter. Remember that you are better at
everything than you think you are—it's important to keep trying to
improve. But give yourself a little bit of a break. Everyone in your life
will benefit from you not beating yourself up all the time.

WHAT'S THE WORST THAT COULD HAPPEN?

Some of the best advice I ever got from the President was after he left
office. When he saw me in April 2009, he asked all about how I was
doing. He is a good career counselor. I tried to put a good spin on
things, but he saw right through me.

I'd joined Burson-Marsteller, a global public relations company, and it wasn't a good fit (mainly because I really didn't want
to do PR). The other problem was that I didn't match the culture at
Burson. The top leadership of the company was from the Clinton
Administration, and they were smart and fun to talk to. We liked
to trade political war stories and gossip about Washington. But our
styles were so different—where the Bush White House was like a
smooth ocean liner, the Clinton White House was more of a scrappy
fishing boat. I got seasick.

The President didn't let me off the hook when I tried to change
the subject. "You worked way too hard to be unhappy after the

White House. Why don't you start your own company, a consulting business?" he asked.

I went through a list of why I thought I needed to be a part of an established global firm, but it felt pretty weak.

And then he asked, "What's the worst that could happen? Your business doesn't succeed and you have to go back to work for a PR firm? Is that the worst thing that could happen to an educated woman in the United States who served in the White House as the press secretary? Doesn't seem like too big a risk to me."

I knew he was right, but there were those butterflies again. I worried what people would think of me if I left so soon after just starting a job. I didn't want to disappoint them. I went home and asked myself again, "What's the worst that could happen?"

Once I thought that through, I realized he was right. I got up the courage to tell my new bosses I wasn't going to stay. They were disappointed but they didn't hold a grudge; in fact, Burson became my first client and I worked as a consultant instead of an employee. That certainly wasn't the worst outcome.

Risk-taking isn't supposed to feel comfortable, but trying to protect myself from that discomfort closed my mind to new opportunities. No risk, no reward. If the worst that can happen is that you have to try something else, then there's really no excuse for not taking a chance.

WHAT DO YOU DO FOR FUN?

Here's a question you want to be ready to answer: What do you do for fun?

I was asked that in an interview right before we moved up to New York when I was busy building a career after the White House. I said that I exercised with a trainer and that I went to a lot of events for Minute Mentoring. The reporter didn't think that was good enough. He pressed me—but what do you do for *fun*? I said, well, I walk my dog. He said that's not for fun, that's a responsibility. Do you do anything *for fun*?

I realized I didn't have an answer that would satisfy him. I didn't really do anything just for fun or that didn't have something to do with work. That was a wake-up call for me, and I vowed to have a better answer the next time I was asked. Now I can say I ride my cruiser bike around my favorite spot in South Carolina, put together dinner parties that aren't work-related, and watch new TV series without working on my laptop at the same time.

Make sure you have an answer to that question—what do you do *for fun*?

LOVE IS NOT A CAREER-LIMITING DECISION

In 1997 when I met Peter, we knew within six weeks that we wanted to be together. He proposed to me at the National Cathedral in October 1997, but I stopped him before he could finish. I was only twenty-five years old and not ready to walk away from my dream job in D.C. and move to England, where I couldn't work.

However, what really held me back was my worry about what my family, friends, and peers would think about my decision. It did seem a little rash—I'd only just met Peter. He was eighteen years older than me and had been married twice. I had a great job and an enviable career track. Everything I'd been told up to then was to keep on the job track so that I kept moving up.

Aside from my career prospects, I worried about getting married too quickly because the relationship might not work out. (I later learned this is not an age-related question, but getting over the fear of a commitment.) Besides, whirlwind romances seemed like something that happened in novels, not in real life. My head and my heart battled it out.

I went home to Colorado and saw a good family friend, Kim Wilkerson. Kim taught the most difficult levels of high school math, coached cheerleading, and organized the prom. She also was the adoptive mom of my biological niece, Jessica. My sister had a baby as a teen, and my family arranged an open adoption with Kim and her husband. It was a very good arrangement, and we stayed close and got together often.

Kim wasn't shy about her opinions, and her advice was about as subtle as a flying axe head. She asked me what I was waiting for. She thought it was an easy decision and she dismissed my concerns about what other people would think; in fact, she told me that most people are so wrapped up in themselves that they don't have time to think about me at all (this is true—keep it in mind).

"If you do anything in life, don't give up on a chance to be loved—he may be the only man who will ever truly love you. Don't miss it."

Kim's advice tipped me into the yes column (sadly she died in an accident a year later in 1999). I made the decision and immediately felt better. When I finally got up the courage to tell everyone I was moving to England to live with Peter, they were thrilled—no one mentioned a single one of my worries. My family and friends had fallen in love with him, too.

Choosing to be loved was the best decision of my life, but I almost talked myself out of it. And it turned out to be the only argument I didn't mind losing.

CHAPTER 6

Civility, Lost and Found

Five Presidents Walk into the Oval . . .

This I wasn't going to miss: five Presidents in the Oval Office together for the first—and perhaps the last—time.

In a few days, President Bush would hand over power to President-elect Obama. The transition had been smooth and was hailed as the most professional in memory. President Bush demanded a much better reception for the Obama Administration than he'd had in 2001 (so out of decency, we left all the O's on the keyboards).

As part of the welcome, President Bush invited the most exclusive club in the world to have lunch in the private dining room off the Oval Office. Former Presidents Jimmy Carter, Bill Clinton, and George H. W. Bush were there with President Bush and President-elect Obama. President Bush told me that during the lunch, they mostly answered President Obama's questions about how best to raise his girls in the public eye. He couldn't have gotten better advice—they all were fathers before they were Presidents.

While the leaders ate, I showed Robert Gibbs, the incoming

press secretary, the secret ceremonial flak jacket in the office closet that's only supposed to be seen by the small fraternity of press secretaries. In the pocket he'd find all the notes written by his predecessors and tied with a red ribbon. I also gave him a couple of my secrets for keeping the workload manageable, like the night note I'd started sending to reporters to ease my mornings. I cautioned him about leaving documents on his desk—there was an open door policy for reporters to just waltz on in anytime they wanted. It was fun to show him around the West Wing, and I was genuinely excited for him and his team—they were about to have the best jobs of their lives.

When the press pool was called in, I grabbed Robert's arm and dragged him with me into the Oval Office. We tucked in behind the reporters and stood together next to the grandfather clock. To our right was the portrait of Lincoln, filling the space where Presidents traditionally hung the portrait of who they considered the most influential President. Eight years before, President Bush had been torn; his dad had been President, after all. But he told his dad that he hung his portrait in his heart, and Lincoln on the wall. He had a way of solving problems.

I felt nostalgic and patriotic as I looked around. Both President Bushes together in the Oval Office was something special to see. It was unlikely we'd see another father and son both serve as Presidents in our lifetime.

But the main attraction, the historical moment I'll never forget, was seeing the first black American elected President there with the others. We all felt proud and hopeful. The Presidents smiled for the cameras and seemed at ease with one another, though Carter had placed himself a bit apart from the group, as if he wanted a smidgen of distance or felt a bit uncomfortable.

The five men stood in front of the *Resolute* desk, which all of the Presidents had used. The desk was made from the planks of an abandoned British Arctic exploratory ship, the HMS *Resolute*, which had been found by an American naval captain. The ship was restored and returned to Britain in a show of friendship. When it was decommissioned, Queen Victoria had the desk made from its timbers and gave it to America. It is sturdy and solid, just like the relationship between the two countries and the five Presidents, and it is a fixture of the Oval Office.

During media interviews leading up to the transition, I'd convinced 41 and 43 to sit together for a couple of interviews. In the pre-briefs, they'd told me that it had been harder to be the father and the son of a President than it was to be the President (because insults and criticisms of your loved ones were harder to take than what was said about you). I learned over the years that they dealt with those slights by forgiving and separating politics from the personal. The toughest thing they'd been through was 41's loss to Clinton in 1992 (in fact, President Bush started running after that to deal with the stress—he ran the Houston Marathon two months later in January 1993).

I imagined all the things that 41 had said about Clinton in that campaign, and the things Clinton had said about 41, and how mad that made 43. Then I thought about the things Obama had said about Bush during Obama's quick rise from Senator to President (and continued to say even after the election), and then the things that Jimmy Carter had said about *all* of them . . . and yet, there they were, standing together for this historic moment, bonded by something untarnished by politics.

The American tradition of Presidential honor, respect, and civility reminds us that there's a reason our country is known as the greatest nation in history. But Presidents can only do so much, and it's up to us not to let those traditions die.

The Heart of the Problem

For a country so blessed, America sure can argue a lot. We've gone from being the confident leader of the free world to bickering about every living thing under the sun. Record numbers of Americans have no trust in the government at all, and the two political parties are so dug in that we can barely agree on a Mother's Day Resolution. In many ways, despite great strides of unity, we are now more divided than ever. A decline of civility is at the heart of the problem.

Why is this happening? As the government gets bigger and less effective, people feel as if they don't have any power, and that breeds frustration. Washington has been dining out on taxpayer money and clinging to special interests, and the government is frequently less responsive to taxpayers. The stakes keep getting higher, and no one meets the public's expectations. Contempt for each other further erodes our ability to solve any problems. And then, a devolving blame game begins and we lose more civility. For many people, the country feels all but lost.

The fights between Republicans and Democrats are somewhat expected, though the rhetoric is depressingly caustic. It's the intra-party fights that are even more debilitating, especially for Republicans. I've always liked the Republican Big Tent approach, and I think it has served us well as a party—we could have big debates within the tent, but we all knew that it was safe under there. I was taught that we don't shoot inside the tent, but not everyone shares that philosophy (with friends like these...). The more time Republicans spend fighting other Republicans, the more damage we do to the Republican brand. If we believe that the conservative approach to governing is superior, then we ought to act like it. I appreciate that conservatives often march to a different drummer (while the Left walks in lockstep), but we're off by half a beat. It's time to get back on the right foot.

An entire book could be written about who's to blame for the loss of civility (the President, the Congress, cable news and talk radio, labor unions, academia, Hollywood... need I go on?), and we could argue about that until the cows come home. The only thing we might be able to agree on is the need to restore civility to public debates. Without some basic manners, we're doomed. There's no hope of reaching agreement if we can't even talk to each other.

Before I go any further, I am aware that some people may say that I'm part of the problem—or if not me specifically, then cable news and talk radio. I think that's a fair criticism, and it's something I've thought about a lot. I recognize there are a few over-the-line communicators (from both ends of the ideological spectrum), and while that's not my style, there's a reason a lot of shows are successful—they're not boring and they keep people coming back. Quiet and cable don't necessarily mix—no one wants to watch paint dry. Cable news revolutionized the industry and gave an outlet to millions of viewers with interest in news and politics that they weren't getting elsewhere. Instead of being monolithic, the number of choices is staggering. It's a competitive business.

While I like the reputation I've gained for being a "voice of reason," some of my critics don't like it. I take a fair amount of heat about civility—but it comes from my right, not from liberals. Believe it or not, conservatives are harsher on one another than they are on their opponents. That's okay—it makes us smarter and better at what we do. The beef that some people have with me is that they think I'm too nice, reserved, and vanilla. They want more spice, spunk, outrage, and bite—they want me to go for the jugular. They point out that being nice and seeking bipartisanship have gotten us nowhere and that we just need to tell it like it is. Fair points, and I don't confuse civility with timidity or passivity.

What I try to point out is that as a Republican, I see our biggest threat as wishful thinking; the second as other Republicans; and the third as Democrats. In fact, I rather like a passionate argument that is well-made. And I get more satisfaction out of winning based on persuasion than name-calling. And to me it's the name-calling that's at the heart of the incivility that is bringing down political discourse (from the right and the left).

Just as civility doesn't mean shrinking from an argument, it also doesn't have to mean "you must agree with me." To the contrary, being civil means that we can argue vehemently and then either find some compromise, call it a tie, or move on to something else. For a long time both sides have felt berated into agreeing with the other side—whether it be the Iraq War or Obamacare. If you disagreed, you were demonized. That's unfair and misses the benefits of having a variety of opinions. As Pete Wehner, a former colleague who is now with the Ethics and Public Policy Center, wrote in an essay about civility in 2010, "Civility does not preclude spirited debate or confrontation. Clashing arguments are often clarifying arguments." We should want more, not less, of this approach to debates.

I think that the best way to be respectful of someone else's point of view is to keep in mind your opponent's intentions—often the end goal is the same (better education, safer streets, more jobs), it's just the method to get there that's in question. So if you don't start off by thinking the opposition is evil, but that they want to get to the same place you do, then you're already on your way to having a more civil and productive conversation.

It's incumbent upon all of us to learn how someone with a different view would think—it's not only polite, but it also can help you win an argument. Use their words to help them come to your way of thinking—I do it to Beckel all the time! And believe it or not, he's come around on some issues.

The scathing language used by many of our elected leaders, candidate hopefuls, and political pundits is beneath them. When did public service turn into a bad episode of *Real Housewives*?

Americans understand that Congress is meant for debate and argumentation. But what bothers them is that it seems that elected leaders can't get along at all. Hateful comments have become normal in Washington, and that's made for some of our greatest disappointments. In their personal lives and businesses, average Americans have to work with people they don't necessarily agree with all the time—but they can set that aside, be constructive, and get results. So, they ask, why can't Members of Congress do the same?

Something has changed in Washington, D.C. Political leaders who used to be held in high regard are now so desperate for attention in a crowded media world that they continually let themselves and their country down by making uncivil and outrageous comments about one another. This has degraded the entire institution. The more hateful the personal attacks get, the more difficult it is to work together. I know that members of Congress used to solve political disputes with pistols on the streets; in the modern world we don't use guns to solve debates, we shoot off different weapons—our mouths.

During the second term of the Bush Administration, the nature of the attacks on President Bush shocked us in the White House—especially when they came from Democratic Congressional leadership. They said things about a President that had not been said before and rarely said in polite company, like "liar" and "loser." And whereas political put-downs used to be thinly veiled insults, these new attacks were crass and undignified.

One could admire the skill and humor certain politicians displayed in criticizing their opponents; today the rhetoric has sunk to the level of schoolyard name-calling. A fine example was when Governor Ann Richards at the Democratic Convention of 1988 tried to frame Vice President George H. W. Bush as an elitist: "Poor George. He was born with a silver foot in his mouth." She made her point *and* she made people laugh. Even the Vice President chuckled. I miss the days of witty political insults. By the time I was press secretary, the language had coarsened, and I balked at responding to the baser comments, and too often I was saying, "I won't dignify that comment with a response." But at some point, if your opponent is doing all of the attacking and you're constantly ducking, you end up with a bruised and battered boss.

It could be just my perspective, but it seems that a tactless comment from a conservative is sure to draw more outrage than something a liberal says. Conservatives spend an inordinate amount of time trying to defend or distance themselves from what another conservative has said or done. Liberals don't seem to feel that they own every other liberal's comments. I almost admire that—they just move on as if nothing was ever said and flip the attack back onto Republicans. It's masterful and maddening.

Let's take my favorite example of the worst offender: Senate Minority Leader Harry Reid. It is astounding the things that he has said—mostly about, but not only to, his political opponents. He regularly calls people liars, losers, anarchists, and radicals. He makes up stories like the one about Mitt Romney not paying his taxes, rails on others for their political views and wealth (the Koch brothers), and says they are "un-American." He called Republicans his enemies and cowards, questions their integrity, and labeled Sen. John McCain an "old snake-oil salesman." He even told President Bush that his dog Barney was fat!

And these are things said in public, in front of the press, often at a microphone. He doesn't limit his insults to Republicans, however. He called a reporter a sleazeball (I almost let him off on that one) and said that D.C. tourists stink. The list goes on and on. But this was as the *Majority Leader* of the United States Senate. This should be unacceptable. America deserves better, and our policy debates are way too important to allow him to demonize everyone. I'm surprised (okay, not really) that no one in his party raises a hand to say, "Stop!" There are many reasons that citizens have such a low opinion of the Congress, and I'd wager that Harry Reid is a major cause of that. His comments are inexcusable and should be condemned.

During the onslaught of Reid's (and others who followed him) personal slander against President Bush, I'm proud to have worked for a leader who didn't respond in kind. He regularly turned the other cheek and instructed us to do the same. He led by example, even in private. Though there was a time when holding back all of the retaliation started to physically wear on my face.

One day when Peter picked me up from the White House, I caught a glimpse of myself in the mirror of our Jeep and didn't like what I saw—I was all sharp corners and hard edges; all the softness had disappeared from my face. It was ugliness from the inside coming out. I believed that we were letting the President down, and I felt trapped and powerless to help. I took every hit personally on his behalf.

But as with many other approaches to leadership, the Bushes were right not to lash out at their critics, even though it would have been very understandable had they done so. Every action can cause an overreaction, and giving someone more attention for being outrageous can exacerbate the problem. I could not have been a counterattack dog at the podium—it's not in my nature and I wouldn't have looked myself in the mirror—but I wonder if things may have been different if once in a while I'd bared some teeth.

Since I left the White House, the rhetoric has gotten worse. So I wrestle with bigger picture questions: Have we lost our ability to be civil to one another in the public square? Whatever happened to manners and dignity, graciousness and kindness? Do any of those virtues even matter anymore? Is there anything we can do to restore civility?

After all of these years in communications, speaking on behalf of other people, I no longer feel that I own anyone else's comments. Being responsible for my own remarks is enough work for me. And with a public job, where all of my words are broadcast to millions each night and recorded, tweeted, and posted for eternity, I am conscientious about how I frame my comments and opinions. I try to be sensitive to how people will react to my words, but not so timid that my commentary is sanitary and ineffective.

I look at it this way—I don't ever want to apologize for something I've said, but I want to be gracious enough to be ready to apologize if I ever need to.

My answers to those questions have come gradually and after some trial and error. In my own life, personally and professionally, I've realized that being civil is an active decision that I get to choose to make several times a day. That's why I believe there's hope—civility is not extinct. It is a choice.

Civility in Practice

Being more civil does not just apply to Presidents (though that would be a good place to start). As Charles Krauthammer said in his book

Things That Matter, manners are the keys to civility. Without them, we're hopeless. Manners make everything else work.

The good news is that there are things we can do right now to restore civility. But it starts with a personal choice to change bad habits—being more congenial, communicating better, anticipating concerns; the following are all ways to improve every aspect of life—personal relationships, friendships, families, bosses, and dealing with your crazy uncle (everyone has one—ours is called Uncle Bob).

Conversation Stranger Danger

There's a reason people should not discuss religion or politics in polite company. That doesn't mean that these topics should *never* be discussed (they're two of the most important issues that affect us), but they shouldn't be your conversation starter.

I'm a little paranoid about being a Republican in New York. I don't expect anyone to agree with me, and I don't pick fights. I have no idea of the political ideology of people I live around, because I don't care what it is. I'm not a conservative evangelist that's going to try to convince people on the merits of Republican policy principles—I do that for a living, so I don't need to do it socially.

I like meeting people, but the last thing I want to do is be lectured about the Bush Administration or how horrible this or that Republican is. I'm sure a liberal would say the same about their experiences when they go to a party and are accosted by someone who dislikes Democrats. I know it goes both ways (I'm just pretty sure that it doesn't happen in Manhattan very often).

That's why I practice conversation stranger danger. When I meet someone new, I rarely volunteer what I do for a living. If I'm asked, I never lie about it, but I try to change the subject. For the most part, people are polite if they recognize me, even if they're not fans of *The Five* or had threatened to move to Canada if Bush won re-election. But I'm amazed by how some people think it's perfectly okay to insult my former boss or Fox News. I've learned to just smile, nod, or give them my signature response, "The Look" (Kimberly Guilfoyle loves it).

I really dislike it when people spoil my night because they're rude. Once at a family-style dinner in a restaurant, a bunch of us were seated together. We didn't know each other, and I looked forward to making some new friends.

A mom, dad, and their college-age son sat across from us, and the woman must have missed the part of the introductions when her son asked me what I did in New York.

While the salads were being served, her son said he'd just heard a speech by Stephen Colbert who said that Bill O'Reilly was just acting on *The O'Reilly Factor*, that he was not being himself. His mom then jumped in and said, "O'Reilly is a buffoon. A total buffoon! He's a fool!"

"Well, I don't see him that way," I said.

She scoffed and repeated how dumb she thought he was.

"Well, you may not like him, but he's not dumb. And he's had the number one cable news show for over eighteen years."

She rolled her eyes. "Well, I guess I have to give him that."

An awkward silence passed.

"So," she asked, smiling, "What do you do in New York City?"

"I work at Fox News," I said deadpan.

She was mildly embarrassed, but I didn't try to bail her out.

"Oh..." she said.

"Yep," I said. At that point, I just wanted to go. I'd lost my appetite. I was bummed the evening started so poorly, because on many levels we had lots in common to discuss since she was from D.C, and had worked at the Justice Department when I had.

The night proved my point—we all make choices about what we're going to say. If you don't want to ruin an evening, find a way to talk about things other than politics to start off. Or provide an unexpected compliment and disarm them—the best defense is a charming offense.

Oh, and just to make sure it's clear: Bill O'Reilly is very, very smart.

How to Respond

Criticism is part of life. You can't escape it forever unless you're not doing anything interesting. Social media has taken criticism to a different level—it can be immediate, vicious, and unfair.

I've seen people obsessed and harassed by their smartphones alerting them about any and all mentions of their names online. It drives them insane, and on balance it's negative—compliments are rare. Learning to manage reactions to criticism is really important in all aspects of life (especially if you're a manager for an organization or running for elected office).

The first thing you need to do is turn off any alerts about yourself when you're mentioned anywhere online (go on, do it now—you know who you are). If you're concerned you'll miss something important or that you need to correct, then assign someone in your office or a trusted friend to check the Internet for you. This will add years back to your life.

When I became the White House press secretary, my mom looked me up and was shocked and upset by the things she read. I told her that we needed a rule—she could not put my name in any search engine under any circumstances. And she couldn't go searching for the criticism either.

My advice is to ignore the chatter. (It's amazing—if you're not listening, you can't hear it!) If criticism builds to a point where you or someone on your behalf needs to respond, the chances are it will be brought to your attention. You don't need to go searching for negativity. Trust me—it'll find you.

Another way to handle it is to anticipate the criticism. If you're planning to post something to social media or giving a speech that is provocative, you can guess what your detractors might say about it. "Scuttle the rebuttal." Try to outwit them in your original comments, or if the goal was to start a debate, participate in a positive and professional way. Take some time to figure out how to disarm your critics without them even realizing it, and you'll be more effective and persuasive. Plus they'll be flattered that you even bothered to find out their point of view—there's value in doing a little bit of investment before you make comments.

When you do react to criticism, try not to be overly defensive. If someone attacks you, just like a bully on a playground, what he really wants is for you to react so that he can hit you again. Keeping your head held high is the best way to drive them crazy and make them look small (think nerds versus bullies—the nerds always win in the end). You can acknowledge criticism without responding negatively, and in fact, there are some critics who may have a point now and then. Is there anything you can learn from what someone thought of your presentation? Feedback can help us improve, if it's taken in a good way. But if you feel that you need to respond to a criticism, try to do so with grace and maybe even with a sharp point of humor that could take a second for the critic to realize he's been bested. Humor, really, is the best trump card.

Additionally, if you have a job that puts you in the public eye (or even hope to one day), build a network of defenders that can deploy on your behalf. Having someone stick up for you can be an effective way to respond to criticism without having to stoop to the attacker's level. Some in your network may do this naturally and without prodding, but there could come a time when you need to ask someone to stand up for you. Even if you don't have a public persona yet, it's not too early to start thinking about who that would be, and offer to do the same for them if they ever need it. We all need a proxy now and then.

I had to learn all this the hard way. In 2007 when I'd just been appointed as the press secretary, I got invited to appear on *Wait Wait—Don't Tell Me!*, the wonderful weekend news quiz show on NPR hosted by the very funny Peter Sagal. Everyone knew I loved the show and I was excited to be a guest. During the program, I was asked what it was like to be the White House spokesperson at such a young age. I rolled with the joke and said I knew what he meant—that most of the White House reporters were so much older than me that they'd actually covered the Cuban Missile Crisis and I pretended I'd never heard of it. I was joking, but the "dumb Republican blonde" die had been cast. Since then, it's the Left's favorite criticism of me, and it doesn't matter that I said it in jest. Pointing that out isn't a battle I've won with fanatics who want to hate me. I had to choose to ignore the barbs and to not let vicious attacks overwhelm me.

And all of that leads me to a final point: Try to keep some perspective about your role in the world. Whatever is being said about you, whatever criticism you're facing, it probably isn't as bad as a million other things that happened in the world that day. That helps me keep some perspective—remember, most of us are really not that big of a deal.

Just Pay a Compliment

A pet peeve of mine is with people who give backhanded compliments. If you don't have something nice to say, just don't say it. A weak compliment is worse than not saying anything at all.

What do I mean by that? Well, I get these kinds of comments a lot:

"I hated everything about the Bush Administration, but I like you."

"I hate your politics, but your dog is awesome."

"I can't stand Fox, but I never miss *The Five*."

It's a mystery to me why people don't think comments like that are offensive and why their compliments fall flat. Compliments are neutralized with underhanded jabs. I'd rather have just a polite hello than an insult about my ideology, past employers, and colleagues folded into a halfhearted compliment. By the time they get to the comma, I've already stopped listening.

Imagine what it would be like if they just swallowed their negativity and said:

"I love listening to you on Fox."

"I think your dog is awesome."

"You were a good press secretary."

See, that's not so hard, is it? Giving someone a compliment doesn't mean that you then are associated as a Republican or Democrat sympathizer. Try it—if you are afraid you'll get conservative or liberal cooties, or that you'll get hit from friendly fire if you praise someone of the other party, then the problem rests with you or the people you call friends. Consider it civility karma. It could come back to benefit you another time.

President Bush and I once bonded over someone's slight of me at a commencement speech. In 2008, I was invited to speak to the graduates of my alma mater, Colorado State University–Pueblo. I felt honored and the President kept asking what I was going to say. He even gave me some advice: "Keep it short."

When I got to campus, the university president, Joe Garcia, met me at the door. He had earned a law degree from Harvard and was working in higher education when the Clinton Administration asked him to serve in a regional role for Housing and Urban Development. So he was fairly involved in politics and should have had better people skills than what he showed to me.

From the start he wanted to needle me about Republicans. I don't know whether he thought he was being clever or funny, but it was rude. I had no idea what anyone's political affiliation was at the school, but at the luncheon he started labeling everyone as this or that, as if I cared. The guests were gracious and a bit embarrassed by his behavior, but he was neither.

The next morning at the commencement, we put on polyester gowns and got ready for the ceremony. Garcia and I had a nice chat in the sunshine outside the venue, and it was a pretty good morning until he got up to introduce me. I felt nervous because I hadn't given a speech in a while (outside of the press briefings) and I really wanted the students to like what I was going to say. Then Garcia slapped me in the face.

At the lectern in front of thousands gathered for the ceremony, Garcia finished a short description of my career thus far, and then he said, "And now, *despite* her party affiliation, I'm pleased to introduce to you Dana Perino."

I kept a smile on my face but thought, "Did I hear that right?" I felt burned. Traveling all that way, taking time off when the White House team needed my help, and being insulted in front of the audience wasn't what I'd expected. I decided to blow him off and gave the speech with as much enthusiasm as I could muster, though I should have taken President Bush's advice more to heart. And my speech was too long so I rushed to the end. I could tell the graduates just wanted to get their diplomas and on with their celebrations.

After the event, I made my way to where my family and friends were sitting and was stopped along the way by people apologizing to me for Garcia's behavior. I pretended that it hadn't affected me and said, "So I wasn't the only one that noticed?" Apparently not. The university started getting lots of complaints, as did the local newspaper, *The Pueblo Chieftain*. They printed some of the messages, and it was clear people in the community were mad at him.

When I got back to Washington, President Bush asked me about the speech and I told him what happened. The President said that Garcia was going to call me to apologize.

He was right. Garcia called. My assistant Chris Byrne asked me if I wanted to take it. I declined.

Over the next three days, the President and I had running banter about it:

"Did he call you?"

"Yes, sir."

"Did you take the call?"

"No, sir."

"Good."

On the third day and after three more calls, the President asked me again.

"Did he call you back?"

"Yes, sir."

"Did you take the call this time?"

"Yes, sir."

"Good."

When you're insulted, be gracious in how you handle it. I didn't need to call up and yell at Garcia, because other people were already doing that for me. But I didn't need to let him off the hook before making him squirm for a while.

When I finally took the call, Garcia's apology was sincere and I told him not to worry about it and then I quickly changed the subject. I thanked him *so very much* for the opportunity to return to Pueblo for the commencement.

Garcia went on to serve as the Lieutenant Governor of Colorado. I hope he's a bit more diplomatic now.

Disagree Without Being a Jerk

One of the keys to being a positive person is learning how to disagree without being a jerk about it. You can be assertive without being aggressive; you just need to find a pleasant tone that is gracious while also being persuasive. That way your boss is more likely to listen to you, and your colleagues will look to you to help solve problems.

Imagine at the White House podium how often a press secretary has to disagree with a reporter—it never ends. Nearly every answer requires some restating of the facts, providing context, or challenging the premise or tone of the question.

As a press secretary and on *The Five*, I've learned that I have a choice in how I answer a question. There's combative or productive—I get to take my pick. I usually chose productive. To do that, I came up with some phrases that were useful tools, such as, "I understand why you're asking the question that way, but look at it from another point of view..." or "You make a fair point, but let me tackle this from another angle...." They made me sound reasonable and encouraged people to be more willing to listen.

These types of phrases work well in an office, too. No matter how frustrating a meeting might be, it's better not to roll your eyes, scowl and frown, put your pen down, and cross your arms over your chest while staring at the floor. Instead, practice your best poker face and put it on when you need to mask a feeling. Then, to make a constructive argument, summarize what you believe the person has just said before you start responding. I would do this with reporters to try to avoid a disagreement over a misunderstanding. In my experience, as soon as voices are raised productivity is lost. Disagreeing for disagreement's sake won't get you very far.

To win a heated argument, you have to keep your cool.

Swallow Your Sarcasm—Save Your Job

Sarcasm is like cheap wine—it leaves a terrible aftertaste. When we were teenagers, we learned how a sarcastic remark could get us noticed. We could make our friends laugh and our parents mad—anything to get a rise out of them.

In the workplace, using sarcasm can get you the kind of attention you don't want. There's a difference between something that's clearly funny and something that's rude. Since it's not always possible to gauge where that line is, it's usually better just to keep your mouth shut.

I relearned this lesson right after I left the White House. I was invited to give a speech for my speaker's bureau in front of a large group of potential clients, and I made a humorous but stinging remark about President Obama. No one laughed. It was just way too soon for a person like me to say something like that. I immediately regretted my mistake, not only because I felt terrible for saying it, but also because I knew I'd just blown a potential business opportunity. Since then, I just use self-deprecating humor in speeches—that way the only person I might offend is myself.

I swallowed plenty of sarcastic remarks when I was the White House press secretary. Imagine how hard it is to keep from biting someone's head off when you're on the ropes every day. But I constantly asked myself, "If President Bush was watching me right now, would he be proud of what I'm saying?" and that kept me from getting into trouble for saying something that might sound funny to my friends but rude to anyone else. I had this regular self-imposed sarcasm monitor and I knew it wasn't charming or persuasive to be nasty to the press. I think that disdain from the podium comes off terribly and hurts the press secretary and his or her boss.

That doesn't mean I wasn't above getting frustrated, but I tried to keep it hidden.

But I have a confession about something I did to get me through a few of my briefings.

The first person I ever told about this was Sean Hannity when he came for a tour of the White House in December 2008. When we stood at the podium for photographs with his kids, he asked me how I didn't ever lose my cool.

"Didn't you ever want to just walk over and punch one of them?" he asked.

I said I never contemplated physical altercations, but that I did have a secret weapon that helped me get through some of the tougher exchanges with reporters.

I showed him how the podium has a little shelf just below where I'd set my notes. On the rare occasions when the briefing was getting too intense or testy and a reporter was showing off for the cameras, I'd just rest my hand next to my water, out of view of anyone, keep a pleasant look on my face, and flip 'em the bird. (I'm sorry, Mr. President! But it got me through some tough briefings.)

Sean loved that—I think it humanized me for him. I asked him to keep my secret until I was ready to spill it myself. In all the years I've been on his show, he never said a word even though it's one of his favorite stories from Washington.

Let me apologize to anyone in the press corps who is offended that I may have secretly told them to read between the lines—I didn't mean it personally. Besides, put yourself in my size 5.5 shoes—it's a tight squeeze. What would you have done? And for all I know, maybe you were flipping me off, too.

Democrats Are Humans, Too

Here, let me prove that you can be a Republican and praise a Democrat, even be friends with them, without melting. Some of my favorite lessons in civility are ones of bipartisan cooperation and understanding.

One of the most sought after invitations in Washington is to the Gridiron dinner. The Gridiron started in 1885 and is one of the oldest and most prestigious media clubs in the country. Membership is by invitation, and reporters know they've really made it if they get to join. And for politicians, diplomats, press secretaries, and policy wonks, invitations are hard to get.

In 2005, I'd been the deputy press secretary for about a month when the Gridiron took place at the Capitol Hilton in Washington, D.C. *USA Today* invited me to sit at their table. "Now I've really made it," I thought.

It was a white tie and tails event—really fancy, especially for someone who had two formal dresses for the entire Bush Presidency (one short, one long—both black. I just rotated them to every event. For this dinner, I wore the long one).

Every year the ballroom is packed with narrow tables lining the room, a stage on one side for the skits the press puts on, and another for the head table. The entire event is supposed to be off the record so that people can say anything they want and not worry about it showing up in the paper the next morning (it's a great concept, but trust isn't what it used to be in Washington).

I found my seat. The chair across from me was empty when I sat down, so I made small talk until the other invited guest arrived. To my delight and surprise, it was the junior Senator from Illinois, Barack Obama.

Count me among his many admirers after his Democratic National Convention speech in 2004. I was quite pleased to be sitting with him. He was the talk of D.C., and he'd only been there a month.

I didn't know enough to be intimidated by him as a future President, so Senator Obama and I talked and talked. We laughed our butts off for four hours. At one point during a break, he took me over to meet his wife, Michelle, who couldn't have been kinder to me.

We had a great time, and I gushed about my new friend to my husband that night.

"I think he could be a really good President in, like, twenty years," I said.

Well, three years later, when I was the press secretary, Senator Obama was the Presidential nominee for the Democratic Party. And he was in the pole position to win it. And so we met again.

In September 2008, the Republican candidate, Senator John McCain, suspended his campaign in the middle of the financial crisis and headed to Washington to help broker a deal on the bank bailout bill. The President then had to invite the Presidential candidates, and the Congressional leadership to the White House. It was high political theater and everyone had a role to play (though some played theirs better than others).

President Bush and his team met in the Oval Office for a prebrief before the meeting. I was one of the last people to file into the Cabinet Room for the meeting. When I crossed the threshold, I saw

Senator Obama shaking hands with everyone. His energy filled the room. Senator McCain seemed more of a bystander than a participant, but I took that as him being polite and understanding the gravity of the moment—not just for his campaign but also for the country.

As Senator Obama turned toward me, I stuck out my hand to introduce myself, but he threw open his arms and said, "Dana Perino! It is so good to see you!" And he wrapped me in a brief hug. I blushed.

I said, "Sir, you may not remember, but—"

He interrupted me, his hands on my shoulders. "Not remember? That was my favorite night in all my time in Washington!"

Then I really turned red—especially since I wasn't sure everyone else knew what he was talking about!

I took my seat with the rest of the senior staff on the side of the Cabinet Room, behind the President, flattered that Senator Obama even knew who I was, let alone remembered the Gridiron as fondly as I did.

The deputy chief of staff, Joel Kaplan, leaned over and whispered to me, "What was that all about?"

"I'll tell you later," I said. "But I just might vote for him, too!" (Note: I didn't.)

The Most Likable Guy in Town

Vice President Joe Biden has led a remarkable life as a public servant. And he's one of the few people in Washington that's accumulated friends rather than losing them over his career.

In the spring of 2010, the Vice President invited the newly

confirmed Broadcasting Board of Governors over to his place to be sworn into our new roles. The BBG was a bipartisan board, and I was one of the Republicans that President Obama nominated.

I was nervous to go back to the White House—I had that concern about being unwelcome because I'd worked for President Bush (so I was paranoid—but it wasn't without merit). My Democrat friends insisted I go with them, and I brought Peter along for moral support.

The Vice President made his entrance. He rounded the corner and said, "Where's that Dana Perino? Oh, there she is!" He came toward me with his arms outstretched and gave me an enthusiastic hug.

He had me all wrapped up and said, "I watch you every day on TV. You're fantastic! Won't you come over to our side? I listen to everything you say!"

Still locked in his hug, I said, "Well, sir, I listened to everything you say, too . . . so that I can make fun of it later."

He howled and put an arm around Peter and chatted to us for several minutes. I learned that day why most everyone in Washington likes Joe Biden—he's one of the most personable and friendly politicians you'll ever meet.

The Most Likable Gal in Town

One of the privileges of having worked in the White House is talking about the experience in front of audiences interested in politics. My frequent partner at speaking opportunities over the years has been Donna Brazile. Donna's middle name could be "Civility" when we're together.

Donna was the first woman and first African-American to manage a Presidential campaign—Al Gore hired her for the job in 1999. I laugh every time she starts a speech, "First of all, I've omitted everything of a partisan nature from this speech, so I'm left with 'Thank you, and good-bye,' followed by, 'I'm Al Gore's former campaign manager, so no matter how well things go this afternoon, I can't win.'"

Anywhere we go, Donna brings the house down. In airports, I have to act like her campaign staffer to fend off the fans so we can make our flights.

Donna and I got to know each other after Hurricane Katrina. She'd grown up the third of nine children in New Orleans and she was devastated by the storm and its aftermath. She took a lot of heat from her fellow Democrats when she decided to reach out a hand to help President Bush rather than to use it to slap him politically, but her efforts were a big part of getting the aid New Orleans needed to rebuild. She put results ahead of partisanship, and that's the best way to be measured.

When our audiences see us together, they're reminded that two people born and raised in very different circumstances can grow up to share experiences and motivations. So what if we disagree on the best policies for a better economy, education system, or national defense? We start with the same goal, and then we work out how best to achieve it. This is not a novel approach to problem solving, though sometimes Washington can make it seem like a foreign concept.

And if we can't agree on anything else, at least we know we share a true love—our dogs, Jasper and Chip.

In 2013, Donna was in New York City and came over to watch *60 Minutes* (I really know how to show someone a good time). Jasper climbed all over her—his new best friend. I always trust my dog's judgment.

After the show, Jasper and I walked Donna to her hotel. We had to cross Broadway at Sixty-Third Street, going toward Lincoln Center. It was Fashion Week, which in NYC means lots of traffic, tons of stilettos, and even more glitz and glamour than usual.

As we were crossing the street and chatting, Jasper started to have a poop with only fourteen seconds left to cross the street (the streetlights in New York City show the countdown). I was slightly humiliated and worried that with all the traffic the drivers wouldn't see us. So Donna, controlling her laughter, went into the middle of the street with her hands up shouting to the drivers to make sure they saw Jasper.

She yelled, "Hey, hey, watch out, that's America's Dog—give us a little bit of time here, folks!" While she created the diversion, I scooped up the deposit and we got across the street with one second to spare (my glamorous big-city life!). The taxi and bus drivers were laughing and honking.

It was one of life's funny moments. Friendship and dogs—perfect.

No Politics at the Dog Park

And while we're on the subject of canines and civility, the dog park should be a politics-free zone. Seriously, folks, if you are hanging with the dogs, give it a rest.

My refuge in the last several years has been the dog park. It's where I don't wear makeup and get to talk about how cute our dogs are, the weather, and what was on TV last night. On my walks at the dog park, I try not to check my e-mail (but I do send pictures). I go out in any weather and walk about three miles. I don't talk about my job, and for the most part my fellow dogwalkers have no idea what line of work I'm in. I'm known as Jasper's Mom (my best title).

I have met many friends at the dog parks over the years—in San Diego, it was Del Mar Dog Beach; in Washington, Lincoln Park and Congressional Cemetery; and in New York, Central Park (leash-free until 9 a.m.—it's the best part of Manhattan). It's usually a politics-free zone. But there are exceptions.

People who don't work in politics but follow and enjoy it love to find someone to talk to. On occasion at the dog park, if one of these folks recognizes me or I finally reveal in conversation what I do, they want to get some insight into the news of the day and sometimes they want to have an argument. I have different ways of dodging such discussions, but it isn't always easy. Sometimes I have to be blunt.

At Central Park there was a guy from my building who started coming every morning with his two little dogs. He was a wealthy man who worked in high finance. I knew he was wealthy because it was just a very natural thing for him to say. He wasn't showing off, it was just a fact.

He recognized me from the Bush White House and from Fox News. He had been hosting a lot of Democrats for high-dollar fundraisers at his apartment and would try to impress me with people he'd met. I smiled and nodded but didn't encourage discussion. I didn't want to get drawn into any arguments, and for weeks he tried to goad me into conversation and I politely dodged his overtures.

Soon I started avoiding him altogether, but dogs will be dogs and Jasper liked to play with his so sometimes I couldn't help but talk with him. One day after a particularly newsy week, I saw him making a beeline for me. It was a beautiful sunny day and the humidity had just broken and all I wanted to do was spend an hour enjoying the morning. I immediately tensed and looked for someone else to talk to, but he was waving both arms to get my attention and said he'd been dying to talk to me.

I snapped. I put up my hand and said, "I'm sorry, I don't discuss politics at the dog park."

"But there are so many interesting things to talk about...."

"No, I'm serious. I don't talk politics here. I'll talk about anything but politics."

He looked wounded and I felt bad. He said he just would love to hear my opinion on the news of the day. But I had to draw a line, to have one place where politics couldn't intrude on the civility of a place I truly love—the dog park.

Since that day, my neighbor never brings up politics at the park and we have perfectly pleasant chats about…nothing. It's the best way to spend a morning, and I actually look forward to seeing him now.

Civility Unveiled

Three years after the administration ended, I got a cream-colored envelope in the mail in Manhattan. The handwriting looked familiar, but I couldn't place it at first. It had been a long time since I'd received anything from the White House Social Office. The President and Mrs. Obama were asking me to attend the official portrait unveilings of President and Mrs. Bush. It was an honor to be invited, but I didn't want to go.

By then, I was full-time on *The Five*, living in New York City, and had few ties to Washington. As a critic of the new administration, though a pretty measured one, I felt it might be hypocritical to accept hospitality from them. I decided not to go, but I woke up in the night thinking it wasn't fair for President Bush to be there without his strongest supporters in the audience. I changed my mind and asked for the day off the show. Then I called Karl Rove and asked him to be my date. It was our first time back to 1600 Pennsylvania Avenue since January 2009.

There are many magical things about the White House, and that day was no different. We saw lots of friends we hadn't seen in years. The Obamas were actually throwing us a reunion, and they were very generous to do so.

Karl and I sat next to General David Petraeus, then the CIA director. One of the rumors around town at the time was that

Obama and Petraeus didn't have much interaction. I whispered to him, "Would you like me to introduce you to President Obama?" The General smiled and winked at me. It was like old times (without the pressure to get back to work).

As the event got started, another President stole the show. At eighty-eight years old, former President George H. W. Bush was the star attraction. He was wheeled into the East Room to a standing ovation. He waved at everyone, and showed off his bright-colored socks. He stood for a moment and let us cheer him on.

Part of 41's enduring charm is that he always looks surprised by the warm, genuine receptions he gets everywhere he goes. One example was when I was in Houston on business, the President's chief of staff, Jean Becker, suggested that we all go to dinner. We hadn't made reservations and he said he didn't think we'd get a table. I said he could get a table anywhere in the world. But when we stepped inside, the young hostess didn't recognize the name and said there wasn't a table inside but that she could put us on the patio (it was only 50 degrees outside).

The President had his hand on my shoulder and shook it and said, "See. I told you no one remembers me." And right about then one of the patrons at the bar turned and started clapping. Others joined in and soon the whole restaurant was on its feet. I elbowed him in the ribs and said, "See, I told you they would." As you can imagine, we got a table.

At the White House, we settled into our seats as the President and First Lady were announced along with the Bushes. The speeches were gracious and President Bush's was emotional and hilarious. In it, he made sure Mrs. Obama knew where his portrait would be hanging, so that she could do for his painting what Dolly Madison did to save the portrait of George Washington in case the British tried to burn down the White House again.

At the end of the event, everyone was milling around a bit and the guests were invited to a reception in the State Dining Room. Karl and I were just chatting away, waving to some of the White House staff that we'd come to know over the years. I thought we were being ushered to the exit, but we were actually in line for a photograph with the Presidents.

I tugged on Karl's sleeve and said, "Come on, we shouldn't go— it's too awkward."

Karl said, "Oh no, it'll be fine...." And just as I was about to bail, we were at the front of the line.

President Obama greeted Karl warmly, saying to President Bush, "This is the guy who wants to put my portrait up here early!"

While they were shaking hands, President Bush saw me. He reached out his arms and wrapped me in a hug and kissed the top of my head. He looked at President Obama and said, "This one...."

President Obama said, "Oh, you don't have to tell me. Everybody loves Dana, and I've got Jay Carney." He was joking and having fun and we all laughed and talked for a minute before we were whisked into the reception area, where 41 was holding court by the mantel.

Again that day I learned the lesson to which I have constantly returned—that projecting my own anxieties onto what others will think of me is always much more negative than reality. The good news is that people aren't necessarily as partisan as you may think they are. For an event I really didn't want to go to, it sure holds a spot as one of the most memorable days of my life. And I will always appreciate the civility shown to the entire Bush team that day.

~~~~~~~

CHAPTER 7

Unafraid to Be Right

Why am I a conservative?

That's a question I get a lot. I don't know if liberals are ever asked to explain themselves, as if liberalism is a natural state of being and conservatism is an aberration that must be examined and defended.

Usually when I'm asked this, it's with some sort of disbelief or even disdain: "How could you *possibly* be a Republican?"

It actually comes quite easily to me.

I don't know if people are born with a worldview or if their thinking is a product of their environment. Many university studies are being done to figure that out (probably with the hope of finding a cure for conservatism). The answer is probably a little bit of both.

Like most conservatives, my path was a bit meandering. I grew up around people who mostly held conservative or libertarian views. The liberals I knew were fairly quiet about it, or at least I don't remember it being very heavy-handed. At the time I didn't know how liberal the media was, but looking back at clips, I'm amazed that after all the news I consumed, I still emerged as I did.

The first Presidential election I really paid attention to was in 1988 when George H. W. Bush ran against Michael Dukakis. I grew up admiring Ronald Reagan and Vice President Bush, and if I were old enough, I would have voted for 41. I was glad he won.

But four years later when I was in college, I almost voted for Bill Clinton. I went to one of his campaign rallies in Pueblo, Colorado, and I don't recall what Clinton said but I remember the energy, the music, "I'm Walking on Sunshine," and all that *felt* new and optimistic. It felt like hope…and, well, change (I later learned this is what all campaigns try to make you feel—no one runs on despair and the status quo). There was no substantive reason for supporting Clinton in my mind—it was more about wanting to feel reinvigorated, something new. Which, I learned later, can be very seductive. And dangerous.

My first Presidential election vote was important to me. It was a big moment, and I thought my decision would determine something about my future (that if I voted for one party, I'd be wedded to that party forever—which is nonsense, but I was dramatic about it). So I started reading a bit more about the policy positions and took part in the debates about the two candidates in my political science class. It was a tough call, but in the end I voted for 41. I trusted him. I was disappointed when he lost.

My politics didn't define me then, but because of my interests and what I do for a living, it somewhat does now. When I first left college and worked in the news business for a while, I hid my conservatism. I didn't want to start fights with people who had visceral reactions against conservatives. I even wondered, "What is *wrong* with me?"

But as you read in Chapter 1, after I read Peggy Noonan's book, I found my ideological footing and increasingly gained confidence in my beliefs. Gradually, I shook off my fear of talking about it.

I'm a conservative because everything else seems easy by comparison. And when something is too easy, it's too good to be true or it's sure to fail and disappoint. I wasn't impressed by the alternatives to conservatism—I gravitate to facts, logic, and reality, whereas to me, liberalism is based on theory, and feelings, and fantasy.

I respect tradition, learn from history, and adhere to a code of ethics that has helped me make sense of the world. By definition, then, I reject situational ethics. I have standards, and I stick to them. For instance, conservatism is where I can fully express my support in the individual rather than the state, and where my belief in self-governance and responsibility isn't in conflict with policies I support.

Far from limiting what I can do or think, being a conservative gives me great freedom. I govern my thoughts by a set of principles. I will listen to arguments, even be persuaded by them—I'm willing to be convinced, but you have to prove it to me. Sanctimony and cynicism don't change my mind—proof does.

And while everyone's principles differ, I find that most conservatives share my approach. In my experience, liberals have to check a lot of boxes to be included—"do you believe this, that, and the other"—and there's a rigidity that gives them very little room to win arguments. They are doctrinaire and rely on sanctimony while ignoring facts. I find that very unattractive. And when the facts on the ground don't match up to reality, that's when I've experienced liberals lashing out at conservatives for being "mean," as if that's going to solve anything. These are like arguments that children have with their parents—conservatives are mean because they deny a third scoop of ice cream. But feelings don't change facts, and it is not "mean" to point them out. I want hard, practical truths—and then I apply my principles to them.

Conservative caricatures are everywhere in the media, but the descriptions of angry, cruel, old-fashioned conservatives just do not match my experience. I find most conservatives to be cheerful and clear-eyed, which really irritates a lot of liberals. Of course, almost *everything* irritates a lot of liberals, nothing more so than a happy conservative. Which is why I always smile and say hello when I'm proudly wearing my George W. Bush Institute jacket around New York City. I love it when people do a double take when they see it.

Being a conservative does not mean I reject compromise. My nature is to seek agreement, to bring people together, and to help them see that they have more in common than they think. I believe that's a better way to win arguments. And I've always found much more "give" in this area among conservatives than among the Left.

Conservatism by its very nature is compassionate—that's one of the things that drew me to President George W. Bush. Conservatives are charitable, forgiving, and are always—*always*—more willing to laugh at themselves (and yes, we have plenty to laugh at). I understand why some conservatives rejected his phrase of "Compassionate Conservative"—perhaps they found it redundant—but that spoke to me, and it opened the door for me to be more active in participating in the public arena.

Being a conservative has given me clarity. And it's given me freedom—my mind is free; therefore, my heart is lighter. And that's a gift from God that I believe we have an obligation to share with others around the world.

Besides, I love to be right. Just ask Peter.

One More Thing

Of all the advice I've ever been given, Margaret Spellings telling me to "put my big girl panties on and deal with it" is my favorite. She was telling me to stop worrying myself to death and to put aside my self-doubt. She reminded me that I'd been given an opportunity to shine, and that it was my choice whether I did.

In writing this book, I remembered another time when I had to be pushed out of my shell. It was at one of the press awards dinners, and I was seated at the head table in place of Tony Snow, who was recovering from exploratory surgery. My mind was preoccupied, and I knew that work was piling up while we sat through the speeches. I just wanted the night to be over and to get off the stage. When I was recognized by the emcee, I kind of half stood, barely looked up, and gave a little nod. I felt shy and like I didn't really belong there anyway—I was only the acting press secretary.

At the end of the evening, John Warner, the longtime Senator from Virginia, waved at me and asked for a word.

He said, "Now I saw you sitting there, and I know that you're not comfortable. But if you'll permit me to give you just a little piece of advice—you see, you earned your place here tonight. And you'll be at many more of these events. So when the announcer calls your name, stand up proudly, flash them a big smile, and wave—give them a reason to applaud. They *want* to be happy for you. Let them have a moment."

It was kind of him to take an interest in me. I realized what he meant, but I didn't think of myself in that light. Still, I did as he said even though it doesn't feel natural to me. Gradually, I've become more comfortable and enjoyed the opportunity to be in the spotlight sometimes. I appreciate that Senator Warner and so many others gave me advice that would help me advance and enjoy my work— they passed on things that they'd learned in their careers, and I'm grateful to be able to do the same for others now.

All of my mentors along the way have helped me achieve, for the most part, what I crave now. I call it "productive serenity." Like millions around the world, I'd been inspired, calmed, and guided by the Serenity Prayer—asking God to help me with acceptance, courage, and wisdom. Serenity doesn't come easily to me—I have to work at it. So I made a decision to try to be actively calm, generous, dignified, and gracious. I look for a balance—to be sharp but not snappy, tough but not aggressive, understanding but not a pushover—all with a sense of humor and a healthy perspective for my very small role in the world.

For a long time I didn't have a defined Dana doctrine to describe this approach; it was more a ball of string. Then one morning at a hotel I came back to my room for bed after a speaking event, and the hotel staff had placed a Zen card with a Buddhist saying on my pillow (this will make Gutfeld roll his eyes). It read, "Say little. But when you speak, utter gentle words that touch the heart. Be truthful. Express kindness. Abstain from vanity. This is the way."

I had an "Aha!" moment when I read those words, because it

captured how I was trying to live my life most productively and happily. I carried the card with me for months until I tacked it in my medicine cabinet, and I still see it every morning and night when I brush my teeth. The card is a little worn, but its message never gets old. In the morning it helps set my intention for the day, and at night it reminds me to forgive myself if I haven't lived up to it (usually because I've let Bob Beckel push my buttons).

On the morning of January 20, 2009, I made my way to the White House for the last hours of the Bush Administration. I took the Metro because the roads were all blocked off for the Inauguration's security. Almost every passenger on the train was headed to the National Mall to witness President Obama take the oath of office. They were so joyous, and I was genuinely happy for them. No one recognized me or knew that I was going into my last four hours of work at the White House—it was like Cinderella approaching midnight and the Metro was about to turn into a pumpkin.

I went into the press office and checked in on the reporters gathered in the briefing room. Everyone was getting ready for the Obamas to arrive. I took the reporters and crew some of my last boxes of White House peanut M&M's and said good-bye for the hundredth time—we'd been together many years and they'd helped me grow into the job.

My last stop was the Oval Office. The President was there, taking some last-minute calls of farewell. He had written the traditional letter for the next President and left it in the desk—addressed to "44."

I walked in and he put his arm around me and said, "You know, the first day I was President, I came in here and I said I wanted to be able to look myself in the eye and say I'd been true to my principles every day that I had the privilege to be the Commander in Chief. I feel like I can do that." He squeezed my shoulder and my nose stung as I sniffed back tears of pride and nostalgia.

With that, the President said he was going to take a final walk around the South Lawn and then head over to join Mrs. Bush. As he left the Oval Office, White House photographer Eric Draper took one last photo of him. I marked that moment in my memory—there went a great President.

A few hours later we met up with him after the inauguration, this time at Andrews Air Force Base. He and I made eye contact as he was about to board the plane that would take him back to Texas, to a place he calls the "Promised Land" and to what Mrs. Bush calls the "Afterlife." He summoned me over and then cupped his hands around my face and bent down to kiss my forehead. I felt like everything was ending, and it was. But so much was beginning as well, which has been the good news. I was ready for it.

And the Good News Continues...

On January 7, 2009, I stepped up to a podium at the DAR Constitution Hall (a beautiful building founded by the Daughters of the American Revolution that is now the capital's largest concert hall) in front of an audience of presidential appointees from across the federal government. These were the hardworking people who didn't have daily interaction with the president, and yet were among the most loyal of his team. The president gathered them all together at least once a year to thank them for their service.

I didn't remember this event until I was on my book tour and met up with a former colleague who told me he'd never forget how I broke down at the podium that day. He said it was one of the sweetest things he had witnessed while working for the president. Then it came back to me. I recall I was tired, stressed, and tied up in knots about having to say good-bye to the president and to the team I'd worked with for so many years.

I was in a rush to get to the event and never thought I'd get emotional. I spoke in front of groups all the time. But when I looked out into the audience and saw the earnestness of the employees, many of them my friends and people who had helped me do my job as the press secretary, I was overwhelmed with appreciation and gratitude.

When it was clear I wasn't going to make it through my short speech, I was rescued onstage by the chief of staff, Josh Bolten, who took things from there and introduced the president.

So, yes, I did cry at the office. Sometimes an occasion calls for tears.

White House Stories

Throughout *And the Good News Is...* I shared behind-the-scenes moments with President George W. Bush to show what kind of a leader he was when the cameras weren't there. These stories elicited the majority of the feedback, and so in the paperback edition, I decided to include more of them. Since I'd already told all of my best stories, I asked former colleagues and new friends if they had anything they'd like to share.

I could have filled another book with their memories. I heard from people who have traveled with the president and Mrs. Bush to Africa on a trip to raise awareness about cervical cancer and to work on preparing a facility for patients there. During that trip, my friend said that the Bushes did more manual labor that week than everyone else combined. He said the president arrived at the work site before others and stayed long after everyone had gone home. He would not allow cameras in to capture the moment; instead, he worked quietly. Occasionally he would say, "To whom much is given, much is required."

Another former colleague remembered how the president made sure that he was given some special attention during an interview, not because he wanted someone else in the shot but because he wanted his staffer's children to be able to see their dad on television with the president of the United States. He knew just when to give someone a boost.

I also heard from a former press office employee who in the years after the White House had children of his own and adopted a young boy from Uganda. The president painted the little boy's portrait, a priceless gift and recognition of his appreciation for the special love an adoption brings to a family.

The policies and politics of any administration are fully documented and will be pored over for years to come. But these glimpses behind the scenes help give you the full measure of a leader. It was a joy to connect with some of my former colleagues, and here is a sampling of their stories as told to me that will give readers even more awareness of the kind of leader and boss President Bush was, and the kind of man he continues to be today.

THE PRESIDENT KNOWS HIS MOST IMPORTANT AUDIENCE

In the spring of 2007, President Bush invited Ed Gillespie to his private study in the residence to ask him to serve as counselor to the president for his last eighteen months in office. The study is a beautiful, dark-paneled room off the Truman Balcony, and Ed settled into a black leather wingback chair across the president's desk from him. The counselor position has a wide-ranging purview, including the White House press office, media affairs, communications, speechwriting, and events.

"You're very good at communicating with American voters," the president said, complimenting Ed's time as chairman of the Republican National Committee. "But in this job you'll need to understand that the president has more audiences than the American people.

"Our allies are an important audience. They listen closely to everything I say, and if they detect uncertainty or lack of resolve, they'll be gone tomorrow."

He snapped his fingers to emphasize the point. This was in June

2007, and America was in the thick of combat in both Afghanistan and Iraq (pre-surge).

"The third audience is our enemies," the president continued. "They listen closely to whatever the American president says, and if *they* detect a lack of resolve, equivocation—they will become emboldened, and ramp up on us.

"The fourth audience is our troops in the field. They listen carefully to what their commander-in-chief says. And if *they* detect uncertainty, lack of resolve, equivocation...Well, it will hurt their morale.

"Now, there will be times when you will want me to say something that would be popular with that first audience, the American people, but what you won't realize is that it would have the effect of hurting the morale of our troops in the field."

As those words were sinking in, he leaned forward across his desk and with his eyes steeled he said, "And you just need to understand: I will never do that."

And Ed thought to himself, *Where do I sign?*

"HISTORY WILL JUDGE YOU FAIRLY"

Standing in between the West Wing and the Old Executive Office Building, Jenny Korn looked at her Blackberry for the hundredth time that day, seeing whether she'd missed a call and checking to make sure the phone was working. She calculated the time of day in the Middle East and said a little prayer.

It was day number five of the five-day period when her husband, who was deployed in a combat zone in Iraq, might have been able to contact her, and she was sick to her stomach that she might miss his call...again. All deployments are different, and this one was during the height of violence in Ramadi. They would have no contact for twelve days at a time while he was at the forward operating base, then there would be a five-day window when he would be back at their main base to take a shower and possibly send an e-mail or make a call. But that wasn't a guarantee. The Internet or phone service might be down and the window would close, leaving her to count down another twelve days until the next window opened. She said she felt like she was holding her breath for those seven months, waiting for a call or an e-mail, hoping for good news and pushing negative thoughts away.

She closed her eyes, took a deep breath, and then tried to refocus on the task at hand. She was in charge of a White House event with over 200 guests and would soon need to brief the president. She shook her head because she still couldn't believe that she had the honor of working for President Bush. When she would see him at these events, she says the president made sure to ask how her husband was doing. And he always said the greatest honor he had was being commander-in-chief.

Jenny said that despite the stress, there couldn't have been a better place during wartime. She had the support of the president and her White House colleagues. She knew they were committed to keeping our country safe and that the president had the Marines' backs. Her husband agreed.

At one of the White House's congressional picnics, after Jenny's husband had returned home safely, they had a chance to visit with the president. She knew how he appreciated military families like theirs, and they all stood there hugging, knowing how much the war had changed all of their lives.

"History will judge your work fairly," the president said, getting a bit choked up.

Capturing the moment, Jenny's marine husband replied, "History will judge you fairly, too, Mr. President."

Indeed.

"YEAH, BABY!"

Chad Pfeifer met President Bush after the White House years and after serving as an army corporal in Operation Iraqi Freedom in 2006 and 2007. During his deployment, Chad was injured by an improvised explosive device, and his left leg was amputated below the knee. He convalesced in a hospital back in the States, and a fellow soldier, also an amputee, suggested they try playing golf. His friend thought it would be good for both body and spirit, as posttraumatic stress was clouding their days. Chad had never played golf and didn't think it was much of a sport, but he started swinging the club and fell in love.

In 2008 he was medically discharged and moved to Arizona to attend the Golf Academy of America. Soon after, he started winning tournaments, including President Bush's annual Warrior Open thirty-six-hole golf tournament three years in a row. Today, he plays professionally on the Web.com PGA Tour, the first veteran amputee ever to do so.

"Golf saved my life," Chad said.

The Warrior Open is part of the president's Military Service Initiative at the Bush Center. It is an event to honor U.S. service members, and the proceeds go to support service members and their families.

Chad told me that President Bush is one of the most down-to-earth and humble men he's ever known—especially for someone who has had that much power. He said the president is a competitor throughout the Open and that while he loves to see the guys succeed, he isn't shy about commenting on a bad shot. Chad said the president has a unique ability to joke around with wounded warriors that also makes them feel respected.

"It feels like the president would do just about anything for us," he said. "It's a feeling you want with your commander-in-chief."

He said that the president's actions after 9/11 and throughout Operations Iraqi Freedom and Enduring Freedom have shown he loves and appreciates the military, and that these feelings have even grown since he left office.

"The president is committed to bettering the lives of wounded soldiers and providing the opportunities to live successful and meaningful lives," he said.

The annual golf tournament is just one of the ways the president honors U.S. servicemen and -women and their families.

"The Warrior Open has given me confidence like I've never had before," Chad said. "I picked up golf in 2008 after losing my leg a year earlier. I struggled with what I wanted to do, who I would become, and how I would keep going forward. But golf was the constant in my life and was my stress reliever and therapeutic tool."

Chad participated in the first Warrior Open in 2011 and won that year. In 2012, he won again, and this win included one of his greatest golf memories: he aced the par-3 fourth hole while President Bush was watching.

"For someone who struggles with memory loss and PTS it is an event I will be certain to remember for the rest of my life," Chad said.

In 2013, he successfully defended his title again and would get the opportunity of a lifetime shortly after.

"I remember getting a phone call from President Bush, and he asked me if I would like to join him at the Presidents Cup, which was being held at Muirfield Village in Dublin, Ohio.

"As I accepted the offer I heard the two words from President Bush that I have come to know and love, 'Yeah, baby!' He was so excited he sounded like a kid on Christmas Day.

Chad says when he hears the president say that, it tells him that he acknowledges the successes and triumphs of the adversity we faced on the battlefield and even after we returned home.

"So, I'm at the Presidents Cup surrounded by the biggest names in the game and President Bush was introducing me like I was a celebrity and that everybody needed to meet me," Chad said. On that trip, President Bush introduced him to Tiger Woods, Phil Mickelson, and Jack Nicklaus.

"I am truly blessed that I was able to go to the Presidents Cup. I got to meet many of my favorite golfers and idols," he said. "The best part of the trip, though, was not the people I got to meet or flying on a private jet or watching the Presidents Cup live. It was seeing the genuine emotions of a president who was so delighted to have a wounded soldier go with him to something he knew I would enjoy.

"After winning the Warrior Open, I had a lot of other wounded vets tell me how I inspired them by not giving up and facing adversity," he said. In turn, Chad has dedicated himself to reaching as many other veterans and persons with disabilities as he can.

"The Warrior Open and President Bush gave me the confidence and drive to be able to reach my goals. I am having an impact and touching lives with my newfound purpose and am able to help out many great nonprofit organizations that help wounded soldiers and people with disabilities.

"I am excited to see what the future holds and how many people I can help, but I would be remiss if I didn't thank President Bush for hosting the Warrior Open and encouraging me both in wins and losses. I greatly appreciate the support and can't help but to sum up my experiences with him with a great big enthusiastic, 'Yeah, baby!' "

"YOU DID A GREAT JOB, MOM"

Lucas Boyce was born six weeks premature and weighed just over four pounds. His mother was a young teen who struggled with substance abuse and would sell her body to support her habit. That's how Lucas was conceived. It was a miracle he lived to be born. And his life has been a miracle, too.

At ten days old, Lucas was sent to the foster-care home of Dorothy

Boyce. Dorothy, a white woman from the Midwest, took care of over forty foster-care children over fifteen years. Lucas says his mother is someone who doesn't see color—she's not color blind; she actually just can't see anyone's skin color. She just sees the person.

Dorothy adopted six of the children and had four of her own. At one point she was the single mother of eleven foster-care and adopted children. She married when Lucas was in elementary school, and she became the stepmother of her husband's three girls, too.

To keep the children focused, Lucas says that his mom taught them to believe in what was possible even when challenges seemed insurmountable. She encouraged them to reach for their goals even if they didn't seem plausible. Little did she know that Lucas would one day work at the White House for President George W. Bush.

Fast-forward to March 2002, when Lucas, as one of the interns in the Office of Presidential Personnel, was invited to the South Lawn of the White House as part of a photo opportunity in support of volunteer service. After the photo, Lucas stepped aside and, as he did, the president gestured to him and said, "Come on, let's get a picture," and he called over his official photographer, Eric Draper.

Overcome with excitement, Lucas threw his arm around the president in kind of a brotherly hug. An obviously bold move and, he thought, probably a breach of protocol, but, being a rookie, he didn't know any better.

The next day Lucas's boss, Ed Moy, came back to their office and said, "So, you made a real impression on the president," and immediately Lucas got a sinking feeling that he'd gotten too chummy with the president and that his internship was over.

He began to apologize, but Ed said that after the meeting the president called him over to his desk and said, "Hey, I met this kid on the South Lawn yesterday. He said he works for you. What's his name again?"

Moy said, "Lucas Boyce."

"Yeah, well, I really enjoyed meeting him."

Moy shot back, "Probably not as much as he enjoyed meeting you, sir."

The president laughed and asked, "What's his story?" Moy told him a little bit about Lucas and his background, and the president said, "Well, what can we do for him? Let's bring him onboard."

And that was how Lucas got his start: from a random chance encounter with the president on the South Lawn of the White House. Lucas said from that he learned that a measure of someone's character is how they treat people who can do nothing for them.

"George W. Bush didn't have to do anything for me. I wasn't anybody special, yet he took the time to chat, had a personal photo taken, and then asked his staff to help me out the next day. I was of no value to him, yet he influenced my life in more ways than I'd ever be able to repay," Lucas said.

Lucas went on to work on the president's reelection campaign and then at the White House in a number of different roles. A few years after his first encounter, he was on his first trip on *Air Force One* and made the innocent mistake of sitting in the president's chair in the conference room. When the president walked in and looked at him, then at his chair, then back at Lucas, and gave him a little smile, Lucas leaped out of the chair, full of apologies.

"What the heck are you doing in my chair?" the president barked, jokingly. Lucas kept apologizing but the president said, "Don't worry about it. I'm not staying. I was just stopping by." Then he gave Lucas that look again, which of course initiated a fresh round of "I'm so sorry, sir!"

"Really. It's okay. Don't worry about it, man," Bush said. He paused. "It's just the president's chair."

The aides in the room burst into laughter. The president started laughing as well. Lucas wasn't sure whether to laugh or apologize again. The next day, Lucas had an opportunity to introduce his parents to the president for the first time at a fund-raising event in his hometown of Kansas City. Lucas found his parents in line to meet the president. He gave them a big hug and then proceeded to tell them to not embarrass him.

"Dad, straighten your tie. Mom, you look great. No, your lipstick is not smudging. It's perfect. Yes. Your hair is perfect, too. Just don't embarrass me!" He gave them another hug and had started to walk away when White House advance director Jason Recher turned Lucas around and pushed him back toward them.

"Introduce your parents to the president," Jason said.

Lucas said his heart started beating a little bit faster. He felt a sense of pride to be able to introduce his mom to the commander-in-chief, but he was unprepared. He stepped forward and, at a loss for anything profound to say, said, "Mr. President, this is my mom and dad, Dorothy and Larry Boyce."

The president got this big smile on his face as he shook their hands. Lucas wondered if President Bush had ever considered that his parents were a different color than Lucas was.

After the photo, the president draped his arms around Lucas's parents, pulling them closer for a quick chat.

"Your son is doing a fantastic job for us and you should be proud of how he turned out. You did a great job in raising him," the president said.

Then he gave Lucas one of his sideways smiles and said, "The only thing about your son is...well, he likes to sit in my seat on *Air Force One*."

Lucas looked on sheepishly as his parents laughed.

Then the president gave him a wink and said, "Just kiddin'."

Lucas said he'll never forget that moment or the lesson of that trip that built on his first encounter with President Bush: your character is also measured by how you treat those who dare to sit in your chair.

PLAY BALL

In 2005, President Bush was scheduled to throw out the first pitch to open the Washington Nationals' new ballpark. The president grew up playing baseball, and he was a former owner of the Texas Rangers before running for office. He takes great pride in his ability to pitch—not throw or toss, but to pitch—a real, hard strike, from the top of the pitcher's mound. He most famously threw a beautiful pitch at Yankee Stadium during the 2001 World Series following 9/11, so he had a very high standard to meet.

A couple of weeks before the game, Jared Weinstein, the president's personal aide, came to Tony Fratto, the principal deputy press secretary, to ask if he'd like to practice with President Bush a couple of times during the week before the game. Tony said yes and brought his glove to the White House, knowing that this was probably going to be one of the coolest days of his life.

At the appointed hour, Tony went out to the South Lawn, feeling a little awkward wearing suit pants, a tie, and dress shoes to toss around a baseball. The president wasn't so encumbered—he'd just finished his biking workout, so he was warmed up and wearing athletic gear. Tony tried to focus. No matter how much fun it was to play ball with the president, the outcome was important. We needed the president to throw a strike.

The first thing Tony discovered while tossing the ball with President Bush is that he does it like he does everything else physical—running, biking, golf, whatever: hard and fast, with no warm-up. So they started throwing and the president was throwing hard. Tony had to figure out what to do.

"I had the president throwing bee-bees at me like we were kids back home," Tony said. "Now, I can throw hard, too, and it was like the president was challenging me to throw harder. So I threw it harder. And we're going back and forth when all of a sudden I remembered I needed to keep my ego in check. I thought, 'The only way I can screw this up is if I injure the president.' So I focused—good catches, good throws, don't injure President Bush."

Out there on the South Lawn, the moment became extremely emotional and meaningful to him, Tony said. And he's not talked about it until now.

"After the shock of President Bush's hard throws, and the sheer coolness of catching ball with him on the South Lawn, I realized it was really the first time I'd ever played catch with someone like a father figure," Tony said. "I love my dad, and he was an important role model for me growing up, but he was not a sports guy. I was a very good baseball player as a kid, but I never played catch with my dad. I literally never caught baseballs with any adults—only other kids.

"I realized this after about twenty or thirty throws with President Bush, and at that point I wasn't at the White House with the president—I was just in the backyard with dad. I don't think of President Bush as a father figure, but as the president, and my friend. But that was a really special personal moment for me. And I have the pictures to prove it!"

On opening night, Tony was able to bring his eight-year-old son, Antonio, to Nats Park for the game. Antonio got to ride in the motorcade, and President Bush had him join him in visiting the teams in their dugouts before the game. Antonio even joined the president and his dad on the field for the pitch.

Everyone had their eyes on the president. Would he or wouldn't he throw a strike?

Of course he did.

Even now, years later, President Bush and Antonio always have something to talk about. In 2013, Antonio visited the president with Tony in Dallas at the Bush Center, and they hadn't seen each other in about six years. Antonio was sixteen by then. But they picked right up talking baseball. President Bush even remembered what position Antonio played.

"There are a lot of reasons I loved working with President Bush, and his love for baseball—and for making it such a special moment for me and my son—is one of them," Tony said.

"HOLD YOUR FIRE!"

Near the end of his time at the White House as the chief speech-writer, Bill McGurn and his wife, Julie, were invited to Camp David for the weekend. At the lunch table two things happened.

"What do you want to do today?" the president asked.

"Shooting," Julie said.

"Have you ever fired a weapon?" he asked.

"No."

Always competitive, the president said, "I bet you twenty dollars you hit nothing."

What the president didn't know is that Bill had never fired a weapon, either. They went to the range. There were ten marines there to teach them how to shoot. Bill told his marine, "Look, all I have to do is three things: I have to hit something. It can't be the president. And I have to beat my wife or the president will never let me hear the end of it."

Julie got way out in front with her score, but finally Bill passed her. He said they were all pretty awful. At one point, the president passed by on his bicycle and shouted, "Hold your fire!"

"We did. And my honor was saved," Bill said.

THE PRESIDENCY IS A LONELY OFFICE

The January 2007 "Surge" speech, in the words of former chief speechwriter Bill McGurn, was such a mess, but it turned out to be a triumph. The speech had been postponed many times over; it was originally supposed to be delivered before Christmas. Then everything kept changing.

The decision to send more troops to Iraq and change the strategy was unpopular, and most of the president's senior advisers were skeptical. Some were more than skeptical—they were opposed. But the president pressed on and convinced them. Then he had to try to convince the American people it was the right decision.

Chris Michel and Bill were working in a tiny little alcove off of Bill's office literally from 6 a.m. until 11 p.m. during that time. Bill remembers living on chicken nuggets from the White House Mess and could not look at one afterward.

Everyone and his brother chimed in on the speech. So on a Saturday morning at six thirty, Chris and Bill were in the Oval Office with President Bush, Condoleeza Rice, Raul Yanes, and others. The president read it through.

"Page one is terrible. But it is not the disaster page two is," the president said.

Bill knew the reason.

"We were not allowed to describe the surge as counterinsurgency, even though that's what it was. The reason was that classic counterinsurgency requires a ten-to-one troop advantage and we didn't have it," Bill said. "General David Petraeus argued the Iraqis made up for the rest. So it's like trying to describe a red tie without saying the word red. And the president liked to see the logic explained."

That night everyone deserted the speechwriters—they often had to stay late as the final work was left to them. Bill told Chris, "If we're going to get in trouble again, let's at least get in trouble for the way we think he wants it." So they just chopped a good chunk of page two.

The next morning, as they handed the draft to Bush, Bill stood in front of the desk and said, "Mr. President, you didn't like page two yesterday. We mostly took it out. So when you look at page two now, if you think of it as page three, it will go down a lot better." The president gave Bill a look while putting his glasses at the end of his nose.

The editing and approval of the speech went well after that, but the delivery was a disaster: bad television feed, bad delivery. Everyone hated it. Even the conservatives dumped on it. But it still holds up today as one of the most courageous and correct decisions of the presidency.

What Bill remembers is how, after a bad read-through, instead of doing it over, the president just went to the South Lawn with Barney to relax. It impressed on Bill how lonely the presidency is at key moments—and this was one of the biggest moments in Bush's administration. And yet he was willing to stand alone.

"The president used to say to me, 'Billy, we are not going to abandon the people of Iraq the way we did the people of Vietnam, from the rooftop of an embassy.' And I loved him for it."

More Good News: Questions for Dana from Readers

HAS PRESIDENT BUSH'S LESSON THAT FORGIVENESS WILL SET YOU FREE STAYED TRUE? DO YOU FORGIVE AND FORGET THE NASTY THINGS PEOPLE SAY ABOUT YOU?

The advice President Bush gave me about forgiving a former colleague is something I use regularly, and not just in the workplace. He taught me how freeing it is to have a forgiving spirit. I try to put that lesson to work for me every day. For example, since I live in Manhattan and walk to work or take the subway, everyone is constantly bumping into each other. Sometimes it can really hurt. I suppress my irritation and instead say, "That's okay," while taking a breath and smiling. I try to think, "Well, that's New York!" That may sound like a small thing, but think about how many little irritations and grievances can build up all day long in your professional and personal lives. If you let them pile up, they can suffocate you. But if you're constantly letting things go, being forgiving and focusing on yourself, you free up your mind and heart for more productive activities and a calmer existence.

I'm also not above asking forgiveness, especially when I snap at someone for something that isn't that big a deal or was just a mistake. The sooner I ask for forgiveness, the better I feel. And I try never to say I'm sorry as a way to slip in that someone else is to blame. I say I'm sorry and then bite my tongue if I'm tempted to undermine my apology and cause more damage.

As to dealing with criticism, I've learned that it comes with the job. I am offering my opinions, and, naturally, many people will disagree with me. My job in television commentary invites criticism, which can be concentrated, relentless, and brutal. It can be all consuming. At first I was alarmed, even wounded, by the comments, but over time I grew numb to them. Eventually, some of the attempted insults made me laugh. Being a part of the daily political conversation has given me a new appreciation for online bullying and what people go through. I especially think of parents and how they're helping their kids deal with it. This will be an ongoing issue for all of us going forward. And while forgiveness is important, I've found that sometimes walking away from my phone and laptop is the best thing I can do.

Try an experiment: delete your social media apps from your phone for twenty-four hours (it is easy to reinstall them). You'll soon see that instead of panicking, you start to feel better, more free. And you don't miss the conversations that much. You realize that if you're not immersed in your phone, you don't have to wallow in the negativity. You're not missing much that you can't get caught up on the next day. Whenever I do this, especially when I'm under attack by a group of trolls, they get bored and eventually stop and I've not ruined my day by worrying about them.

WHAT TYPE OF ADVICE DO YOU HAVE FOR PEOPLE WITH LOW SELF-ESTEEM?

My heart hurts when I hear that someone has low self-esteem, because it's an emotion that can be crippling. Often, the destructive voice that we use to criticize ourselves is our worst enemy. Pushing that voice out of your head is the first step for overcoming the power of that negativity.

When I was going through my quarter-life crisis, I found a few things that helped me:

First, I learned to make lists, and I would write down all the things that I thought I needed to do to be a better, more successful person. I would then take each thing and mark whether it was something I could control. If it was, then I made a list of the things I could do to improve, and if it wasn't, I tried to recognize that and let go of the responsibility of fixing something I had no control over.

Second, I found that belonging to my singles' group at church was a source of support and stability. If you're not a part of a church, there are other groups outside of work that you could join. I'm a fan of the Junior League, which does so much good in communities across America, and, in addition to offering volunteering opportunities, it provides a good way to network with people you wouldn't otherwise meet.

Third, even today, I like to have a range of goals in mind. They can even be small. For example, at the gym, pull-ups always seemed impossible to me. Recently, I set a goal with my trainer to be able to do five pull-ups within a three-month period. It was ambitious, and even my husband gently tried to lower my expectations. Maybe because I didn't think I could do it, I ended up doing better than I thought—I felt little pressure to succeed because there were no consequences if I didn't meet the challenge. But within six weeks, I was able to do eight. It was a small accomplishment, but it helped me think I was still able to achieve things. I like that feeling.

If you're struggling in your daily life, it's important that you make an appointment to see a professional who can help you. There's no shame in seeking advice; in fact, you might find that a professional is able to turn around your outlook, and then you'll wonder why you waited so long to ask.

And remember what Tony Snow told me on his last day at the White House when I fretted about not being able to fill his shoes: You are better at this than you think you are. That is undoubtedly true about all of us.

WHAT ADVICE CAN YOU OFFER TO A WOMAN TRYING TO REENTER THE WORKPLACE AFTER STAYING AT HOME FOR FIFTEEN YEARS TO RAISE CHILDREN? SO MUCH HAS CHANGED.

This is one of the most interesting issues to me because I have many friends who are deciding whether to stay home to raise their children or to keep working, and they are wondering whether and how they will be able to go back to work someday.

So much of the advice in *And the Good News Is...* is based on the benefits of networking—building, growing, and keeping a network of people you can rely on. Making friends over the years and keeping in touch with them is what eventually led me to my position as the White House press secretary. I never would have been on anyone's list for the Justice Department job after the 9/11 attacks if my friend hadn't known that I was interested in moving back to Washington. When I got the call from her asking if I would join her team, I started packing that night and started work a couple of weeks later.

A friend of mine who has three young boys and runs the human resources team for a global public relations firm says that anyone thinking of returning to the workforce should keep in touch (or get back in touch) with people they worked with before. She encourages people to lean on the positive relationships they have made throughout their careers before they took a break from the workforce. She also says that if there's not a full-time role available, you should be willing to consider freelance or consulting work. Sometimes it's getting a foot back in the door that leads to larger opportunities.

Also, if you're engaged in some projects, you're likely to have more confidence and you won't feel you have to jump at the first thing that comes along. You can take more time to think about what you want to do and to look around for other opportunities.

Being out of the workforce for a significant period can put up some hurdles where you might not have had them before. Technology and the way work gets done changes, so keeping yourself relevant to the latest things in your field can help you clear those hurdles. There are online classes to take if you want to freshen up your technology skills.

Finally, ask for advice. People like to help, and they can't help if you don't ask.

YOU HAVE A SHORT SEGMENT ABOUT NOT WEARING UGG BOOTS AROUND THE OFFICE BECAUSE IT GIVES THE APPEARANCE THAT YOU'RE SHUFFLING THROUGH YOUR DAY. DO YOU HAVE ANY TIPS FOR HOW TO DRESS IN MORE CASUAL BUSINESS ENVIRONMENTS SO THAT YOU FIT IN WITH THE REST OF THE TEAM?

I've lived by the motto that you should dress for the job you want, not the job that you have. Think about it. What you're wearing is the first thing everyone sees, and they can't un-see it. Before you walk out the door in the morning, look in the mirror and ask yourself, "Would I buy something from this person? Can I trust her to provide a good service? Does this person look like she's excited to be here?"

Some additional practical tips include choosing shoes you can walk in without teetering or stumbling, making sure shoes are polished, and having a nice pedicure if you wear open-toed shoes. Also, if you have to tug on your skirt every time you stand up, it is too short for the office. Wear clothes that you feel comfortable in and that will earn you compliments. Of course, the best topper of any outfit is a great attitude, so smile—you're going to work!

DO YOU HAVE ANY REGRETS ABOUT ANY OF THE CAREER CHOICES YOU MADE UP UNTIL THIS POINT? WHAT ABOUT YOUR LIFE CHOICES?

One of the best lessons I learned from President Bush is "You don't get do-overs." So I've learned to let go of regrets. But of course, I look back and wish that I'd worked harder, studied more, taken better care of my health, and not been so rushed that I missed a lot along the way. In my speeches on the book tour I would tell audiences, "Don't worry your young lives away," and I could see in their faces that they knew exactly what I meant.

All of my career choices have built on one another, from being a waitress and a country music deejay to working as a reporter and then as a spokesperson. And now, I can see how all of those experiences culminated in allowing me to have one of the best jobs for me, as a contributor to Fox News Channel and a frequent public speaker about policy and politics. Oh, and I'm an author. That still surprises me—I actually wrote a book and people read it. What an honor!

The hardest question I get now is "What's next for you?" And I don't have an answer. I have to remind myself not to worry my midlife away—every time I make a plan, something better comes along. So I'm going to sit back for while and try to live in the right now.

DO YOU HAVE ANY ADVICE FOR GOING BACK TO WORK AFTER BEING RETIRED? I'M TURNING SIXTY, FEEL FORTY, AND I WANT TO GO BACK. I MISS THE SOCIAL INTERACTIONS AND SENSE OF ACCOMPLISHMENT THAT I HAD FROM YEARS OF WORKING.

I love to hear from people with ambition and excitement about adding another chapter to their lives. Since you may have more flexibility to explore a new line of work, you might consider doing an exercise such as the one Peter and I did in San Diego. We called it "The White Board Incident."

I was bored in public relations and feeling a pull back to Washington, D.C., and I missed working in public policy communications and my friends. But I knew Peter wouldn't want to leave the great weather of San Diego (and I was reluctant to put on a winter coat again, too, believe me!). But Peter sat me down and had me list everything I wanted and didn't want to do in a job. Then we assigned a numerical value to each item. The results were very clear, and it helped me realize that my instincts about moving back to D.C. were correct. A similar exercise can help you narrow down some options.

One of the most important things to consider is the people you'll be working with—that can make all the difference. If you're surrounded by interesting, good people who are working together as a team, it almost doesn't matter what kind of work you're doing. This is a great chance to try something totally new to you. And if you're concerned about getting locked into something too quickly, consider working part time or on a freelance basis. That will give you some flexibility.

And once you find something, remember that younger workers are hungry for advice and mentoring. See if there's a way for you to help them learn by example in the early part of their careers.

DO YOU HAVE ANY TIPS TO SUSTAIN A FRIENDSHIP BETWEEN TWO PEOPLE WITH VERY DIFFERENT OPINIONS?

I cherish my friends and try to avoid talking politics with people outside of work. When you argue for a living, it's the last thing you want to do when you're off the clock. But with social media, everyone's opinions are constantly on display. Sometimes people you really like are so aggressive on social media that it can wear you down and even make you think differently about the person.

I have a solution for this that I've tried: unfollow them. That may sound cruel, but it actually is the best way to preserve a friendship. You can let them know that you're not following them anymore and tell them why, but say it in a way that shows you have a sense of humor about politics, that you don't take it that seriously. Or don't mention it to them. They probably won't even notice.

If politics is getting in the way of your enjoyment of one of your friends, then detach emotionally from the opinions they're expressing. Remember that our intentions are the same. We all want a strong, vibrant America—we just have different ways of achieving that goal.

DID YOU HOPE MANAGERS WOULD GET SOMETHING OUT OF YOUR BOOK, TOO?

I heard a great story about a young woman working as a personal assistant in the financial sector who read my book and then told her manager, "I think you need to read this." I loved imagining that scene.

I was somewhat surprised but very pleased to hear from several people in management positions that the book helped them understand and look out for their younger staffers. A new congresswoman sent me a note saying it was particularly helpful as she worked to train her new team. Advice such as letting them sit in on meetings and conference calls, letting them be around the big boss once in a while, and actually looking at them (and not at the computer or phone) while talking to them were good reminders.

I think one of the most important aspects for managers to recognize is that their employees have ambition and want to do a great job, and they want to contribute to the bottom line. I am concerned when younger staffers aren't encouraged to move on after a couple of years in an entry-level job. One of the measures of a good manager should be facilitating the upward mobility of his or her employees. Let's not hold anyone back because it would be inconvenient to us to have to train someone else for that position.

The other part of the book that I think was important for managers was the portion that included stories about what leadership looked like at the White House under President George W. Bush when the cameras weren't rolling. He set such good examples, including taking an interest in his younger staff's lives, encouraging them to take risks, and even helping them deal with personal difficulties. The feedback on the Bush anecdotes was so positive that I am including more of them from other White House staffers here.

WAS THERE ANYTHING YOU LEARNED OR THAT SURPRISED YOU WHILE YOU WERE TRAVELING AROUND THE COUNTRY ON YOUR BOOK TOUR?

The book tour blew me away. It was so humbling. Americans love books, and I was honored to see people coming to the bookstores and events, having stood in line for hours, just for a chance to meet me for a few brief seconds and to get their books signed. I enjoyed watching people make friends in the line, and I was even the reason two young people met and decided to go on a date. I like to imagine that they fell in love and are planning a wedding. I met long-lost family members and friends of my grandparents, including a surgeon who had saved my grandfather's life when he had heart trouble. Occasionally, fans of President George W. Bush or *The Five* came up to the table with tears in their eyes, which made me start to cry. I completely lost it when I looked into the eyes of a Gold Star mother who had lost her son at war who had waited for so long to shake my hand; I had to stop the book signing line for a while to gather myself.

I was encouraged to see the broad appeal of the book. I noted that people were buying it for nieces and nephews, grandparents, mothers "who watch me every day," fathers who were in the military and on deployment, teachers, and more. I was given handmade gifts for Jasper, and eventually I had to ask people not to bring him any more treats or he would become Fatsper. One person in Chicago made him a quilt, and now we take it with us on weekends so that we can protect our friends' linens when Jasper inevitably winds up on the bed.

Here's what I learned on the book tour: America is better and kinder, more savvy, intelligent, and honorable than the media on the coasts portrays. It was such a good reminder for me. Our nation is exceptional in so many ways.

AND THE GOOD NEWS IS . . . WAS YOUR FIRST BOOK. WILL THERE BE A SECOND?

My parents started reading to me at a young age, and I have loved books ever since. As a kid, I dreamed of being an author, and I thought I'd write fiction. I wanted to come up with characters like Ramona Quimby, Pippi Longstocking, and Sheila the Great. My career took me in another direction, but I have always appreciated good writing and storytelling. After I left the White House, I helped edit and publicize several other books. I didn't really think I'd ever write my own.

Growing up, possibly because I read so much, I was a decent storyteller, and that helped me in my public speaking competitions. My husband is an even better at keeping an audience's attention (of course, the British accent is to his advantage on that score), and I would learn from him how best to tell a joke. While I didn't keep notes from my White House days, I have an exceptionally strong memory for detail—I can picture scenes in my mind and remember full quotes—and I found myself telling the stories of my life over and over to audiences. I was repeatedly asked about my upbringing on the ranch, meeting a guy on an airplane and leaving my job and my country to go to be with him, and being the first Republican woman to be the press secretary. All of those are good stories embedded with career and life lessons. So when I thought of the kind of book I would want to write, I knew it was also one that I would want to read. The result is a collection of stories full of lessons learned through experiences with an encouraging tone and practical advice.

I was also fascinated by the writing process. I'm a fairly social person, and I had never spent much time alone. Writing the book was very solitary, but not in a bad way. Time went by so fast—entire Saturday afternoons would pass and I would feel like I'd put in a good day's work. And then I'd realize just how much more was left to do. I forced myself to take some breaks, though my instincts were always to power through. I recognized that my writing was better when I was fresh and had enough white space in my brain to let ideas roll around for a while.

I had to type with my laptop at an angle because my dog, Jasper, would insist on sitting on the rocking chair with me, but there isn't quite room for the two of us. I felt so much satisfaction when I wrote a sentence I thought was just right, only to read it again and think it was terrible. So I'd try again. And again. When I felt good about it, I'd pause for a moment and scratch Jasper behind the ears. He'd sigh and push against me to get even more of the chair for himself.

When I finished, I felt a real sense of accomplishment. I was ready to deliver the final draft. We were in the kitchen in our home in South Carolina, and I had some tears in my eyes. It was hard to say good-bye since it had been my companion for so long. And it's a little scary because you don't know how your work is going to be received. I said to Peter, "Well, here it goes..." and the publisher very ably took it from there.

I'm grateful for everyone who read, edited, and supported the book, and I hope to be able to write more in the future. Besides, I need some more cuddle time with Jasper.

Acknowledgments

On a train in the summer of 2009, I wrote down some ideas for a book of my own. I tore out the page, put it in my wallet, and forgot about it.

Three years later, when Sean Desmond and I worked together on *Decision Points*, he asked if I'd ever thought of writing a book. I gave him several reasons why I didn't consider it seriously, but then I remembered the note. He said, "Leave this with me," and set out to publish the book I wanted to write. I'm grateful for his dedication, steady guidance, and gentle humor. Sean, Susan, and Daniel have made encouraging me one of their family projects.

Deb Futter, the publisher of Twelve, trusted me and Sean from the beginning, and she gave us room to run. Brian McLendon, head of publicity, won my heart when he said he loved my dog. Catherine Casalino and I envisioned the cover, and she made an excellent choice in photographer Melanie Dunea. Libby Burton's edits were specific and smart—she's a mind reader with a bright future. Thanks also to Paul Samuelson and Tony Forde—doing public relations for a former White House press secretary isn't easy but they stand out. And Joan Matthews and Mari Okuda's copyediting is a lifesaver.

Bob Barnett and I have worked together for years, mostly on behalf of other authors. Like Sean, he believed in this book even before I did. I've benefited from his advice and sometimes I pinch myself to think I'm actually one of his clients.

Paul Mauro is the best editor and writer you've never heard of—he and his wife, Joan McNaughton, are friends I stole from Greg Gutfeld. Paul has a very demanding day job, and in his limited spare time he edited three drafts and kept me laughing with his commentary in the margins. I'm at a rare loss for words to describe my gratitude to him.

There were several people in my trusted readers program: Tim and Michele Chase, Spence Geissinger, Darcy Gulbin and her son John, Ingrid Henrichsen, Jamie Horowitz, Barry Jackson, Joshua McCarroll, Emily Schillinger, Tracy and Jeff Schyberg, Don Stewart, and Chris and Mary Stirewalt.

Many of my friends from the Bush Administration have kept me company, and I thank especially Hannah Abney, Charles Blahous, Trey Bohn, Freddy Ford, Tony Fratto, Keith Hennessey, Ken Lisaius, Jeanie Mamo, Sally McDonough, Mike Meece, Chris Michel, Brent McIntosh, Bill McGurn, Scott Stanzel, Justine Sterling, and Raul Yanes.

Nicolle Wallace also gave me encouragement, treating me as an author—not just as another press secretary who was writing a book.

Chris Byrne, Rachel Ellis, Stuart Siciliano, and Carlton Carroll helped me remember specifics from the White House years.

I wrote about my co-hosts on *The Five*, and in addition to thanking them for filling my days with laughter, I need to thank those at the Fox News Channel who were instrumental in giving me a shot and supportive of my additional pursuits: Roger Ailes, Bill Shine, Suzanne Scott, Dianne Brandi, and John Finley.

Sean Hannity was the first to invite me on the channel after leaving the White House, and we've been friends since. Megyn Kelly and her husband, Doug Brunt, were enthusiastic about the project.

And the crew, makeup artists, and hair stylists are some of my best friends, and I appreciate their talents.

Particular thanks go to Gutfeld. He gave me a shot in the arm to punch up the language and to trust my writing instincts. He was the net under my tightrope as I wrote, and he was patient when I had questions. His first love and best talent is his writing—we're fortunate that he's willing to share his gifts with us on television, too.

The people I can never thank enough are President George W. Bush and First Lady Laura Bush. I learned so much from them in eight years—about politics, loyalty, and love. They are remarkable leaders, and I'm well aware I'd not be writing this without the opportunities they afforded and the trust they placed in me.

My mom, Jan Perino, read all the drafts and has an eagle eye for typos. My dad, Leo, and my aunt Patty Sue Schuler helped me tell the story of my family's start in America. My cousin Preston Perino answered questions while on horseback. A long-lost distant cousin, Arlene Vaught, shared her extensive family research with me. My sister, Angie Machock, should get an Oscar for best sister in a supporting role.

And finally there's Peter, the love of my life that I married after sitting next to him on a plane in 1997. At that point, I'd never even met President Bush, so this is not at all the life we imagined. Peter's given me room to grow and supported me with enthusiasm, moving here and there and dealing with long hours, distraction, and more than his fair share of the chores. And it's because of him that I've had the joy of raising two Hungarian Vizslas, Henry, who died at nearly fourteen years old in 2012, and Jasper, the silly puppy that delights my fans and followers.

I've had a blessed life so far and I'm constantly humbled by it.

About the Author

DANA PERINO is a Fox News contributor and co-host of one of the most popular shows on cable television, *The Five*. Perino was the first Republican woman to serve as the White House press secretary, and served for over seven years in the administration of President George W. Bush, including at the Department of Justice after the terrorist attacks on 9/11. Perino lives in Manhattan with her husband, Peter McMahon, and their dog, Jasper.

ABOUT TWELVE

TWELVE was established in August 2005 with the objective of publishing no more than twelve books each year. We strive to publish the singular book, by authors who have a unique perspective and compelling authority. Works that explain our culture; that illuminate, inspire, provoke, and entertain. We seek to establish communities of conversation surrounding our books. Talented authors deserve attention not only from publishers, but from readers as well. To sell the book is only the beginning of our mission. To build avid audiences of readers who are enriched by these works—that is our ultimate purpose.

For more information about forthcoming TWELVE books, please go to www.twelvebooks.com.